INDEX TO PLAYS

SUPPLEMENT

INDEX TO PLAYS

SUPPLEMENT

COMPILED BY

INA TEN EYCK FIRKINS

NEW YORK
THE H. W. WILSON COMPANY
1935

PREFACE

This supplement to the *Index to Plays* issued in 1927 is offered as a bridge between the period covered by the first volume and the present date. The greater part of the material now made available represents the work of play writers since 1927 but a fraction of it is made up from the work of authors not included in the earlier volume but who have since become of sufficient importance to warrant the inclusion of their names in the *Supplement*. Also a few inadvertent omissions from the first list have been indexed in this one. The attention of the user is therefore called to the fact that it will be desirable to consult both volumes in looking up a reference irrespective of the actual date of publication unless that date is later than 1927 in which event obviously it could be found in the *Supplement* only.

In compiling such a bibliography it is difficult to decide exactly what should be included. To index all published plays would be impossible even were it desirable. The choice cannot be made on merit only because not infrequently a play which has neither literary nor technical dramatic merit may be desired for a quite legitimate reason. No consistent method of choice can be claimed for the present volume but in a general way the following points have been decisive in the compiler's selection:

All plays of well-known dramatists whether published in separate books, in collections or in magazines.

Collections of plays by less well-known authors when numerous enough or interesting enough to have secured a publisher of recognized standing.

When a play by an obscure author appears in a composite collection important enough to be indexed, other works by the same writer have been looked up and usually included.

Published plays which have had a popular run on Broadway.

Translations of plays by foreign authors whether found in books or magazines.

Many titles which appeared in the first volume, reappear in the *Supplement*. When that occurs the original entries are not repeated but additional entries are given, that is to say, references to reprints in collections or periodicals, or new editions of the author's works.

A mere repetition of the entries given in the *United States Catalog* or in lists of well-known publishers of plays has been deemed unnecessary.

There have been indexed in the *Supplement* the works of 1335 authors and 3284 titles.

The matter of an extensive index to subjects requires a more elaborate explanation than may properly be given here. Suffice it to say that it is my opinion that no satisfactory subject index can be compiled because no selection from title or subject, even with notes as to length, number of characters and generic classification is an adequate basis for selection for production in relation to a given group. There are for instance, indexed in this volume, sixty plays about Christmas; it is doubtful if from this number, two would be found that might meet the requirements of any special class of amateurs. A play must always be examined before it is selected for production or reading and no library will have the sixty plays listed in this volume to offer its client. This fact alone creates an immediate and insurmountable *impasse*. The difficulty of the amateur group is a real one but it is not to be solved by the publication of subject lists.

The arrangement of the entries in this volume is the same as that in the *Index to Plays,* i.e. it is in two parts, an Author Index, and a Title and Subject Index. The order of entry under the author's name is as follows:

Separate publication of a play.
Collected works of the author.
Composite collections.
Periodicals.

When a separate edition of a play has been issued, the full bibliographical information has been given—title, publisher, place and date of publication under the outdoor entry. After this, or after the title of the play if it has appeared in collected editions or magazines only, is given, first a word or two of description—comedy, tragedy, social, domestic—enough to suggest the character of the play, and then the number of acts. Occasionally when it has been impossible to obtain a copy of a play for examination this information will be found incomplete.

In the Title and Subject Index has been given the title of the play, followed by the author's name. To locate the place of publication it is necessary to refer to the Author Index. Subject entries are given in bold-face type; there follows an indented list of plays upon the given subject. The subject list is not complete; it is intended merely to suggest a few titles to those seeking plays for special occasions or upon special subjects.

In Appendix A only those works of an author which contain more than one play have been entered. The separate editions of the single plays have been entered as noted above, with full bibliographical information in the Author Index. Appendix B contains the list of composite collections indexed.

It is a pleasure to acknowledge the many courtesies extended to me during the preparation of this volume by the Library of Congress and my publishers.

INA TEN EYCK FIRKINS

May 20, 1935

List of Periodicals Referred to in this Index

CONTENTS

INDEX TO PLAYS

SUPPLEMENT

———•———

AUTHOR INDEX

Abbott, George and Bridgers, Ann Preston
Coquette; a play in three acts. N.Y. Longmans. 1928. 8°. 137p. Comedy
Same in Mantle, B. ed. Best plays of 1927-28 (abridged)

Abbott, George and Gleason, James
·Fall guy; a comedy in three acts. N.Y. French. c1928. 12°. 97p.

Abbott, George, *joint author. See* Burnett, Dana and Abbott, George

Abdullah, Achmed
Black tents. N.Y. Liveright. Orient. 7 scenes. 1930. 12°. 218p.

Ackland, Rodney
Strange orchestra, a play in three acts. London. Gollancz. 1932. 112p.
Same in Famous plays of 1932-33

Adair, T.
Bean boy. 1 act
In Jagendorf, M. A. ed. Nine short plays written for young people to stage

Ade, George, 1866-
College widow. Comedy. 4 acts
In Cordell, R. A. ed. Representative modern plays

Ahearn, T. J.
Twelve before three. 1 act
In Nicholson, K. ed. Hollywood plays

Aikins, Carroll C. C.
God of gods. Indian. 2 acts
In Massey, V. ed. Canadian plays from Hart House theatre. v. 2

Akins, Zoë, 1886-
Old maid. Dramatized from the novel of Edith Wharton. N.Y. Appleton. 1935. 12°. 188p. 5 episodes
Portrait of Tiero. Tragedy. 1 act
In Isaacs, E. J. ed. Plays of American life and fantasy
Such a charming young man. N.Y. French. 1933. 17p.

Alarcón, D. Juan Ruiz de
Truth suspected. Comedy. 3 acts
In Poet Lore 38:475

Alden, Alice Wight, 1865-
Dickon goes to the fair. Juvenile. 1 act
In Dickon goes to the fair, and other plays

Aldington, Hilda Doolittle (Mrs. Richard Aldington) (H. D. pseud.)
Hippolytus temporizes; a play in three acts. Boston. Houghton. 1927. 12°. 139p. Lyrical tragedy

Aldis, Mary (Reynolds) 1872-
Mrs. Pat and the law. Boston. Baker. 1923. 12°
St. Patrick's day. 1 act
In Schauffler, R. H. and Sanford, A. P. eds. Plays for our American holidays. v. 1
Two plus two; or, Two and two make four. Chicago. Dramatic pub. co. [c1929] 12°

Alehin, Alexander Fedor, 1891-
Boaster. 1 act
In First sin, and other one act plays
First sin. 1 act
In First sin, and other one act plays
Glutton. 1 act
In First sin, and other one act plays
Secret. 1 act
In First sin, and other one act plays

Aleichem, Sholem, 1859-1916
Gymnazie. 1 act
In White, B. F. trans. Nine one-act plays from the Yiddish
Liars. Comedy. 1 act
In Shay, F. ed. Fifty more contemporary one-act plays

Alexander, Hartley
Kills-with-her-man
In Isaacs, E. J. ed. Plays of American life and fantasy

Alger, Esther Marion
In 'ependence; a one act play
In Poet Lore 41:140

Allen, Inglis, 1879-
Suffragette's redemption, a play in one act. N.Y. French. c1913. 12°. 16p.

Álvarez Quintero, Serafín, 1871- **and Álvarez Quintero, Joaquín,** 1873-
Don Abel wrote a tragedy. Comedy. 3 acts
In Four comedies
Doña Clarines. Comedy. 2 acts
In Four comedies
Fortunato. Tragic farce. 2 scenes
In Four plays
Grief (La pena); a drama in two scenes
In Poet Lore 41:391
Hundred years old. (El centenario) Comedy. 2 acts
In Four plays
Plays of to-day
Lady from Alfalqueque (La consulesa) Comedy. 2 acts
In Four plays
Love passes by. Comedy. 2 acts
In Four comedies

Álvarez Quintero, S. and J.—*Continued*
Malvaloca. Andalusian life. 3 acts
  In Dickinson, T. H. ed. Chief con-
    temporary dramatists. ser. 3
Peace and quiet. Comedy. 2 acts
  In Four comedies
Sunny morning; a comedy of Madrid in
  one act. . . 1932. N.Y. French. [1914]
  18p.
  Same in Webber, J. P. and Webster,
    H. H. eds. One-act plays for sec-
    ondary schools
Widow's eyes; a comedy in one act
  In Poet Lore 40:552
Women have their way. (Women's
  town) (Pueblo de las mujeres)
  Comedy. 2 acts
  In Four plays

Ament, William Sheffield
Duel about nothing. 1 act
  In Hughes, G. ed. Short plays for
    modern players

Andersen, Madge
Fairy ring. 1 act
  In Jagendorf, W. A. ed. Nine short
    plays

Anderson, Lee
Arabesque. 1 act
  In Ten one act plays
Bed for three. 1 act
  In Ten one act plays
Dawning. 1 act
  In Ten one act plays
Give the audience a chance. 1 act
  In Ten one act plays
In the thousands of years to come. 1 act
  In Ten one act plays
Is peculiar. Revenge. 3 scenes
  In Players book of one act plays.
    ser. 1
"Man wants—". 1 act
  In Ten one act plays
Manhood. 1 act
  In Ten one act plays
Mutiny. Tragedy. 1 act
  In Players book of one act plays.
    ser. 1
Rondo. 1 act
  In Ten one act plays
Simple soul. 1 act
  In Ten one act plays
Strategy; a prevarication in one act
  In Players book of one act plays.
    ser. 1
Such is love. 1 act
  In Ten one act plays

Anderson, Maxwell, 1888-
Both your houses; a play in three acts.
  N.Y. French. 1933. 12°. 180p.
  Same in Mantle, B. ed. Best plays
    of 1932-33 (abridged)
Elizabeth the queen, a play in three acts.
  N.Y. Longmans. 1930. 8°. 168p. His-
  torical
  Same in Mantle, B. ed. Best plays of
    1930-31 (abridged)
Gypsy. Comedy. 3 acts
  Same in Mantle, B. ed. Best plays of
    1928-29 (abridged)

Mary of Scotland; a play in three acts.
  N.Y. Garden City. 1933. 12°. 202p.
  Historical
  Same in Mantle, B. ed. Best plays of
    1933-34 (abridged)
Night over Taos; a play in three acts.
  N.Y. French. 1932. 12°. 200p. His-
  torical
Outside looking in. Hobo comedy.
  3 acts
  In Anderson, M. and Hickerson, H.
    Gods of the lightning. . . Outside
    looking in
Saturday's children; a comedy in three
  acts. N.Y. Longmans. 1927. 8°. 166p.
  Same in Mantle, B. ed. Best plays of
    1926-27 (abridged)
          Tucker, S. M. ed. Modern
    American and British plays
Valley Forge, a play in three acts. Wash-
  ington [D.C.] Anderson House. 1934.
  8°. 169p. Historical.
What price glory. War. 3 acts
  In Chandler, F. W. and Cordell, R. A.
    eds. Twentieth century plays

**Anderson, Maxwell, 1888- and Hickerson,
Harold**
Gods of the lightning. Sacco-Vanzetti
  case. 3 acts
  In Gods of the lightning. . . Outside
    looking in
Outside looking in
  In Gods of the lightning. . . Outside
    looking in

Andreas, Eulalie
Divorce specialist. Comedy. 1 act
  In Four one-act comedies
Lure of the stage. Comedy. 1 act
  In Four one-act comedies
Modern David Garrick. Comedy. 1 act
  In Four one-act comedies
Woman of it. Comedy. 1 act
  In Four one-act comedies

Andreas, Eulalie and Hurrie, Jane
Yes, yes! go on; a comedy in three
  acts. . . Boston. Baker. c1928. 8°.
  122p.

Andreev, Leonid Nikolaevich, 1871-1819
He who gets slapped. Satire. 4 acts
  In Dickinson, T. H. ed. Chief contem-
    porary dramatists. ser. 3
    Moses, M. J. ed. Dramas of mod-
      ernism and their forerunners
    Tucker, S. M. ed. Modern conti-
      nental plays
    Tucker, S. M. ed. Twenty-five mod-
      ern plays
    Watson, E. B. and Pressey, B. eds.
      Contemporary drama. European
      plays

Ankrum, Morris and Duffey, Vincent
Mystery man; a mystery play in three
  acts. . . N.Y. French. c1928. 12°.
  97p.

Annunzio, Gabriel d' 1864-
Francesca da Rimini. Tragedy. 3 acts
  In Tucker, S. M. ed. Modern conti-
    nental plays
    Tucker, S. M. ed. Twenty-five
      modern plays

Anonymous
At the ferry. 1 scene
 In Johnson, T. ed. More plays in miniature
Punch and Judy. Puppet. 1 act
 In Moses, M. J. ed. Treasury of plays for children
Shakespeare, the playmaker
 In Sanford, A. P. ed. Plays for graduation days
Taking the picnic to the shut-in. Red Cross. 1 act
 In Schauffler, R. H. and Sanford, A. P. eds. Plays for our American holidays. v. 4

Ansky, S. A. pseud. *See* Rappoport, Solomon

Anspacher, Louis Kaufman, 1878-
Unchastened woman. Comedy. 3 acts
 In Mantle, B. and Sherman, G. P. eds. Best plays of 1909-19

Anthony, C. L. pseud. (Smith, Dorothy Gladys) 1896-
Autumn crocus, a play in three acts. London. Gollancz. 1931. 12°. 127p. Social
 Same in Famous plays of 1931
 Plays of a half-decade
Service; a play in three acts. London. Gollancz. 1932. 12°. 126p.
 Same in Famous plays of 1932-33

Archer, William, 1856-1924
Beatriz Juana. Renaissance. 3 acts
 In Three plays
George Washington's wedding. Historical. 1 act
 In Schauffler, R. H. and Sanford, A. P. eds. Plays for our American holidays. v. 3
Lidia [based on Rowley's Great duke of Florence]. Comedy. 4 acts
 In Three plays
Martha Washington. Historical. 8 scenes
 In Three plays
War is war; or, The Germans in Belgium, a drama of 1914. N.Y. Doran. [c1919] 12°. 117p.

Aristophanes, 440-380 B.C.
Lysistrata; a comedy; il. by Norman Lindsay. N.Y. Illustrated Editions Co. 1933. 114p. Feminism. 3 acts
 Same in Plays of the Moscow Art Theatre musical studio. 1925

Arkell, Reginald
Columbine: A fantasy; and other verses. London. Benn. 1911. 12°
 Same in Hampden, J. ed. Ten modern plays
 Webber, J. P. and Webster, H. H. eds. One-act plays for secondary schools
Sending grandpa to heaven; a play in one act. N.Y. French. [c1929] 12°. 19p.

Arkwright, Ruth
Baby New Year. 1 act
 In Schauffler, R. H. and Sanford, A. P. eds. Plays for our American holidays. v. 2

Olaf and the trolls; a Norwegian fairy-play in three scenes. 193-? London. National Society's Depository. 12°. 35p.

Arlen, Michael, pseud. (Kuyumjian, Dikran)
Acting version of the Green Hat; a romance. N.Y. Doran. c1925. 8°. 108p.

Arlen, Michael and **Hackett, Walter**
Good losers; a play in three acts and a prologue. N.Y. French. c1933. 8°. 99p.

Arlen, Michael and **Smith, Winchell,** 1871-
Zoo; a comedy in three acts. N.Y. French. c1927. 8°. 99p.

Arlett, Vera Isabel, 1896-
Corner in dreams; a comedy in one act. London. Gowans. 1927. 12°. 57p.
Gardener; a play in one act
 In Poet Lore 41:305
Last man in; a play in one act
 In Poet Lore 41:410
Making it pay; a comedy in one act. N.Y. French. c1931. 12°. 27p.
Visitor; a play in one act. London. Gowans. 1929. 8°. 30p.

Arliss, George, *joint author. See* Hamlin, Mary P. and Arliss, George

Armstrong, Anthony
Ten-minute alibi. Detective. 3 acts
 In Famous plays of 1933

Armstrong, L. van V.
Late Captain Crow. 1 act
 In One-act plays for stage and study. ser. 5

Armstrong, Noel
Marthe. Character. 1 act
 In Shay, F. ed. Fifty more contemporary one-act plays

Arnold, J. and **Burke, E.**
Good medicine
 In Twelve one-act plays

Asch, Shalom, 1880-
Sabbatai Zevi; a tragedy in three acts and six scenes with a prologue and an epilogue. Authorized trans. from the Russian version by Florence White and George Rapall Noyes. Philadelphia. Jewish publication society of America. 1930. 12°. 131p.

Ash, Shalom. *See* Asch, Shalom

Ashton, Winifred (Clemence Dane, pseud.)
Adam's opera, the text of a play . . . set to music by Richard Addinsell. Garden City, N.Y. Doubleday. 1929. 8°. 134p. 2 acts
Bill of divorcement. Problem. 3 acts
 In Recapture; a Clemence Dane omnibus
 Cordell, R. A. ed. Representative modern plays
 Marriot, J. W. ed. Great modern British plays
Granite. Tragedy. 4 acts
 In Recapture; a Clemence Dane omnibus
 Tucker, S. M. ed. Modern American and British plays
Mariners. N.Y. Macmillan. 1927. 12°. 72p. Problem. 3 acts

Ashton, Winifred—Continued
  Mr. Fox, a play for boys, N.Y. French.
    c1927. 8°. 21p. 1 act
  Shivering shocks; or, The hiding place;
    a play for boys. N.Y. French. c1923.
    12°. 22p. 1 act
  Traveller returns; a play in one act, by
    Clemence Dane. N.Y. French. c1927.
    12°. 22p.
  Wild Decembers. London. Heinemann.
    1932. 8°. 97p. Brontës. 3 acts
  Will Shakespeare. 1 act
    In Recapture; a Clemence Dane om-
      nibus

Ashton, Winifred and Addinsell, Richard
  Come of age. Garden City, N.Y. Double-
    day. 1934. 12°. 116p. Thomas Chat-
    terton

Atlas, Leopold L.
  House we live in. Character. 4 acts
    In Wednesday's child and House we
      live in
  "L." 1 act
    In Baker, G. P. ed. Yale one-act plays
  Wednesday's child. Domestic. 2 acts
    In Wednesday's child and House we
      live in
    Same in Mantle, B. ed. Best plays of
      1933-34 (abridged)

Averchenko, Arkady
  Man with the green necktie; a Russian
    comedy
    In Golden Bk 17:449

Bacon, Leonard
  Dream and action. N.Y. Harper. 1934.
    71p. Jean-Arthur Rimbaud

Bagg, Helen
  Left overs. Comedy. 3 acts
    In Prize plays of 1927

Bailey, Loretto Carroll
  Cloey. Comedy. 1 act
    In Koch, F. H. ed. Carolina folk
      comedies
  Job's kinfolks, a play of the mill people.
    1 act
    In Koch, F. H. ed. Carolina folk-
      plays. ser. 3

Bain, Ethel
  Glowing cross; a miracle playlet for
    Easter. Briggsville, Wis. Catholic
    drama movement. c1931. 12°. 10p.
  He is risen; a play for Easter week, in
    six scenes with prologue. N.Y.
    Avondale press. 1929. 12°. 31p.
  Road to Bethlehem; a Christmas play for
    children in one scene. N.Y. Avon-
    dale press. [c1927] 12°. 13p.

Baker, Elizabeth
  Bert's girl; a comedy in four acts. Lon-
    don. Benn. 1927. 12°. 98p.
  Faithful admirer. Comedy. 1 act
    In Shay, F. ed. Fifty more contem-
      porary one-act plays
  Miss Tassey. Suicide. 1 act
    In Clark, B. H. ed. Representative
      one-act plays by British and Irish
      authors

Balderston, John Lloyd, 1889-
  Berkeley Square; a play in three acts. . .
    (The plot suggested by Henry
    James's posthumous fragment, "The
    sense of the past") N.Y. French.
    c1928. 8°. 96p.
    Same in Mantle, B. ed. Best plays of
      1929-30 (abridged)
  Morality play for the leisured class.
    1 act
    In Shay, F. ed. Fifty more contem-
      porary one-act plays

**Balderston, John Lloyd, 1889- and Hoarre,
J. E.**
  Red planet, a play in three acts. N.Y.
    French. 1933. 12°. 99p.

Ball, Jack and Scribner, Edwin
  Have patience, doctor; a merry medical
    mix-up in three acts. N.Y. French.
    c1933. 12°. 103p.

Ballard, Frederick, 1884-
  Ladies of the jury, a comedy in three
    acts. N.Y. French. 1931. 12°. 147p.
  Rainy day, a comedy in three acts. N.Y.
    French. [c1931] 12°. 110p.

**Banning, Kendall, 1879- and Kellock, Har-
old, 1879-**
  Copy; a comedy-drama in one act. N.Y.
    Longmans
    Same in Twelve one-act plays

Barbee, Lindsay, 1876-
  Making of a king. Biblical
    In Gaw, A. et al. Pharaoh's daughter
      and other Biblical plays of the
      contest, 1927

Baring, Maurice, 1874-
  After Euripides' Electra. 1 act
    In Golden Bk 17:257
  Aulis difficulty. Travesty. 1 act
    In Tucker, S. M. ed. Twelve one-act
      plays for study and production
  Calypso. Comedy. 1 act
    In London Merc 18:245
  Catherine Parr. Historical. 1 act
    In Hampden, J. ed. Eight modern
      plays
  Don Juan's failure. 1 act
    In Golden Bk 13:69 Ap '31
  Drawback. Duologue
    In Johnson, T. ed. More plays in min-
      iature
  Gaston de Foix; a play in three acts.
    Oxford. Blackwell. 1913. 12°. 72p.
  Greek vase. Comedy. 1 act
    In Johnson, T. ed. Miniature plays for
      stage or study
  King Alfred and the neat-herd. 1 act
    In Modern short plays. ser. 3
  Rehearsal. Shakespeare. 1 act
    In Hampden, J. ed. Nine modern
      plays
      Webber, J. P. and Webster, H. H.
      Typical plays for secondary
      schools
      Golden Bk 9:104 Mr '29
  Xanthippe and Socrates. Duologue.
    1 scene
    In Johnson, T. ed. More plays in min-
      iature

Barnard, Charles, joint author. See De Mille,
  W. C. and Barnard, C.

Barnes, Eleanor
Close to the wind. 1 act
In Poet Lore 40:588
Barnouw, Erik
Open collars; a play of undergraduate
life in Kingston University. Prince-
ton Univ. press. 1928. 8°. 83p. 3 acts
Baronian, Hagop H., 1842-1891
Gentlemen beggars; a comedy in five
acts; tr. from the Armenian and
dramatized by E. D. Megerditchian.
Boston. Bruce Humphries. 1932.
118p.
Barrett, Frank Wilson, *joint author. See*
Brandon-Thomas, Jevan, and Bar-
rett, Frank Wilson
Barrie, Sir James Matthew, 1860-
Admirable Crichton. Comedy. 4 acts
In Plays of J. M. Barrie
Alice-sit-by-the-fire. Comedy. 1 act
In Plays of J. M. Barrie
Barbara's wedding. World war. 1 act
In Plays of J. M. Barrie
Dear Brutus. Comedy. 3 acts
In Plays of J. M. Barrie
Watson, E. B. and Pressey, B. eds.
Contemporary drama: English and
Irish plays
Half an hour. Comedy. 1 act
In Plays of J. M. Barrie
Shall we join the ladies?
Kiss for Cinderella. Comedy. 3 acts
In Plays of J. M. Barrie
Mary Rose. Fantasy. 3 acts
In Plays of J. M. Barrie
New word. Comedy. 1 act
In Plays of J. M. Barrie
Old friends. Heredity. 1 act
In Plays of J. M. Barrie
Shall we join the ladies?
Old lady shows her medals. Comedy.
1 act
In Plays of J. M. Barrie
Pantaloon. Comedy. 1 act
In Plays of J. M. Barrie
Peter Pan; or, The boy who would not
grow up. N.Y. Scribner. 1928. 12°.
162p. Fairy. 5 acts
In Plays of J. M. Barrie
Quality street. Comedy. 4 acts
In Plays of J. M. Barrie
Rosalind. Comedy. 1 act
In Plays of J. M. Barrie
Seven women. Comedy. 1 act
In Plays of J. M. Barrie
Shall we join the ladies?
Shall we join the ladies? N.Y. Scribner.
1928. 12°. 21p. [This is the first act
of an unfinished play] Mystery
Same in Plays of J. M. Barrie
Shall we join the ladies?
(Hodder)
Asquith, C. ed. Black cap;
new stories of murder and
mystery
Twelve-pound look. Comedy. 1 act
In Plays of J. M. Barrie
Well-remembered voice. **Supernatural.**
1 act
In **Plays of J. M. Barrie**

What every woman knows. Comedy.
4 acts
In Plays of J. M. Barrie
Watson, E. B. and Pressey, B. eds.
Contemporary drama: English
and Irish plays. v. 1
Will. Comedy. 1 act
In Plays of J. M. Barrie
Barrows, Marjorie
Clown of Doodle Doo
In Jagendorf, M. A. ed. Nine short
plays
Barrows, Thomas, *joint author. See* Nichol-
son, Kenyon and Barrows, Thomas
Barry, Philip, 1896-
Animal kingdom; a comedy. N.Y. French.
1932. 12°. 198p.
Same in Mantle, B. ed. Best plays of
1931-32 (abridged)
Holiday, a comedy in three acts. N.Y.
French. 1929. 12°. 205p.
In Mantle, B. ed. Best plays of 1928-
29 (abridged)
Hotel universe, a play. N.Y. French.
1930. 12°. 166p. Psychoanalysis.
1 act
In a garden; a comedy in three acts.
N.Y. French. 1929. 12°. 133p.
Same in Tucker, S. M. ed. Twenty-five
modern plays
John, a play. N.Y. French. 1929. 12°.
173p. St. John the Baptist
Joyous season. N.Y. French. 1934. 12°.
168p. Social climbers. 3 acts
Paris bound, a comedy. N.Y. French.
1929. 12°. 193p. 3 acts
Same in Mantle, B. ed. Best plays of
1927-28 (abridged)
Tomorrow and tomorrow, a play. N.Y.
French. 1931. 12°. 173p. Problem.
3 acts
Same in Mantle, B. ed. Best plays of
1930-31 (abridged)
White wings; a comedy in three acts.
N.Y. French. 1929. 12°. 149p.
You and I, a comedy in three acts. N.Y.
French. 1929. 12°. 160p.
Barry, Philip, *joint author. See* Rice, Elmer
L. and Barry, Philip
Barry, William Edwin
Jade god, a mystery play in three
acts. . . dramatized from the novel
of the same name by Alan Sullivan.
N.Y. French. c1930. 12°. 77p.
Barton, Lucy
New Salem days
In Sanford, A. P. ed. Lincoln plays
Susan should marry. 1 act
In Sanford, A. P. ed. One-act plays
for women
Basshe, Emanuel Jo, 1899-
Centuries; portrait of a tenement house;
a New playwrights theatre produc-
tion. N.Y. Macaulay. 1928. 12°. 227p.
Earth; a play in seven scenes. . . N.Y.
Macaulay. [c1927] 12°. 17-122p.
Invitation. 1 act
In One-act plays for stage and study.
ser. 4

Batchelder, Clara Burbank (Barbara Burbank, pseud.)
  Anne, of old Salem. A drama in three acts. Chicago. Dramatic pub. co. c1906. 12°. 41p.
  Symphony in black; a comedy in two acts for female characters only. . . Boston. Baker. 1901. 12°. 21p.
Bate, Richard Alexander, 1871-
  Robert Edward Lee. Boston. Stratford. 1927. 12°. 83p. Historical. 4 acts
Bates, Arlo, 1850-1918
  Yes and no. Duologue. 1 scene
    In Johnson, T. ed. More plays in miniature
Bates, Esther Willard
  Evacuation of Boston. Historical
    In Johnson, T. ed. Washington anniversary plays
  Tree of life. Easter. 1 act
    In Schauffler, R. H. and Sanford, A. P. eds. Plays for our American holidays. v. 1
Bates, Herbert
  King's English. Fantasy. 1 act
    In Goldstone, G. A. ed. One-act plays
Baum, Vicki, 1888-
  Grand Hotel; tr. by Basil Creighton. Garden City, N.Y. Doubleday. 1931. 8°. 309p. Tragi-comedy. 3 acts
    Same in Mantle, B. ed. Best plays of 1930-31 (abridged)
Baumer, Marie, 1905-
  It's an ill wind. 1 act
    In One-act plays for stage and study. ser. 5
  Jobyna steps out, a comedy in three acts. N.Y. French. c1932. 12°. 100p.
  Town. 1 act
    In Clark, B. H. and Nicholson, K. eds. American scene
Bax, Clifford, 1886-
  Apricot tree. Comedy. 1 act
    In Twelve short plays
  Aucassin and Nicolette. Romance. 1 act
    In Twelve short plays
    Marriott, J. W. ed. One-act plays of to-day. ser. 5
  Cloak. Fantasy. 1 act
    In Twelve short plays
  Immortal lady; a play in three acts. N.Y. French. [1931] 8°. 70p.
    Same in Valiant ladies
  Poetasters of Ispahan, a comedy in verse. Boston. Baker. [c1929] 12°. 39p.
    Same in Hampden, J. ed. Nine modern plays
    Twelve short plays
  Prelude and fugue. Love. 1 act
    In Twelve short plays
  Quaker's 'cello. Character. 1 act
    In Bourne, J. ed. 8 new one-act plays of 1933
  Rose and the cross. 5 pts.
    In Twelve short plays
  Rose without a thorn. N.Y. French. c1931. 8°. 67p. Historical. 3 acts
    Same in Valiant ladies
    Famous plays of 1932
    Plays of a half-decade

  Silly Willy. Marionette play. 6 scenes
    In Twelve short plays
    Hampden, J. ed. Seven modern plays for younger players
  Socrates, a play in six scenes. London. Gollancz. 1930. 12°. 135p.
    Same in Six plays
  Square pegs; a rhymed fantasy for two girls. London. Hendersons. 1920. 12°. 27p. 1 act
    Same in Twelve short plays
    Marriott, J. W. ed. One-act plays of to-day. ser. 4
  Summit. Love. 1 act
    In Twelve short plays
    Johnson, T. ed. Diminutive comedies
  Unknown hand. Satire. 1 act
    In Twelve short plays
  Venetian, a play. N.Y. Farrar. [c1931] 12°. 235p. Renaissance. 3 acts
    Same in Valiant ladies
  Volcanic island. Freudian comedy. 1 act
    In Twelve short plays
  Wandering scholar. Comedy. 1 act
    In Twelve short plays
Baxter, A.
  Brother Donald. Comedy
    In Snook, L. O. ed. Comedies seven
Beach, Lewis, 1891-
  Merry Andrew; a comedy in three acts. N.Y. French. 1930. 12°. 180p.
Beatty, Willard W. *joint author. See* Cuddy, L. A. and others
Beck, Warren
  Affairs of men. Comedy. 1 act
    In Six little theatre plays
  After all these years. Comedy. 1 act
    In Six little theatre plays
  Apostrophe in modern dress. Comedy
    In Snook, L. O. ed. Comedies seven
  Fine frenzy. Comedy. 1 act
    In Six little theatre plays
  Fixed canon. Law. 1 act
    In Six little theatre plays
  Heart too soon made glad. 1 act
    In Six little theatre plays
  It's no use to argue. Future. 1 act
    In Six little theatre plays
Beecher, Betty B.
  Inner urge. Comedy
    In Snook, L. O. ed. Comedies seven
Behrman, Samuel Nathaniel, 1893-
  Biography, a comedy. N.Y. Farrar. [c1933] 12°. 241p. 3 acts
    Same in Mantle, B. ed. Best plays of 1932-33 (abridged)
  Brief moment, a comedy in three acts. N.Y. Farrar. [c1931] 12°. 235p.
    Same in Mantle, B. ed. Best plays of 1931-32
  Meteor. N.Y. Brentano's. 1930. 12°. 178p. Egoism. 3 acts
    Same in Three plays
  Rain from heaven; a play in three acts. N.Y. Random House. 1935. 250p.
  Second man; a comedy in three acts. Garden City N.Y. Doubleday. 1927. 12°. 195p. Also N.Y. French. c1928
    Same in Three plays

Serena Blandish; or, The difficulty of getting married. Comedy. 2 acts
In Three plays

Beith, John Hay (Ian Hay, pseud.) 1876-
Blank cartridge, a farce. N.Y. French. c1928. 12°. 24p.
Happy ending; a play in three acts. N.Y. French. c1927. 8°. 83p.
Mr. Faint-heart, a romantic comedy in three acts, by Ian Hay [pseud.] N.Y. French. c1931. 8°. 67p.
Personally or by letter, a little comedy. N.Y. French. c1928. 12°. 20p. 1 act
Treasure trove, a fantasy. N.Y. French. 1928. 12°. 24p. 1 act

Beith, John Hay, 1876- and Armstrong, Anthony, 1897-
Orders are orders; a military diversion in three acts. N.Y. French. c1933. 8°. 101p.

Beith, John Hay, 1876- and Bolton, Guy Reginald
Song of six pence; a Scottish comedy. N.Y. French. c1930. 8°. 80p. 3 acts

Beith, John Hay, 1876- and King-Hall, Stephen
Midshipmaid; a naval manoeuvre in three acts. N.Y. French. c1932. 8°. 95p. Also Houghton. 1933

Beith, John Hay, 1876- and Wodehouse, Pelham Grenville, 1881-
Baa, baa, black sheep; a farcical comedy in three acts. N.Y. French. 1930. 8°. 81p.
Damsel in distress; a comedy of youth, love and adventure in three acts. N.Y. French. 1930. 8°. 89p.
Leave it to Psmith; a comedy of youth, love and misadventure, in three acts. N.Y. French. c1932. 8°. 87p.

Belasco, David, 1859-1931
Adrea. Tragedy. 5 acts
In Six plays
Darling of the gods. Japanese. 5 acts
In Six plays
Du Barry. Historical. 5 acts
In Six plays
Girl of the golden West. Melodrama. 4 acts
In Six plays
Madame Butterfly. Tragedy. Japan (From story of John Luther Long) 1 act
In Six plays
Quinn, A. H. Representative American plays
Return of Peter Grimm. Supernatural. 3 acts
In Six plays

Bell, Florence Eveleen Eleanore (Oliffe), Lady
Angela; a play in three acts. London. Benn. 1926. 12°. 101p.
Dean of St. Patrick's; a play in four acts. London. Arnold. 1903. 8°. 94p.
Heart of Yorkshire, a play in three parts and an epilogue. London. Humphreys. 1923. 12°. 75p.
Kirstin. 3 scenes
In Four short plays

Parachute. Comedy. 1 act
In Four short plays
Second-class duke. Comedy. 1 act
In Four short plays
Story of Rachel. 1 act
In Four short plays
Way the money goes, a play in three acts. London. Sidgwick. 1910. 12°. 104p.

Bell, Florence E. E. and Cecil, Arthur
Time is money; a comedy in one act. N.Y. French. 1905. 12°. 27p.

Bell, James Wallace
Symphony in illusion. 1 act
In Marriott, J. W. ed. Best one-act plays of 1932

Bell, John Joy, 1871-
Thirst. Mediaeval episode. 1 act
In Eight one-act plays

Bellamy, Frederica Lefevre
Darkness and dawn; a mystery play of Easter even. N.Y. Woman's press. [1930] 12°. 38p.
Same in Schauffler, R. H. and Sanford, A. P. eds. Plays for our American holidays. v. 1

Belser, Gertrude L.
Deliverer; a legend of Washington; a short play. Philadelphia. Hall-Mack. [c1932] 8p.

Benavente y Martínez, Jacinto, 1866-
Bonds of interest; tr. from the Spanish by John Garrett Underhill. N.Y. Scribner. 1929. 12°. 112p. Comedy. 3 acts
La malquerida. Tragedy. 3 acts
In Tucker, S. M. ed. Modern continental plays
Tucker, S. M. ed. Twenty-five modern plays
Saturday night; tr. from the Spanish with a preface by John Garrett Underhill. N.Y. Scribner. 1927. 12°. 129p. Symbolic. 5 tableaux

Benelli, Sem, 1877-
Love of the three kings. Tragic poem. 3 acts
In Dickinson, T. H. ed. Chief contemporary dramatists. ser. 3
California Univ. Chron. 25:1

Bennett, Arnold, 1867-1931
Bright island. Comedy. 3 acts
In Three plays
Cupid and commonsense. Comedy. 4 acts
In Three plays
Don Juan de Marana; a play in four acts. London. Laurie. 1923. 12°. 178p.
Flora. 3 acts
In Five three-act plays
Good woman; a farce in one act. London. Gowans. 1930. 8°. 39p.
Great adventure. Comedy. 4 acts
In Church, V. ed. Curtain!
Cordell, R. A. ed. Representative modern plays
Question of sex; a farce in one act. London. Gowans. 1930. 8°. 45p.
Sacred and profane love. Comedy. 4 acts
In Three plays

Bennett, Arnold—*Continued*
Snake charmer. 1 act
In Eight one-act plays
One-act plays for stage and study.
ser. 6
Stepmother; a farce in one act. London.
Gowans. 1929. 24°. 46p.
**Bennett, Arnold, 1867- and Knoblock,
Edward, 1874-**
Milestones; a play in three acts. London.
Methuen. [1912] 16°. 126p.
In Marriott, J. W. ed. Great modern
British plays
Pence, R. W. ed. Dramas by
present-day writers
Tucker, S. M. ed. Modern plays
Mr. Prohack; a comedy in three acts.
London. Chatto. 1927. 12°. 121p.
Also Garden City, N.Y. Doubleday.
1928
Bennett, Charles
"Return", a play in a prologue and
three acts. London. Benn. 1928. 12°.
115p.
Bennett, Mabel Keightley
My Dixie Rose; a comedy drama in three
acts. Chicago. Denison. 1927. 12°.
96p.
Bennison, Louis
"Johnny get your gun"; a comedy in
prologue and three acts. . . N.Y.
French. c1927. 12°. 112p.
**Benrimo, Joseph Henry, 1871- and Rhodes,
Harrison, Garfield, 1871-**
Willow tree, a Japanese fantasy in three
acts. . . N.Y. French. c1931. 12°.
91p.
Benton, Rita, 1881-
Carrots may be golden; a play; with
preface by Mrs. A. S. Best. N.Y.
Longmans. 1932. 68p.
**Beresford, Hugh and Seale, C. S. St.
Brelade**
Second guest. Fear. 1 act
In Eight one-act plays
Berkeley, Reginald Cheyne, 1890-
Dweller in the darkness, a play of the
unknown, in one act. Boston. Baker.
[Anthology of one-act plays] 1926.
12°. 4p.
Same in Phillips, Le R. & Johnson, T.
Types of modern dramatic
composition
Lady with a lamp. London. Gollancz.
1929. 12°. 136p. Also French
Same in Famous plays of today
Plays of a half-decade
White chateau. London. Williams. 1925.
12°. 79p. 6 scenes
In Marriott, J. W. ed. Great modern
British plays
Berkowitz, I. D.
Landsleit. 1 act
In White, I. D. trans. Nine one-act
plays from the Yiddish
Berman, Henry
Age of discretion. 1 act
In Life demands! and other plays
Law of compensation. 1 act
In Life demands! and other plays

Life demands! 4 acts
In Life demands! and other plays
Out of the dark. 1 act
In Life demands! and other plays
Time's fool. 1 act
In Life demands! and other plays
Vestiges. 1 act
In Life demands! and other plays
Bernard, Jean Jacques, 1888-
Glamour. 3 acts
In Katzin, W. ed. Eight European
plays
Martine, a play in five scenes. Boston.
Baker. [c1932] 8°. 57p. Genre
Same in Katzin, W. ed. Eight Euro-
pean plays
Poet's secret. (Le secret D'Arvers) Ro-
mantic. 1 act
In Vernon, V. and F. eds. Modern
one-act plays from the French
Unquiet spirit; a play in three acts;
tr. by J. L. Frith. Boston. Baker.
1932. 8°. 55p.
Bernard, Tristan, 1866-
Free treat. (Franches lippées) Comedy.
1 act
In Vernon, V. and F. eds. Modern
one-act plays from the French
French without a master; a farce in one
act; tr. by Barrett H. Clark. N.Y.
French. [c1915] 12°. 20p.
I'm going! a comedy in one act; tr. by
Barrett H. Clark. N.Y. French. c1915.
12°. 12p.
Besier, Rudolf, 1878-
Barretts of Wimpole street; a comedy in
five acts. Boston. Little. 1930. 8°.
165p. Historical
Same in Famous plays of 1931
Mantle, B. ed. Best plays of
1930-31 (abridged)
Plays of a half-decade
Virgin goddess. Tragedy. 1 act
In Marriott, J. W. ed. Great modern
British plays
**Besier, Rudolf, 1878- and Edginton, May
(Helen Marion) 1883-**
Secrets, a play in a prologue, three acts
and an epilogue. N.Y. French. c1930.
8°. 84p.
Biddle, (Frederick) Arnold
Lord of life. Parish play
In Two plays
Verdict of the people. Parish play
In Two plays
Bimko, Felix, 1890-
Liars! Comedy. 1 act
In Block, E. ed. One-act plays from
the Yiddish. ser. 2
Binyon, [Robert] Lawrence, 1869-
Boadicea, a play in eight scenes. London.
Benn. 1927. 12°. 71p.
Godstow nunnery. 1 act
In Three short plays
Love in the desert. 1 act
In Three short plays
Memnon. 1 act
In Three short plays

Paris and Œnone; [a tragedy in one act].
London. Constable. 1906. 12°. 23p.
Same in Modern short plays. ser. 1
Sophro the wise; a play for children. . .
London. Benn. [1927] 8°. 63p.

Björnson, Bjornstjerne, 1832-1910
Beyond our power. Problem. 2 acts
In Tucker, S. M. ed. Modern continental plays

Blackmore, Madeline
"I'm over forty," a comedy in one act.
N.Y. French. c1933. 12°. 18p.
To die with a smile. 1 act
In Nicholson, K. ed. Hollywood plays

Blair, Philip
Drumgarth; a play in one act. London.
Allen. [1931] 12°. 32p.

Blair, Wilfrid
Consarning Sairey 'Uggins, a one-act
farce. N.Y. French. [c1914] 12°. 19p.
Death of Shakespeare; a chronicle play in
two scenes. Oxford. Blackwell. 1916.
8°. 24p.

Bland, Margaret
Pink and patches; a play in one act. N.Y.
French. 1928. 12°. 24p.

Bland, Margaret and Duls, Louisa
Lighted candles, a tragedy of the Carolina highlands. 1 act
In Koch, F. H. ed. Carolina folkplays. ser. 3

Blaney, Charles E. *joint author. See*
Spooner, Cecil and Blaney, Charles E.

Bloch, Bertram
Gas, air, and earl. Comedy. 1 act
In Nicholson, Kenyon, ed. Appleton
book of short plays. ser. 2
Morals and circumstance; a one act play
In Smart Set 58:87

Blom, Eric, 1888-
Trouble factory, a tragi-comedy in four
acts. London. Benn. 1928. 12°. 101p.

Boatright, Mody Coggin, 1896-
Age of accountability; a tragedy in one
act
In Poet Lore 40:295
C. C.; a tragedy in one act
In Poet Lore 41:124

Boker, George Henry, 1823-1890
Nydia; a tragic play; ed. by E. S. Bradley. Press of Univ. of Penn. 1929.
12°. 102p. Pompeii. 5 acts

Bolitho, William, 1890-1930
Overture—1920, a play, foreword by
Gabriel Beer-Hofmann. N.Y. Simon.
1931. 8°. 136p. Labor. 3 acts
Same in Mantle, B. ed. Best plays of
1930-31 (abridged)

Bolton, Guy, *joint author. See* Marcin,
Max and Bolton, Guy

Bolton, Ivy
King of Sherwood. April Fool. 1 act
In Schauffler, R. H. and Sanford, A. P.
eds. Plays for our American
holidays. v. 2

Bomstead, Beulah
Diabolical circle. Cotton Mather. 1 act
In Goldstone, G. A. ed. One-act plays

Bond, Frank Fraser
Woolly lamb of God, a play in one act.
N.Y. French. c1932. 12°. 27p.

Bonneschky, Guido
Dr. Faust. Puppet. 4 acts
In McPharlin, P. ed. Repertory of
marionette plays

Booth, Hilliard
Forget-me-knots; a farce in three acts.
N.Y. French. 1927. 12°. 56p.
Her radio Romeo; a comedy in two acts.
N.Y. French. c1927. 12°. 35p.
His majesty, the queen; a comedy in two
acts. N.Y. French. 1927. 12°.
Letters; a comedy in three acts. N.Y.
French. 1928. 12°. 61p.
Nine points of the law; a farce in three
acts. N.Y. French. c1928. 12°. 73p.
Rookie and the rules; a comedy in one
act. N.Y. French. 1929. 12°. 20p.
Sally's ship comes in; a comedy in three
acts. N.Y. French. c1927. 12°. 75p.
White carnations; a comedy in three
acts. N.Y. French. c1927. 12°. 67p.

Bordeaux, Henry, 1870-
Shattered. (L'écran brisé) Intrigue. 1
act
In Vernon, V. and F. eds. Modern
one-act plays from the French

Borsook, H.
Three weddings of a hunchback. Comedy.
1 act
In Massey, V. ed. Canadian plays from
Hart House theatre. v. 1

Bottomley, Gordon, 1874-
Acts of Saint Peter, a cathedral festival
play. London. Constable. 1933. 12°.
85p.
Ardvorlich's wife. Historical. 1 act
In Scenes and plays
Bower of Wandel. 1 act
In Lyric plays
Crier by night, a play in one act. Tragedy
In Bibelot 15:297
Culbin sands. 1 act
In Lyric plays
Kirkconnel lea. 1 act
In Lyric plays
Marsaili's weeping. 1 act
In Lyric plays
Merlin's grave. Legendary. 1 act
In Scenes and plays
Parting. 1 scene
In Scenes and plays
Return. 1 act
In A parting and The Return
Scenes and plays
Singing sands. Historical. 1 act
In Scenes and plays
Sisters. 1 scene
In Scenes and plays
Suilven and the eagle. 1 act
In Lyric plays
Towie castle. Historical. 1 act
In Scenes and plays
Widow. Biblical. 1 scene
In Scenes and plays
Woman from the voe
In Lyric plays

Bouchor, Maurice, 1855-
Noël, or The mystery of the nativity.
4 scenes
In McPharlin, P. ed.   Repertory of
marionette plays
Bouchor, Maurice. *See also* Harper, H.
Christmas tale
Boulton, E. *joint author. See* Jennings,
Gertrude E. and Boulton, E.
Bourdet, Édouard
Sex fable, a play. . . English text by
Jane Hinton. N.Y. Brentano's. 1931.
12°. 188p.
Bourne, John
Black night. 1 act
In Bourne, J. ed. 8 new one-act plays
for 1933
Down the Crocus tunnel
In Bourne, J. ed. Eight new plays for
boys and girls
Puck's good deed for the day; or, Shake-
speare is so modern! Romantic. 1
act
In 8 new one-act plays of 1933
Second visit. Supernatural. 1 act
In Marriott, J. W. ed. Best one-act
plays of 1932
Bowie, Walter Russell, 1882-
Christmas pageant of the Holy Grail.
Religious. 1 act
In Eastman, F. ed. Modern religious
dramas
Box, Sydney
Fantastic flight. 1 act
In Bourne, J. ed. 8 new one-act plays
for 1934
Murder trial. 1 act
In Eight one-act plays
Symphonie pathétique. Music. 1 act
In Bourne, J. ed. 8 new one-act plays
of 1933
Boxer, Cecile F.
Call; a play in one act. N.Y. French.
c1929. 18°. 20p.
Boyce, Keith, pseud. (Mrs. Hutchins Hap-
good) 1872-
Winter's night. Character. 1 act
In Shay, F. ed. Fifty more contempor-
ary one-act plays
Bracco, Roberto, 1862-
Phantasms. Pathological. 4 acts
In Tucker, S. M. ed. Modern con-
tinental plays
Bradford, Roark
How come Christmas, a modern morality.
1 act
In Harper's M 162:45
Branch, Anna Hempstead
St. Francis and the wolf. St. Francis.
1 act
In Schauffler, R. H. and Sanford, A. B.
eds. Plays for our American holi-
days. v. 4
Shoes that danced. Fantasy. 1 act
In Webber, J. P. and Webster, H. H.
eds. One-act plays for secondary
schools
Brandane, John, pseud. *See* MacIntyre,
John

**Brandon-Thomas, Jevan, and Barrett, Frank
Wilson**
Patchwork, a play in one act. N.Y.
French. c1927. 12°. 20p.
Braun, Wilbur
Greatest good (for the greatest number);
a comedy in three acts. N.Y. French.
c1933. 12°. 125p.
Brentano, Lowell, *joint author. See* Oursler,
Fulton and Brentano, L.
Bridie, James, pseud. *See* Mavor, Osborne
Henry
Brieux, Eugène, 1858-1932
Because I love you. Jealousy. 1 act
In Vernon, V. and F. eds. Modern
one-act plays from the French
Damaged goods. . . a play in three acts.
tr. by John Pollock, with a preface
by G. Bernard Shaw. N.Y. Bren-
tano's. 1912. 12°. 80p. Heredity
False gods. Superstition. 5 acts
In Tucker, S. M. ed. Modern conti-
nental plays
Brighouse, Harold, 1882-
Bit of war; a play in one act. N.Y.
French. 1933. 18p.
Coincidence; comedy in three acts. N.Y.
French. 1929. 12°. 102p.
Cupid and Psyche. Fantasy. 1 act
In Six fantasies
Dealing in futures, a play in three acts.
N.Y. French. c1913. 12°. 87p.
Doorway; a play in one act. London.
Williams. [19—?] 12°. 16p.
Exiled princess. Fantasy. 1 act
In Six fantasies
Followers. Comedy. 1 act
In Webber, J. P. and Webster, H. H.
eds. One-act plays for secondary
schools
Fossie for short; a comedy in one act.
N.Y. French. c1927. 12°. 35p.
Ghost in the garden. Fantasy. 1 act
In Six fantasies
Ghost of Windsor Park. Fantasy. 1 act
In Six fantasies
One-act plays for stage and study.
ser. 3
Graft, a comedy in four acts.   N.Y.
French. c1913. 12°. 91p.
Hobson's choice. Lancashire comedy.
4 acts
In Marriott, J. W. ed. Great modern
British plays
Tucker, S. M. ed. Modern Ameri-
can and British plays
How the weather is made. Fantasy.
1 act
In Marriott, J. W. ed. One-act plays
of to-day. ser. 3
Little liberty; a comedy in one act. N.Y.
French. c1927. 12°. 20p.
Maid of France. Joan of Arc. 1 act
In Cohen, H. L. ed. One-act plays
by modern authors. 1934 edition
Schauffler, R. H. and Sanford, A.
P. eds. Plays for our American
holidays. v. 1
Night of "Mr. H"; a Charles Lamb
pastiche. N.Y. French. c1927. 12°.
22p.

Oak settle. Comedy. 1 act
In Modern short plays. ser. 3
Oracles of Apollo. Fantasy. 1 act
In Six fantasies
Price of coal. Lancashire. 1 act
In Hampden, J. ed. Nine modern
plays
Prince who was a piper. Comedy. 1 act
In Marriott, J. W. ed. One-act plays
of to-day. ser. 4
Romany road. Fantasy. 1 act
In Six fantasies
Marriot, J. W. ed. Best one-act
plays of 1932
Safe amongst the pigs, a comedy in three
acts. N. Y. French. c1930. 8°. 60p.
Smoke-screens, a comedy in one act.
N.Y. French. c1932. 12°. 25p.
Same in Marriott, J. W. ed. Best one-
act plays of 1931
Sort-of-a-prince, comedy in three acts.
N.Y. French. c1929. 8°. 98p.
Stoker; a play in one act. N.Y. French.
1929. 12°. 20p. Mutiny
Same in Marriott, J. W. ed One-act
plays of to-day. ser. 5
One-act plays for stage and
study. ser. 5
What's bred in the bone; a comedy in
three acts. N.Y. French. c1928. 8°.
64p.
When did they meet again? a play in
one act. N.Y. French. ₁c1927₁ 12°.
25p.
Wish shop. Fantasy. 1 act
In Hampden, J. ed. Four new plays
for women and girls
New plays for women and girls
Witch's daughter. 1 act
In One-act plays for stage and study.
ser. 4

Brighouse, Harold and Walton, John
(Olive Conway, pseud.)
King's waistcoat, a play in one act. N.Y.
French. 1926. 12°. 121-137p.
Mimi. 1 act
In Marriott, J. W. ed. One-act plays
of to-day. ser. 3
Starlight widow, a comedy in three acts.
N.Y. French. c1929. 12°. 86p.
Wireless can't lie. 1 act
In Marriott, J. W. ed. Best one-act
plays of 1932
Women do things like that. Love. 1 act
In Marriot, J. W. ed. Best one-act
plays of 1931

Britton, Kenneth Phillips and Hargrave,
Roy
Houseparty, a play in three acts. N.Y.
French. 1930. 12°. 218p.

Britton, Lionel, 1887-
Brain; a play of the whole earth. N.Y.
Putnam. ₁1930₁ 12°. 129p. 3 acts
Spacetime inn. N.Y. Putnam. ₁1932₁ 12°.
103p. 3 acts

Brody, Alter, 1895-
House of mourning. Folk-play. 1 act
In Lamentations
Lowing in the night. Folk-play. 1 act
In Lamentations

Rapunzel. Folk-play. 1 act
In Lamentations
Isaacs, E. J. ed. Plays of American
life and fantasy
Theatre Arts M 9:257
Recess for memorials. Folk-play. 1 act
In Lamentations

Brooks, Charles Stephen, 1878-
I was talking across the fence this morn-
ing. Comedy. 1 act
In Tragedy of Josephine, and other
one-act plays
Land of nod, an operetta. 1 act
In Moses, M. J. ed. Ring up the cur-
tain!
Man from the dark. Comedy. 1 act
In Tragedy of Josephine, and other
one-act plays
Man who was afraid to die. Comedy.
1 act
In Tragedy of Josephine, and other
one-act plays
Old trouper. Comedy. 1 act
In Tragedy of Josephine, and other
one-act play
Cohen, H. L. ed. One-act plays by
modern authors. 1934 edition
Pine hill. Comedy. 1 act
In Tragedy of Josephine, and other one-
act plays
Please stir the fire, James. Comedy.
1 act
In Tragedy of Josephine, and other
one-act plays
Romance after midnight. Comedy. 1 act
In Tragedy of Josephine, and other
one-act plays
Tea with a wicked lady. Comedy. 1 act
In Tragedy of Josephine, and other
one-act plays
Tragedy of Josephine. Comedy. 1 act
In Tragedy of Josephine, and other
one-act plays

Brooks, George Sprague, 1895-
Fortinbras in plain clothes, a sequel to
Hamlet in modern dress. Comedy.
1 act
In One-act plays for stage and study.
ser. 4
Luca Sarto [a romantic play in four
acts]. N.Y. Harcourt. ₁c1922-24₁ 8°.
186p.
No cause for complaint. Law. 1 act
In Clark, B. H. and Nicholson, K. eds.
American scene

Brooks, George S. and Lister, Walter B.
Spread eagle; a drama and a fiction for
patriots; with a foreword by John
Anderson. N.Y. Scribner. 1927. 12°.
149p.

Broome, Dora M.
Moon. Lancashire. 1 act
In Marriott, J. W. ed. Best one-act
plays of 1932

Brosnan, Alma
At number fifteen; a domestic drama in
three acts. London. Sidgwick. ₁1927₁
12°. 86p.

Brown, Abbie Farwell, 1857-1927
Lantern. Revolution. 2 acts
  In Lantern, and other plays for children
Little shadows. Christmas. 1 act
  In Lantern, and other plays for children
"Quits," a comedy in one act. Boston. Baker. [c1896] 12°. 21p.
Rhoecus. Masque. 1 act
  In Lantern, and other plays for children
Wishing moon. Fantasy. 1 act
  In Lantern, and other plays for children

Brown, C. S.
Modern magi. Religious. 1 act
  In Eastman, F. ed. Modern religious dramas

Brown, Curtis, 1866-
Mrs. Hazenby's health, a play in one act. N.Y. French. c1912. 8°. 15p.

Broun, Heywood Campbell, 1888-
Death says it isn't so. Satire. 1 act
  In Shay, F. ed. Fifty more contemporary one-act plays

Brown, Laurence Oliver (Laurence Oliver, pseud.)
Blind; a play in three acts. N.Y. Harper. 1928. 12°. 130p. Symbolic

Browne, Maurice, *joint author.* See Nichols, Robert and Browne, Maurice

Brownell, John Charles
Gentle rogue, a comedy in three acts. N.Y. French. c1933. 12°. 103p.
Nut farm, a comedy in three acts. N.Y. French. c1930. 12°. 108p.

Bruce, Richard
Sahdji, an African ballet. Negro. 1 act.
  In Locke, A. LeR. and Gregory, M. eds. Plays of Negro life

Bruckner, Ferdinand
Races. tr. from the German . . . by Ruth Langner. N.Y. Knopf. 1934. 12°. 139p. Jews in Germany. 3 acts

Brunton, F. Carmichael
Blind man's bluff. 1 act
  In Eight one-act plays

Brush, Dorothy Hamilton
One-Eye, Two-Eye and Three-Eye, a puppet play for children in three acts. N.Y. French. [c1929] 12°. 26p.
Poor little turkey girl, a play of Pueblo Indian folk-lore. N.Y. French. [c1928] 12°. 59p.

Büchner, Georg, 1813-1837
Danton's death. Historical. 3 acts
  In Plays of Georg Büchner
Leonce and Lena. Comedy. 3 acts
  In Plays of Georg Büchner
    New Europe 13:246
Wozzeck, a fragment. 27 scenes
  In Plays of Georg Büchner

Buckley, Donald
Night in June; a play in three acts. London. Benn. 1929. 12°. 75p.

Bufano, Remo
Orlando Furioso. Marionette. 1 act
  In Shay, F. ed. Fifty more contemporary one-act plays

Burbank, Barbara, pseud. *See* Batchelder, Clara Burbank

Burgess, Katharine Stanbery
God winks; a comedy in one act. Summit, N.J. Swartout. 12°. 31p.
  Same in Schauffler, R. H. and Sanford, A. P. eds. Plays for our American holidays. v. 3. Twelve one-act plays

Burke, Edwin
This thing called love, a comedy in three acts. N.Y. French. c1929. 12°. 104p. Copyrighted in 1928 under title Bed and bored

Burke, Edwin, *joint author.* See Arnold, J. and Burke, E.

Burke, Inez
Two races. Negro pageant. 1 act
  In Richardson, N. ed. Plays and pageants from the life of the Negro

Burnet, Dana, 1888-
Angel food; a comedy in three acts. Philadelphia. Penn. 1927. 12°. 101p.
Boundary line, a drama in three acts. N.Y. Longmans. 1931. 12°. 118p.
Rain, a play in one act. Boston. Baker. [c1926] 12°. 35p. Suicide

Burnet, Dana and Abbott, George
Four walls; a play in three acts. . . Rewritten and revised 1927 (under title The prisoner). French. N.Y. 1928. 12°. 109p.

Burnett, Mrs. Frances (Hodgson) 1849-1924
Racketty-packetty house; a play in prologue and three acts. N.Y. French. c1927. 12°. 65p.

Burrill, Bertha Y.
Rich man, poor man; a farce in one act. N.Y. French. c1927. 12°. 35p.

Burrows, Edith Maie, 1887-
Garden Cinderella. May day. 2 acts
  In Schauffler, R. H. and Sanford, A. P. eds. Plays for our American holidays. v. 2

Burt, Olive F. Woolley
Midsummer night
  In Dickon goes to the fair, and other plays

Butler, Rachel Barton
Prudence in particular; a comedy in three acts. N.Y. French. c1928. 12°. 94p.
West of Omaha; a farce in one act. Boston. Baker. c1909. 12°. 30p.

Byron-Webber, Ronald
100—not out. Comedy. 1 act
  In Eight one-act plays

Cabell, James Branch, 1879-
Jewel merchants. Comedy. 1 act
  In Golden Bk 12:88 S '30

Caldwell, Erskine. *See* Kirkland, John. Tobacco road

Callaway, Emilie H.
Miss Oliver's dollars, a farce in one act. Boston. Baker. [c1908] 18p.
Return of Deborah; a farce in two acts. N.Y. French. c1907. 12°. 23p.
Widow's wiles: a comedy in three acts. N.Y. Dick. c1908. 12°. 34p.

Cameron, Margaret (Mrs. H. C. Lewis)
1867-
Christmas chime, a play in one act. N.Y.
French. c1910. 22p.
Kleptomaniac, a comedy in one act. N.Y.
French. 1903. 12°. 27p.
Loyal renegade, a comedy in one act.
Oakland, Cal. Enquirer pub. co. 1900.
8°. 7p.
One of those days, a play in one act.
N.Y. French. [c1931] 12°. 48p.
Same in New plays for women and
girls

Campbell, Lawton
Girl who slipped. Comedy. 1 act
In Drama 17:203
Shakespeare smiles; a comedy in one act.
N.Y. Appleton. 1924. 12°. 17p.
Solid South, a play in three acts. N.Y.
French. [c1931] 12°. 102p.

Campion, Cyril, 1894-
Absent-minded lady
In Campion, C. et al. Stage door; ten
sketches for revue
Editorial error
In Campion, C. et al. Stage door; ten
sketches for revue
Level crossing
In Campion, C. et al. Stage door; ten
sketches for revue
Oh! Mathilda!
In Campion, C. et al. Stage door; ten
sketches for revue
Reformation
In Campion, C. et al. Stage door; ten
sketches for revue

Campion, Cyril and Dignon, Edward
Ask Beccles; a crook play in three acts.
N.Y. French. 1927. 12°. 75p.

Canfield, Dorothy. *See* Fisher, Dorothea
Frances Canfield

Canfield, Mary Cass
Duchess says her prayers. Historical.
1 act
In Shay, F. ed. Fifty more contemporary one-act plays

Cannelin, Maurice
Stardust children; a sketch in one act
In Players M 8:Ja.-F. '21

Cantillon, Arthur
Pierrot before the seven doors; a play
in one act. London. Gowans. 1930.
12°. 38p.
In Phillips, Le R. and Johnson, T. eds.
Types of modern dramatic composition

Čapek, Josef, 1887- **and Čapek, Karel M.**
1890-
Adam the creator, a comedy in six scenes
and an epilogue. tr. by Dora Round.
N.Y. R.R. Smith. 1930. 12°. 187p.
Same in Moses, M. J. ed. Dramas of
modernism and their fore-
runners
And so ad infinitum. *See* Čapek, K. and
J. World we live in

World we live in (And so ad infinitum;
an insect comedy); a play in three
acts with prologue and epilogue. N.Y.
French. c1922. 12°. 102p.
Same in Chandler, F. W. and Cordell,
R. A. eds. Twentieth cen-
tury plays

Čapek, Karel M. 1890-
R. U. R. [Rossum's universal robots].
Fantastic melodrama. 4 acts
In Dickinson, T. H. ed. Chief con-
temporary dramatists. ser. 3
McDermott, J. F. ed. Modern
plays
Tucker, S. M. ed. Modern con-
tinental plays
Tucker, S. M. ed. Twenty-five
modern plays
Watson, E. B. and Pressey, B. eds.
Contemporary drama. European
plays
Solstice
In Poet Lore 35:475

Carb, David, 1885-
Samson à la mode. Comedy. 1 act
In Nicholson, Kenyon, ed. Appleton
book of short plays. ser. 2

Carb, David, *joint author. See* Delano,
Edith Bernard and Carb, David

Carpenter, Edward Childs, 1872-
Bachelor father; a comedy in three acts.
N.Y. French. [1932] 12°. 144p.
Dumb as a fox; a comedy in four acts.
N.Y. French. c1928. 12°. 117p. (Copy-
right 1916 under title "Jack in the
box.")
Leopard lady; a play in three acts. N.Y.
French. c1928. 12°. 105p.
Pipes of Pan; or The call of spring. N.Y.
French. c1926. 12°. 110p.
Romeo—and Jane; a comedy in four acts.
N.Y. French. c1927. 12°. 94p.
Tongues of men, a comedy in three acts.
N.Y. French. c1913. 12°. 102p.
When your ship comes in; a play in four
acts. N.Y. French. c1927. 12°. 106p.

Carrington, Elaine Sterne
Five minutes from the station. Comedy.
1 act
In Hughes, G. ed. Short plays for
modern players
Good provider; a comedy in one act.
N.Y. Appleton. 1928. 12°. 19p.

Carroll, Philip Henry
Jane McCrae; a tragedy in five acts.
Albany, N.Y. Fort Orange press.
1921. 124p.

Carter, Margaret
Pedro the toreador
In Burne, J. ed. Eight new plays for
boys and girls

Carton, R. C. pseud. *See* Critchett, Richard
Claude

Carver, Ada Jack
Cajun; a drama in one act. N.Y. French.
c1926. 12°. 22p.
Same in Clark, B. H. and Nicholson, K.
eds. American scene

Cavanah, Frances
Glorious wish
In Johnson, T. ed. Plays about George
Washington

Chandler, William
Thirteen eighty one. An English tragedy.
[London. Stylus press. 1927] 8°. 80p.
Tyler's insurrection 1381

Chantel, Lucien
Who killed me? (Qui m'a tué?) Psychological. 1 act
In Vernon, V. and F. eds. Modern
one-act plays from the French

Chapin, Harold, 1886-1915
Augustus in search of a father. Comedy.
1 act
In Webber, J. P. and Webster, H. H.
eds. Typical plays for secondary
schools
Autocrat of the coffee-stall. 1 act
In Isaacs, E. J. ed. Plays of American
life and fantasy
Dropping the baby; a fable in one act.
London. Gowans. 1927. 16°. 36p.
Dumb and the blind. Comedy. 1 act
In Marriott, J. W. ed. One-act plays
of to-day. ser. 3
New morality. Comedy. 3 acts
In Marriott, J. W. ed. Great modern
British plays
Philosopher of Butterbiggins. Comedy.
1 act
In Hampden, J. ed. Nine modern plays
Golden Bk 9:87 Ja '29

Chekhov, Anton Pavlovich, 1860-1904
Anniversary. Comedy. 1 act
In Plays of Anton Tchekhov (Modern
lib. ed.)
Boor. Comedy. 1 act
In Goldstone, G. A. ed. One-act plays
Cherry orchard. Comedy. 4 acts
In Plays of Anton Tchekov (Modern
lib. ed.)
Moses, M. J. ed. Dramas of mod-
ernism and their forerunners
Steeves, H. R. ed. Plays from the
modern theatre
Tucker, S. M. ed. Modern conti-
nental plays
Tucker, S. M. ed. Twenty-five mod-
ern plays
Watson, E. B. and Pressey, B. eds.
Contemporary drama: European
plays
Whitman, C. H. ed. Seven contem-
porary plays
On the high road. (On the highway)
Character. 1 act
In Plays of Anton Tchekhov (Modern
lib. ed.)
Proposal. Comedy. 1 act
In Cohen, H. L. ed. One-act plays by
modern authors. 1928 edition
Sea-gull. Character. 4 acts
In Plays of Anton Tchekhov (Modern
lib. ed.)
That worthless fellow Platinov. Trans-
lated from the Russian by John
Cournos. N.Y. Dutton. 1930. 12°.
279p. Russian life. 4 acts

Three sisters. Russian life. 4 acts
In Plays of Anton Tchekhov (Modern
lib. ed.)
Le Gallienne, E. ed. Eva Le-
Gallienne's Civic repertory plays
Tobacco evil. 1 act
In Theatre Arts M 7:77 Ja '34
Uncle Vanya. Russian life. 4 acts
In Plays of Anton Tchekhov (Modern
lib. ed.)
Wedding. Comedy. 1 act
In Plays of Anton Tchekhov (Modern
lib. ed.)

Chen-Chin Hsuing
Thrice promised bride. Folk-tale. 1 act.
In Goldstone, G. A. ed. One-act plays
Webber, J. P. and Webster, H. H.
eds. Typical plays for secondary
schools

**Chesterton, Ada E. (Jones) (Mrs. Cecil
Chesterton) and Neale, Ralph**
Love game, a comedy in three acts.
London. Benn. 1929. 12°. 108p.
Man who was Thursday; adapted from
the novel of G. K. Chesterton. Lon-
don. Benn. 1926. 12°. 100p.

Chesterton, Gilbert Keith, 1874-
Judgment of Dr. Johnson; a comedy in
three acts. London. Sheed. [1927]
12°. 91p.

Chetham-Strode, Warren
Sometimes even now; a play in three
acts. London. Gollancz. 1933. 12°.
96p.
Same in Famous plays of 1933

Chlumberg, Hans, d. 1930
Miracle at Verdun; tr. from the German
by Julian Leigh. N.Y. Brentano's.
1931. 12°. 161p. 8 scenes
Same in Chandler, F. W. and Cordell,
R. A. eds. Twentieth cen-
tury plays
Famous plays of 1932-33

Church, Virginia
What men live by. Religious. [Drama-
tization of Tolstoi's novel]. 1 act
In Church, V. W. ed. Curtain!
Eastman, F. ed. Modern religious
dramas

Churchill, Winston, 1871-
Crisis; a play in four acts . . . a dramatization of the novel of the same
name. N.Y. French. c1927. 12°. 96p.

Clark, J. Audrey
Quarry. Comedy. 1 act
In Clark, B. H. and Nicholson, K. eds.
American scene

Clarke, Austin, 1896-
Flame; a play in one act. London. Allen. [1930] 12°. 38p.
Son of learning, a poetic comedy in
three acts. London. Allen & Unwin.
[1927] 12°. 68p.

Clarke, Benaiah Franklin
Bless his little heart; a farcical comedy
in three acts. N.Y. French. 1927.
12°. 71p.

Claudel, Paul, 1868-
Book of Christopher Columbus; a lyrical drama in two parts, decorations by Jean Charlot. New Haven. Yale press. 1930. 4°. 57p.
Satin slipper; or, The worst is not the surest. tr. by Rev. Fr. John O'Connor with the collaboration of the author. London. Sheed. 1931. 8°. 310p. Divine purpose. 4 pts.
Tidings brought to Mary. Mystery. 4 acts
In Tucker, S. M. ed. Modern continental plays

Clemens, LeRoy, *joint author. See* Hymer, John B. and Clemens, LeRoy

Clements, Colin Campbell, 1894-
Across the border. Character. 1 act
In Clark, B. H. and Nicholson, K. eds. American scene
Shay, F. ed. Fifty more contemporary one-act plays
Boy through the window; a comedy in three acts. N.Y. French. 1928. 12°. 86p.
Curtain! A comedy in one act. N.Y. French. 1925. 12°. 24p.
Just women. A comedy in one act. N.Y. French. 1919. 12°. 26p.
Mister Punch. 1 act
In Sanford, A. P. ed. Plays for graduation days
Pirates. A comedy in one act. N.Y. French. 1922. 12°. 26p.
Siege. 1 act
In Sanford, A. P. ed. One-act plays for women
Spring! Comedy. 1 scene
In Johnson, T. ed. More plays in miniature
Touchstone. A play in one act for boys. N.Y. French. 1923. 12°. 16p.
Two plum puddings; a pantomime for holidays and any day. Chicago. Old Tower press. [c1924] 12°. 15p.
Same in Schauffler, R. H. and Sanford, A. P. eds. Plays for our American holidays. v. 1

Clements, Colin, 1894- **and Saunders, J. M.** 1897-
Love in a French kitchen. Mediaeval farce. 1 act
In One-act plays for stage and study. ser. 4

Clough, Grace Evelyn, 1876-
Santa Claus on trial. 1 act
In Curtis, A. ed. Christmas plays for one and all

Coates, Dorothy
In our stars. Character. 1 act
In Bourne, J. ed. 8 new one-act plays of 1933
Lonely of heart. 1 act
In Bourne, J. ed. 8 new one-act plays for 1934

Cobb, Mrs. G. H.
Just advertise. 1 scene
In Johnson, T. ed. More plays in miniature

Cocteau, Jean, 1891-
Orphée; a tragedy in one act and an interval. tr. by C. Wildman. N.Y. Oxford univ. press. 1933. 54p.

Coffin, Gertrude Wilson
Magnolia man; a mountain comedy. 1 act
In Koch, F. H. ed. Carolina folk comedies
Shotgun splicin', a mountain comedy. 1 act
In Koch, F. H. ed. Carolina folk-plays. ser. 3

Cohan, George Michael, 1878-
Baby cyclone; a new farce in three acts. N.Y. French. c1929. 12°. 125p.
Pigeons and people
In Mantle, B. ed. Best plays of 1932-33 (abridged)
Prince there was; a comedy in three acts, from Darragh Aldrich's story, "Enchanted hearts." N.Y. French. c1927. 12°. 100p.
Seven keys to Baldpate. Farce
In Mantle, B. and Sherman, G. P. eds. Best plays of 1909-19
Tavern, a play in two acts. N.Y. French. c1918. 12°. 100p. Comedy

Cohen, Bella and Spewack, Samuel, 1899-
Poppa; a comedy in three acts. N.Y. French. c1929. 12°. 107p.

Cohen, Lester
Oscar Wilde; a play. N.Y. Boni & Liveright. 1928. 12°. 179p. Historical. 3 acts

Cohen, Octavus Roy, 1891-
Come seven; a Negro farce-comedy in three acts. N.Y. Longmans. 1927. 12°. 108p.
Melancholy dame. Comedy. 1 act
In Nicholson, Kenyon, ed. Appleton book of short plays. ser. 2

Cohn, A. A.
Semper fidelis. Triangle. 1 act
In Nicholson, K. ed. Hollywood plays

Colby, Gretchen
First Easter bunny. Easter. 1 act
In Schauffler, R. H. and Sanford, A. P. eds. Plays for our American holidays. v. 1

Coleby, Wilfred T.
Truants, a comedy in three acts. N.Y. French. c1913. 12°. 99p.

Collins, Sewell, 1876-
Anne, one hundred per cent; a story in four acts—founded on a short story by Edward Franklin [pseud.] entitled "Rescuing Anne" in *Munsey's Magazine.* N.Y. French. c1927. 12°. 113p. Comedy

Collins, Sewell, *joint author. See* Davis, Owen and Collins, Sewell

Collison, Wilson, 1893-
Farewell to women, a comedy about sex. N.Y. McBride. 1932. 12°. 258p.

Corrie, Joe
Hoose o' the hill. 1 act
In Marriott, J. W. ed. Best one-act
plays of 1931
Coulus, Romain, 1866-
Love and learning. (Les jeux de l'amour)
Comedy. 1 act
In Vernon, V. and F. eds. Modern
one-act plays from the French
Cournos, John, 1881-
O'Flaherty the great; a tragi-comedy.
N.Y. Knopf. 1927. 12°. 335p.
**Courteline, Georges, pseud. (Moinaux,
Georges)** 1860-
Peace at home. (Le paix chez soi) Do-
mestic. 1 act
In Vernon, V. and F. eds. Modern
one-act plays from the French
Cowan, John B. 1882-
Canuck. Vancouver, B.C. Rose, Cowan
and Latta. 1931. 12°. 149p.
Cowan, Sada
Ball and chain; a play in one act. N.Y.
French. 1930. 12°. 36p.
In the morgue; a play in one act. N.Y.
French. 1930. 12°. 13p.
Same in Forum 55:399
Sintram of Skagerrak; a play in one act.
N.Y. French. 1930. 12°. 14p.
Coward, Noel Pierce, 1899-
Bittersweet; a musical play in three acts.
N.Y. French. 1933. 12°. 67p.
Same in Bittersweet, and other plays
Play parade
Cat's cradle. 1 scene
In Collected sketches and lyrics
Cavalcade. Garden City, N.Y. Double-
day. 1933. 12°. 138p. Pageant of
life
Same in Play parade
Conversation piece; a romantic comedy.
Garden City, N.Y. Doubleday. 1934.
120p. 12°
Customs house, Dover. 1 act
In Collected sketches and lyrics
Design for living; a comedy in three
acts. Garden City, N.Y. Doubleday.
1933. 12°. 139p.
Same in Play parade
Mantle, B. ed. Best plays of
1932-33 (abridged)
Easy virtue. Social. 3 acts
In Bittersweet, and other plays
Hay fever. Comedy. 3 acts
In Bittersweet, and other plays
Play parade
Home chat. Social. 3 acts
In Home chat, Sirocco, etc.
Plays. ser. 1
Mild oats. 1 act
In Collected sketches and lyrics
Point Valaine, a play in three acts.
Garden City, N.Y. 1935. 12°. 117p.
Post-mortem; a play in eight scenes.
Garden City, N.Y. Doubleday. 1931.
12°. 112p. World war
Same in Play parade

Private lives, an intimate comedy in
three acts. Garden City, N.Y.
Doubleday. 1931. 12°. 88p. 3 acts
Same in Play parade
Chandler, F. W. and Cordell,
R. A. eds. Twentieth cen-
tury plays
Queen was in the parlour. Melodrama.
3 acts
In Plays. ser. 1
Sirocco. Social. 3 acts
In Home chat, Sirocco, etc.
Plays. ser 1
"This was a man"; a comedy in three
acts. Garden City, N.Y. 1933. 244p.
Same in Home chat, Sirocco, etc.
Vortex. Problem. 3 acts
In Play parade
Tucker, S. M. ed. Twenty-five
modern plays
Weatherwise. Comedy. 2 scenes
In Collected sketches and lyrics
Young idea. Comedy. 3 acts
In Marriott, J. W. ed. Great modern
British plays
Coward, Noel Pierce, 1899- **and others**
Third little show. [A musical comedy
. . .] N.Y. Harms. 1931. 4°. 7 pts. in
1 v.
Cowen, Laurence, 1865-
Biddy; an Irish stew in three helpings.
N.Y. French. 1926. 12°. 86p.
Cowles, Albert
Killer
In Phillips, Le R. and Johnson, T. eds.
Types of modern dramatic com-
position
Cox, Philip
Rani of Jhansi; a historical play in four
acts. London. G. Allen. [1933] 119p.
Cox, William Norman
Scuffletown outlaws, a tragedy of the
Lowrie gang. 1 act
In Koch, F. H. ed. Carolina folk-
plays. ser. 3
Craven, Frank, 1875-
19th hole; a comedy in three acts. N.Y.
French. 1928. 12°. 104p.
Spite corner; a comedy in three acts.
N.Y. French. c1923. 8°. 79p.
"That's gratitude!" a comedy in prologue
and three acts. N.Y. French. 1931.
12°. 191p.
Too many cooks; a comedy in three acts.
N.Y. French. c1927. 12°. 128p.
Creagh-Henry, May
Crib; a Christmas play in one act. N.Y.
French. c1929. 12°. 17p.
Gold, a play in two parts. N.Y. French.
c1925. 12°. 23p.
Way of attainment, a play in a prologue
and one act. N.Y. French. c1927.
12°. 23p.
Crimmins, Agnes, *joint author.* See Mc-
Fadden, E. A. and Crimmins, Agnes
Critchett, Richard Claude, 1853-1928
Mr. Hopkinson, an original farce, by
R. C. Carton [pseud.] . . . N.Y.
French. c1908. 12°. 119p.

Crocker, Bosworth
Josephine. 1 act
  In One-act plays for stage and study.
      ser. 6
Last straw. Suicide. 1 act
  In Clark, B. H. and Nicholson, K. eds.
      American scene
Croisset, Francis de
On with the new. (Ne dites pas Fon-
      taine) Comedy. 1 act
  In Vernon, V. and F. eds. Modern
      one-act plays from the French
Cronyn, George W. 1888-
Lady and the law. Outwitting justice.
      1 act
  In Shay, F. ed. Fifty more contem-
      porary one-act plays
Crothers, Rachel, 1878-
As husbands go; a comedy. N.Y. French.
      1931. 12°. 158p. 3 acts
  Same in Chandler, F. W. and Cordell,
      R. A. eds. Twentieth century
      plays
      Mantle, B. ed. Best plays of
      1930-31 (abridged)
Caught wet; a comedy in three acts.
      N.Y. French. 1932. 12°. 92p.
Expressing Willie. Comedy. 3 acts
  In Cordell, R. A. ed. Representative
      modern plays
He and she; a play in three acts. Bos-
      ton. Baker. 1933. 12°. 126p. Problem
Let us be gay, a comedy. N.Y. French.
      1929. 12°. 172p. 3 acts
  In Mantle, B. ed. Best plays of 1928-
      29 (abridged)
Mary the third. Psychological. 3 acts
  In Tucker, S. M. ed. Modern plays
      Tucker, S. M. ed. Twenty-five mod-
      ern plays
Peggy. Character. 1 act
  In Phillips, Le R. and Johnson, T. eds.
      Types of modern dramatic com-
      position
When ladies meet. N.Y. French. 1932.
      12°. 147p. Triangle. 3 acts
  Same in Mantle, B. ed. Best plays of
      1932-33 (abridged)
**Cuddy, Mrs. Lucy A., McCauley, Mary
      Weaver, and Beatty, Willard W.**
Columbus; a play of perseverance for
      school use. . . . N.Y. Rand. c1927.
      12°. 111p.
Thanksgiving in Plymouth; a play in
      three acts. . . . N.Y. Rand. c1925.
      12°. 167p.
Culbertson, Ernest Howard
Across the Jordan; a comedy in one act.
      N.Y. French. c1929. 12°. 22p.
Color in court; a play of Negro life, in
      one act. N.Y. French. c1933. 12°.
      37p.
End of the trail
  In Clark, B. H. and Nicholson, K. eds.
      American scene
      Isaacs, E. J. ed. Plays of American
      life and fantasy
Rackey. Negro. 1 act
  In Locke, A. Le R. and Gregory, M.
      eds. Plays of Negro life

Cummings, Edward Estlin
Him. N.Y. Boni. 1927. 12°. 145p. Ether
      dream. 3 acts
Cummins, S. Lyle
Sleeping beauty. May day. 1 act
  In Schauffler, R. H. and Sanford, A. P.
      eds. Plays for our American holi-
      days. v. 2
Cuney-Hare, Maud
Antar of Araby. Negro. 4 acts
  In Richardson, W. ed. Plays and
      pageants from the life of the
      Negro
Curel, François, Vicomte de, 1854-
Fossils. [Les fossiles] Hereditary claims.
      4 acts
  In Watson, E. B. and Pressey, B. eds.
      Contemporary drama: European
      plays. v.1
Curtis, Agnes
Back numbers at Christmas. Comedy.
      1 act
  In Christmas comedies
Bringing up the Christmas baby. 1 act
  In Curtis, A. ed. Christmas plays for
      one and all
Christmas candle. Comedy. 1 act
  In Christmas comedies
Christmas comes but once a year. 1 act
  In Curtis, A. ed. Christmas plays for
      one and all
Christmas "gimme." Comedy. 1 act
  In Christmas comedies
Christmas greetings. Comedy. 1 act
  In Christmas comedies
Christmas poet. Comedy. 1 act
  In Christmas comedies
Christmas secret. 1 act
  In Curtis, A. ed. Christmas plays for
      one and all
Facing facts at Christmas. Comedy. 1
      act
  In Christmas comedies
Is there a Santa Claus? 1 act
  In Curtis, A. ed. Christmas plays for
      one and all
Life of the Christmas party. Comedy.
      1 act
  In Christmas comedies
My son Josiah. Christmas. 1 act
  In Curtis, A. ed. Christmas plays for
      one and all
Santa Claus messenger. 1 act
  In Curtis, A. ed. Christmas plays for
      one and all
That troublesome Christmas present.
      Comedy. 1 act
  In Christmas comedies
To the rescue on Christmas eve. Com-
      edy. 1 act
  In Christmas comedies
What the Shining Star club did at
      Christmas. Comedy. 1 act
  In Christmas comedies
Cushing, Catherine Chisholm
Jerry; a comedy in three acts. N.Y.
      French. 1930. 12°. 90p.
Widow by proxy, a farce-comedy in
      three acts. N.Y. French. c1930. 12°.
      115p.

Cushing, Charles Cyprian Strong, 1879-
Barely proper; an unplayable play. N.Y.
Farrar. 1931. 12°. 93p.
Devil in the cheese; a fantastic comedy.
N.Y. French. 1927. 12°. 180p. 3 acts
Out o' luck; a play in three acts, found-
ed on sketches of the Saint Mihiel
drive. N.Y. French. 1932. 12°. 115p.
Saint Martin's summer; a play in one
act. Hartford, Conn. Haylofters.
1927. 12°. 27p.

Daixel, Samuel
After midnight. 1 act
In White, B. F. trans. Nine one-act
plays from the Yiddish

Dane, Clemence, pseud. *See* Ashton, Winifred

Dane, Essex
His only way 1 scene
In Johnson, T. ed. More plays in min-
iature
Red sunset; a drama of the days of the
French revolution (in rhymed verse).
Boston. Baker. [c1930] 12°. 20p.
Tuberoses; a drama for four women.
Boston. Baker. [1933] 12°. 37p.
When the whirlwind blows. Labor.
1 act
In Modern short plays. ser. 3
Wooden leg. Duologue. 1 scene
In Johnson, E. ed. More plays in
miniature
Workers at the loom. 1 act
In Ten fantasies for stage and study

Darmady, J.
Annual jumble sale. 1 act
In Marriott, J. W. ed. Best one-act
plays of 1931
Mousetrap. Shakespeare. 1 act
In Marriott, J. W. ed. One-act plays
of to-day. ser. 5

Davidson, Marion L.
Whipped cream. Comedy. 1 act
In Johnson, T. ed. Diminutive come-
dies

Davies, D. T.
Barber and the cow. N.Y. Brentano's.
1927. 12°. 108p. Comedy. 3 acts

Davies, Mary Carolyn
Cobweb kings. 1 act
In One-act plays for stage and study.
ser. 4
Slave with two faces. Allegory. 1 act
In Pence, R. W. ed. Dramas by
present-day writers
Tables and chairs. Fantasy. 1 act
In One-act plays for stage and study.
ser. 5

**Daviot, Gordon, pseud. (Elizabeth Mack-
intosh)**
Laughing woman, a play. London. Gol-
lancz. 1934. 12°. 103p.
Same in Famous plays of 1933-34
Richard of Bordeaux; a play in two acts.
Boston. Little. 1933. 12°. 153p. His-
torical
Same in Famous plays of 1933

Davis, Dorrance
Busybody; a domestic farcical comedy in
three acts; an adaptation of the
original professional production. N.Y.
Longmans. 1929. 12°. 119p.
Shelf; a comedy more or less polite, in
three acts. N.Y. French. c1928. 12°.
127p.

Davis, Owen, 1874-
Cupid at Vassar; a college comedy drama
in four acts. N.Y. French. c1907.
12°. 70p.
Forever after. . . . N.Y. French. c1928.
12°. 73p.
Old sweetheart of mine; a play in four
acts. N.Y. French. c1911. 12°. 75p.

Davis, Owen, 1874- **and Collins, Sewell,**
1876-
"9:45," a mystery play, or a comedy-
melodrama. . . . N.Y. French. c1927.
8°. 96p.

Davison, John
Shadows of strife, a play in three acts,
with a foreword by Sir Barry Jack-
son. London. Dent. [1930] 12°. 86p.

Day, Holman Francis, 1865-
Along came Ruth; a comedy in three
acts. N.Y. French. c1930. 12°. 98p.

Deane, Hamilton and Balderston, John L.
Dracula; the vampire play in three acts;
from Bram Stoker's . . . novel, Dracula. N.Y. French. 1933. 109p.

Deans, Harris, 1886-
Aren't women wonderful! A comedy in
three acts. N.Y. French. 1929. 12°.
98p.

Dearden, Harold, 1882-
Fall. 1 act
In Three short plays
Flaming sword; a play in three acts.
London. Heinemann. 1929. 12°. 82p.
Poet laureate. 1 act
In Three short plays
Three women. 1 act
In Three short plays
Two white arms; a comedy-farce in three
acts. London. Heinemann. [1928] 12°.
209p.

Dearmer, Geoffrey, 1893-
Man with a cane. London. Yearbook
press. 1929. 16p. Comedy. 1 act
St. Paul; an historical play in three acts.
London. Heinemann. 1929. 12°. 76p.

De Casalis, Jeanne, *joint author. See*
Sherriff, Robert C. and De Casalis,
Jeanne

De Jagers, Dorothy, *joint author. See*
Heyward, Dorothy Hartzell and De
Jagers, Dorothy

De Kay, John Wesley, 1874-
Maid of Bethany, a tragedy in three
acts. Munich. K. Wolff. [1929] 12°.
155p. [Another version was published
by the author in 1910 under title:
Judas]

Delafield, E. M. pseud. *See* De la Pasture,
Edmée Elizabeth Monica

Delano, Edith Bernard and Carb, David, 1885-
Grandma pulls the string
   In Phillips, Le R. and Johnson, T. eds.
     Types of modern dramatic composition

De la Pasture, Edmée Elizabeth Monica (E. M. Delafield, pseud.) 1890-
Glass wall; a play in three acts. London. Gollancz. 1933. 12°. 84p.
To see ourselves; a domestic comedy in three acts. N.Y. French. 1932. 8°. 519p.
   Same in Famous plays of 1931
     Plays of a half-decade

De la Roche, Mazo, 1885-
Come true. Old people's home. 1 act
   In Low life and other plays
Low life; a comedy in one act. Toronto. Macmillan. 1925. 12°. 37p.
   Same in Low life and other plays
Return of the immigrant. Ireland. 1 act
   In Low life and other plays

Delf, Harry
Too much family, a play in three acts. N.Y. French. c1928. 12°. 81p. Originally produced under title "Atlas and Eva"; copyright under title "Six feet under")

Dell, Floyd, 1887- and Mitchell, Thomas
Little accident. Comedy. 3 acts
   In Mantle, B. ed. Best plays of 1928-29 (abridged)

Denison, Merrill, 1893-
Prize winner; a comedy in one act. N.Y. Appleton. 1928. 12°. 35p.
Weather breeder. Comedy. 1 act
   In Shay, F. ed. Fifty more contemporary one-act plays

Denny, Ernest, 1869-
Happy thought, a comedy in three acts. N.Y. French. c1930. 12°. 117p.
Lazy-bones; a comedy in three acts. N.Y. French. c1929. 12°. 124p.

Deseo, Mrs. Lydia May (Glover) 1898-
Never the twain; a play in one act
   In Poet Lore 41:272

De Sola, Alis, *joint author. See* Nicholson, Kenyon and De Sola, Alis

Dickens, Charles, 1812-1870
Christmas carol (dramatized by Frank Shay)
   In Shay, F. ed. Appleton book of Christmas plays
Lamplighter. Farce. 1 act
   In Golden Bk 3:69

Dickens, Charles Stafford
Command performance, a play in three acts. N.Y. French. c1930. 12°. 94p.

Dickey, Paul and Page, Mann
Red trail; a comedy in three acts. N.Y. French. c1929. 12°. 105p.

Dickson, Lee and Hickson, Leslie M.
Whose money? Farce. 1 act
   In Shay, F. ed. Fifty more contemporary one-act plays

Dignon, Edward, *joint author. See* Campion, Cyril and Dignon, Edward

Divine, Charles, 1889-
Post mortems. Comedy. 1 act
   In Nicholson, Kenyon, ed. Appleton book of short plays. ser. 2

Dix, Beulah Marie, 1876-
Allison's lad. Execution. 1 act
   In Hampden, J. ed. Nine modern plays
Girl comes home; a comedy in one act. N.Y. French. 1927. 12°. 22p.
Hundredth trick, a romantic tragedy. 1 act
   In Tucker, S. M. ed. Twelve one-act plays for study and production
Legend of Saint Nicholas. Juvenile. 1 act
   In Legend of Saint Nicholas and other plays
Princess Dayshine. Romantic. 7 scenes
   In Legend of Saint Nicholas and other plays
Weal of Wayland's well. May-day. 4 acts
   In Legend of Saint Nicholas and other plays

Dobson, Austin, 1840-1921
Au revoir. Dialogue. 1 act
   In Johnson, T. ed. More plays in miniature
Secrets of the heart. Dialogue. 1 act
   In Johnson, T. ed. More plays in miniature

Dodge, Henry Irving, 1861-, **Marston, Laurence and Paulton, Edward**
Skinner's dress suit; a comedy in three acts. N.Y. French. c1928. 12°. 106p.

Donahoe, Joseph Aloysius, 1875-
Girl who would not; or, A colonial elopement; a comedy in four acts. N.Y. French. c1928. 12°. 98p.

Donahue, V. and Holmes, L. T.
Elves and the shoemakers. Christmas
   In Schauffler, R. H. and Sanford, A. P. eds. Plays for our American holidays. v. 1 [Christmas]

Dondo, Mathurin Marius, 1884-
Every dog has his day. Marionette. 1 act
   In McPharlin, P. ed. Repertory of marionette plays
Miracle of Saint Martin. 1 act
   In One-act plays for stage and study. ser. 4

Donnay, Maurice Charles, 1859-
Lovers. Comedy. 3 acts
   In Steeves, H. R. ed. Plays from the modern theatre
Lysistrata; a comedy in four acts; tr. from the French by William A. Drake. N.Y. Knopf. 1929. 12°. 140p.

Doran, Marie
Gay co-eds; a comedy in three acts. N.Y. French. c1933. 12°. 85p.
Little flower; a religious drama in three acts. N.Y. London. c1928. 12°. 85p.
Quo vadis; a play in five acts and seven scenes, adapted from the novel of Henryk Sienkiewicz. N.Y. French. c1928. 12°. 102p. Nero

Dortch, Helen
Companion-mate Maggie. Negro comedy. 1 act
In Koch, F. H. ed. Carolina folk comedies

Dos Passos, John
Airways, inc. N.Y. Macaulay. 1928. 12°. 148p. 3 acts
Same in Three plays
Fortune heights
In Three plays
Garbage man; a parade with shouting. N.Y. Harper. 1926. 12°. 160p. 2 pts.
Same in Three plays

Douglas, Eileen
Green broom
In Bourne, J. ed. Eight new plays for boys and girls

Douglass, Vincent
Jeffersons, a comedy in three acts. N.Y. French. c1926. 12°. 94p.
Perfect wife, a dramatic comedy in three acts. N.Y. French. 1928. 12°. 105p.

Downey, June E.
Arrow. Fantasy. 1 act
In Poet Lore 38:297

Downey, T. H.
Paste pearls. Comedy. 1 act
In Johnson, T. ed. Diminutive comedies

Downs, Oliphant
In Cohen, H. L. ed. One-act plays by modern authors. 1934 edition

Dowson, Ernest, 1867-1900
Pierrot of the minute. Fantasy. 1 act
In Cohen, H. L. ed. One-act plays by modern authors. 1934 edition

Doyle, Sir Arthur Conan, 1859-1930
Exile. Christmas. 1 act
In Shay, F. ed. Appleton book of Christmas plays

Dransfield, Jane, 1875-
Blood o' kings. Hudson Valley. 1 act
In Clark, B. H. and Nicholson, K. eds. American scene

Dreiser, Theodore, 1871-
Blue sphere. 1 act
In Smart Set anthology
Girl in the coffin. Tragedy. 1 act
In Clark, B. H. and Nicholson, K. eds. American scene

Drinkwater, John, 1882-
Bird in hand; a play in three acts. Boston. Houghton. 1929. 12°. 88p. Comedy
Same in Theatre M 50:24
Cophetua. Romantic. 1 act
In Pence, R. W. ed. Dramas by present-day writers
God of quiet. War. 1 act
In Goldstone, G. A. ed. One-act plays
Laying the devil; a play in three acts. London. Sidgwick. 1933. 12°. 80p.
Midsummer eve [a play for broadcasting]. London. Sidgwick. 1932. 12°. 80p.
Robin Hood and the pedlar. Masque. 1 act
In Modern short plays. ser. 1

X=O: a night of the Trojan war. 1 act
In Hampden, J. ed. Ten modern plays
Webber, J. P. and Webster, H. H. eds. One-act plays for secondary schools

Drummond, A. M.
Traffic signals. 1 act
In One-act plays for stage and study. ser. 6

Drury, William Price
King's hard bargain. 1 act
In Marriott, J. W. ed. One-act plays of to-day. ser. 3

du Bois, Theodora
Aladdin. 7 scenes
In Moses, M. J. ed. Ring up the curtain!

Duffey, Vincent, *joint author*. *See* Ankrum, Morris and Duffey, Vincent

Dukes, Ashley, 1885-
Dumb wife of Cheapside; a comedy in a prologue and two acts. N.Y. French. c1929. 12°. 42p.
Same in Five plays of other times
Fountain head; a play in three acts. London. Gollancz. 1928. 12°. 118p.
In Five plays of other times
Jew Süss, a drama in five acts based upon Power, the historical romance of Lion Feuchtwanger. N.Y. Viking. 1930. 12°. 178p.
Man with a load of mischief. Comedy. 3 acts
In Five plays of other times
Marriott, J. W. ed. Great modern British plays
Plays of to-day. ser. 3
Matchmaker's arms, a comedy in three acts. London. Benn. 1931. 12°. 80p.
Same in Five plays of other times
Patriot; a play in three acts, by Alfred Neumann. Adapted by Ashley Dukes. N.Y. Boni. [1928]
Song of drums. *See* Dukes, A. Ulenspiegel
Such men are dangerous. (Adapted from "The patriot" by Alfred Neumann). Russian revolution. 8 scenes
In Famous plays of to-day
Tyl Ulenspiegel, or The Song of drums. An heroic comedy in a prologue and three acts
See Dukes, A. Ulenspiegel
Ulenspiegel; a legend in seven scenes. (Tyl Ulenspiegel) N.Y. French. 1933. 57p.
Same in Five plays of other times
Theatre Arts M 10:240

Duls, Louisa, *joint author*. *See* Bland, Margaret and Duls, Louisa

Dunbar, Olivia Howard
Blockade
In Isaacs, E. J. ed. Plays of American life and fantasy

Duncan, Thelma Myrtle, 1902-
Death dance. Negro. 1 act
In Locke, A. Le R. and Gregory, M. eds. Plays of Negro life

Duncan, Thelma Myrtle—_Continued_
Sacrifice. Negro. 1 act
  _In_ Richardson, W. ed. Plays and
    pageants from the life of the
    Negro

Dunning, Philip
Night hostess; a dramatic comedy. N.Y.
  French. 1928. 12°. 164p.

Dunning, Philip and Abbott, George
Broadway; a play in three acts. N.Y.
  Doran. 1927. 12°. 236p. Melodrama
  Same in Mantle, B. Best plays of 1926-
    27 (abridged)

**Dunsany, Lord Edward John Moreton
  Drax Plunkett, 18th baron,** 1878-
Atalanta in Wimbledon. Comedy. 1 act
  _In_ Seven modern comedies
Evil kettle. James Watt. 1 act
  _In_ Schauffler, R. H. and Sanford, A. P.
    eds. Plays for our American holi-
    days. v. 4
Flight of the queen. Fantasy. 4 scenes
  _In_ Marriott, J. W. ed. One-act plays
    of to-day. ser. 4
Glittering gate. After death. 1 act
  _In_ Watson, E. B. and Pressey, B. eds.
    Contemporary drama. English
    and Irish plays. v. 1
Gods of the mountain. Fantasy. 1 act
  _In_ Modern short plays. ser. 2
Golden doom. Symbolic. 1 act
  _In_ Marriott, J. W. ed. One-act plays
    of to-day. ser. 3
His painted grandmother. Comedy. 1
  act
  _In_ Seven modern comedies
Hopeless passion of Mr. Bunyon. Com-
  edy. 1 act
  _In_ Seven modern comedies
In holy Russia. Comedy. 1 act
  _In_ Seven modern comedies
Jest of Hahalaba. Comedy. 1 act
  _In_ Seven modern comedies
Journey of the soul. Comedy. 1 act
  _In_ Seven modern comedies
Lord Adrian; a play in three acts.
  Walthan Saint Laurence in Berk-
  shire. Golden Cockerel press. 1933.
  8°. 73p.
Lost silk hat. Comedy. 1 act
  _In_ Church, V. W. ed Curtain!
    Goldstone, G. A. ed. One-act plays
Night at an inn. Superstition. 1 act
  _In_ Cohen, H. L. ed. One-act plays by
    modern authors. 1934 edition
    Pence, R. W. ed. Dramas by
    present-day writers
    Tucker, S. M. ed. Twelve one-act
    plays for study and production
Old folk of the centuries. London.
  Mathews. [1930] 12°. 66p.
Raffle. Comedy. 1 act
  _In_ Seven modern comedies
Tents of the Arabs. Fantasy. 2 acts
  _In_ Modern short plays. ser. 1

Duranty, Louis Emile
Cataclysterium's medicine. Marionette.
  1 act
  _In_ McPharlin, P. ed. Repertory of
    marionette plays

Duvernois, Henri, 1875-
Bronze lady and the crystal gentleman.
  Comedy. 1 act
  _In_ Vernon, V. and F. eds. Modern
    one-act plays from the French
Harmony, a comedy in one act; author-
  ized translation by Babette and Glenn
  Hughes. Boston. Baker. [c1933] 12°.
  68p.

Dyar, Ralph E.
Horseshoe luck. Comedy. 3 acts
  _In_ Prize plays of 1928

Earnest, J.
Marriage of Isolt. Comedy. 1 act
  _In_ Johnson, T. ed. Diminutive come-
    dies

Eastman, Fred, 1886-
America on trial; a pageant play in one
  act. N.Y. French. [1932] 12°. 26p.
  Same in Plays of American life
America's unfinished battles. Religious.
  1 act
  _In_ Eastman, F. ed. Modern religious
    dramas
Bread. Religious. 1 act
  _In_ Plays of American life
    Clark, B. H. and Nicholson, K. eds.
    American scene
    Eastman, F. ed. Modern religious
    dramas
Courtship. Comedy. 1 act
  _In_ Plays of American life
Doctor decides. 1 act
  _In_ Plays of American life
Great choice, an incident of the next war.
  1 act
  _In_ Plays of American life
Our lean years. 1 act
  _In_ Plays of American life
Ragged edge. Comedy. 1 act
  _In_ Plays of American life
Tinker; a play in three acts. N.Y. Cen-
  tury. [c1930] 12°. 97p.
  Same in Plays of American life

Eaton, Walter Prichard, 1878-
Grandma—old style; a comedy in one
  act. N.Y. French. 1933. 18p.

Edgar, Mary S.
Conspiracy of spring. Arbor day. 1 act
  _In_ Schauffler, R. H. and Sanford, A. P.
    eds. Plays for our American holi-
    days. v. 2

Edmonds, Randolph
Devil's price. 4 acts
  _In_ Shades and shadows
Everyman's land. Death. 1 act
  _In_ Shades and shadows
Hewers of wood. 1 act
  _In_ Shades and shadows
Phantom treasure. 2 scenes
  _In_ Shades and shadows
Shades and shadows. Tragedy. 1 act
  _In_ Shades and shadows
Tribal chief. Tibet. 1 act
  _In_ Shades and shadows

Egerton, Lady Alix
Masque of the three strangers. Symbolic. 1 act
In Cohen, H. L. ed. One-act plays by modern authors. 1934 edition

Ehlert, Mrs. Fay
Undercurrent; a one-act play . . . preface by John Pollock. N.Y. French. 1929. 8°. 97p.

Ehrlich, Mrs. Ida Lublenski, 1886-
Cured; a comedy in one act. N.Y. French. c1928. 13p.
Same in One act plays for stage and study. ser. 4
Helena's boys. N.Y. French. c1927. 12°. 95p.
'Twas ever thus. Farce. 1 act
In Nicholson, Kenyon, ed. Appleton book of short plays. ser. 2
Winners all. 1 act
In Shay, F. ed. Fifty contemporary one-act plays

Eldridge, Florence M.
Growth of a nation. Melting pot. 1 act
In Schauffler, R. H. and Sanford, A. P. eds. Plays for our American holidays. v. 3

Elias, Mrs. Edith L.
Goose and gooseberry; a play in three acts for children. London. Harrap. [1933] 95p.

Eliot, Thomas Stearns
Rock. N.Y. Harcourt. 1934. 12°. 86p. Pageant

Ellis, Edith
White collars; a comedy in three acts,... based on a novelette of Edgar Franklin [pseud.] . . . N.Y. French. c1926. 12°. 134p. Copyrighted 1923 under title "Regular people."

Ellis, Walter W. 1874-
Almost a honeymoon, a farce in three acts. N.Y. French. c1931. 8°. 85p.
Hawley's of the High street; an eccentric comedy in three acts. N.Y. French. c1923. 12°. 107p.
Little bit of fluff; a farce in three acts. N.Y. French. c1922. 12°. 101p.
S. O. S.; a play in three acts. N.Y. French. 1929. 8°. 92p.

Else, R.
It pays to be a Poggle. Comedy
In Snook, L. O. ed. Comedies seven

Emerson, Jerry
Screen. 1 act
In Sanford, A. P. ed. One-act plays for women

Emery, Gilbert, pseud. (Emery Bernsley Pottle)
Delilah. Tragedy. 1 act
In Nicholson, Kenyon, ed. Appleton book of short plays. ser. 2
Hero. Tragi-comedy. 3 acts
In Tucker, S. M. ed. Modern American and British plays
Thank you, doctor
In Twelve one-act plays

Ernst, Alice Henson
Spring sluicing. Yukon. 1 act
In Isaacs, E. J. ed. Plays of American life and fantasy

Erskine, John, 1879-
Helen retires; an opera in three acts. N.Y. Bobbs. 1934. 12°. 107p.

Erskine, Laurie York, 1894-
Three cans of beans. 1 act
In Hughes, G. ed. Short plays for modern players

Ervine, St. John Greer, 1883-
First Mrs. Fraser; a comedy in three acts. London. Chatto. 1929. 12°. 88p.
Same in Mantle, B. ed. Best plays of 1929-30 (abridged)
John Ferguson. Tragedy. 4 acts
In Chandler, F. W. and Cordell, R. A. eds. Twentieth century plays
Mantle, B. and Sherman, G. P. eds. Best plays of 1909-1919
Tucker, S. M. ed. Modern American and British plays
Tucker, S. M. ed. Twenty-five modern plays
Magnanimous lover. Comedy. 1 act
In Four one-act plays
Ole George comes to tea. Comedy. 1 act
In Four one-act plays
Progress. London. Allen. [1931] 12°. 26p. Comedy. 1 act
Same in Four one-act plays
She was no lady. London. Allen. [1931] 12°. 25p. Comedy. 1 act
Same in Four one-act plays

Evréinov, Nicolai Nicolaievich (Yevreinov, Nikolai)
Theatre of the soul. Monodrama. 1 act
In Dickinson, T. H. ed. Chief contemporary dramatists. ser. 3

Eyre, Laurence, 1881-
Merry wives of Gotham; or, Two and sixpence; a comedy in three acts. N.Y. French. c1930. 12°. 101p.
Mis' Nelly of N'Orleans, a comedy of moonshine, madness and make-believe. N.Y. French. c1930. 12°. 105p.
Things that count, a comedy in three acts. N.Y. French. c1930. 12°. 103p.
Two and sixpence. *See* Eyre, Laurence, Merry wives of Gotham; or, Two and sixpence

Fagan, James Bernard, 1873-
And so to bed; a comedy in three acts. N.Y. Holt. 1927. 12°. 145p. Samuel Pepys
Improper duchess; a modern comedy in three acts. London. Gollancz. 1931. 12°. 112p.
In Famous plays of 1931
Plays of a half-decade
Prayer of the sword; a play in five acts. London. Johnson. 1904. 12°. 116p.

Fairbanks, S. von K.
Other voice. 1 scene
In Johnson, T. ed. More plays in miniature

Farjeon, Herbert
Friends. 1 act
In Marriott, J. W. ed.   One-act plays
of to-day. ser. 3
Happy New Year. Revue. 1 act
In Happy New Year—and Your kind
indulgence

Farrar, John Chipman, 1896-
Birthdays come in February. Juvenile
In Indoor and outdoor plays for chil-
dren
God Pan forgotten. Juvenile
In Indoor and outdoor plays for chil-
dren
Grandmother dozes. Juvenile
In Indoor and outdoor plays for chil-
dren
Here are the sailors! Comedy. Sea. 1
act
In One-act plays for stage and study.
ser. 7
House gnomes: a play for a Christmas
tree
In Indoor and outdoor plays for chil-
dren
Moses, M. J. ed. Ring up the cur-
tain!
Kingdom of rose queens. Juvenile
In Indoor and outdoor plays for chil-
dren
Magic sea shell. Juvenile. 1 act
In Indoor and outdoor plays for chil-
dren
Nerves; a play in one act. N.Y. French.
1922. 12°. 27p. World war
Sand castle. Juvenile
In Indoor and outdoor plays for chil-
dren
Swing high. Juvenile
In Indoor and outdoor plays for chil-
dren
Wedding rehearsal. Mystery farce. 1
act
In One-act plays for stage and study.
ser. 5
Worship the Nativity. Juvenile. 1 act
In Indoor and outdoor plays for chil-
dren

Fauchois, René
Late Christopher Bean (adapted by
Emlyn Williams). Comedy. 3 acts
[See also Howard, S. C.]
In Famous plays of 1933

Fenzi, Francesco, 1672-
Jewels of Isabella. Columbus. 2 scenes
In Schauffler, R. H. and Sanford, A. P.
eds.   Plays for our American
holidays. v. 4

Ferber, Edna, 1887-
Eldest. American life. 1 act
In Clark, B. H. and Nicholson, K. eds.
American scene
Nicholson, Kenyon, ed. Appleton
book of short plays. ser. 2
Ferber, Edna, *joint author. See* Kaufman,
George and Ferber, Edna

Ferguson, John Alexander, 1873-
Campbell of Kilmohr. Historical. 1 act
In Hampden, J. ed. Eight modern
plays

Scarecrow. Fantasy. 1 act
In Marriott, J. W. ed.   One-act plays
of to-day. ser. 5
Ferguson, Rachel, 1893-
Charlotte Brontë; a play in three acts.
London. Benn. 1933. 88p.
Fernald, Chester Bailey, 1869-
Mask and the face; a satire in three acts
(based on La maschera e il volto, by
Luigi Chiarelli). N.Y. French. c1927.
12°. 78p.
To-morrow, a play; in three acts of
drama and an epilogue of discovery.
London. Benn. 1928. 12°. 103p.
Ferris, Walter, 1882-
Death takes a holiday, a comedy in three
acts . . . based on a play of the same
title by Albert Casella. N.Y. French.
1930. 12°. 151p.
Same in Mantle, B. ed. Best plays of
1929-30 (abridged)
Feutchtwanger, Lion, 1884-
Oil Islands. Comedy. 3 acts
In Two Anglo-Saxon plays
Warren Hastings. Historical. 3 acts
In Two Anglo-Saxon plays
Field, Rachel Lyman, 1894-
At the junction. 1 act
In Cross-stitch heart, and other plays
Bad penny. 1 act
In One-act plays for stage and study.
ser. 6
Bargains in Cathay. 1 act
In Cross-stitch heart, and other plays.
Clark, B. H. and Cook, T. R. eds.
One-act plays
Chimney sweeps' holiday. Juvenile
In Patchwork plays
Cross-stitch heart. 1 act
In Cross-stitch heart, and other plays
Greasy luck. 1 act
In Cross-stitch heart, and other plays
Clark, B. H. and Nicholson, K. eds.
American scene
"Little Square-toes." 1 act
In Patchwork plays
Londonderry air. 1 act
In Cross-stitch heart, and other plays
Magic pawnshop; a New Year's fantasy.
N.Y. Dutton. [1927] 8°. 125p.
Miss Ant, Miss Grasshopper, and Mr.
Cricket. 1 act
In Patchwork plays
Nine days queen. 1 act
In Cross-stitch heart, and other plays
Patch-work quilt. Fantasy. 1 act
In Marriott, J. W. ed. One-act plays
of to-day. ser. 4
Polly Patchwork. Garden City, N.Y.
Doubleday. 1928. 12°. 56p. 1 act
Same in Patchwork plays
Sentimental scarecrow. 1 act
In Patchwork plays
Field, Salisbury, *joint author. See* Mayo,
Margaret and Field, Salisbury
Fielden, Anne D.
Abraham Lincoln—a pageant
In Sanford, A. P. ed. Lincoln plays

Finnegan, Edward
Danny boy; a comedy in three acts. Boston. Baker. 1926. 12°.
Fool of a man; a comedy in one act. Boston. Baker. [c1926] 16°
Same in Phillips, Le R. and Johnson, T. eds. Types of modern dramatic composition
Singapore spider. 1 act
In Johnson, T. ed. Miniature plays for stage or study
Slippin'; a one-act play. Chicago. Denison. [c1927] 12°. 15p.

Finsterwald, Maxine
Seven against one, a play in one act. N.Y. French. c1930. 12°. 22p.
Severed cord, a play in one act. N.Y. French. c1929. 12°. 22p.

Firkins, Oscar W. 1864-1932
After twenty-five years
In Drama 15:99
Answer. Psychological. 1 act
In Two passengers for Chelsea, and other plays
Bloom on the grape. Social. 1 act
In Two passengers for Chelsea, and other plays
Bride of quietness. Keats' Ode on a Grecian urn. 1 act
In Bride of quietness, and other plays
Columns. Sophocles and Euripides. 1 act
In Revealing moment, and other plays
Divided lives
In Northwest Musical Herald 6:4
Emeralds. Comedy. 1 act
In Two passengers for Chelsea, and other plays
Empurpled moors. The Brontës. 1 act
In Bride of quietness, and other plays
Geoffrey's wife. Psychological. 1 act
In Two passengers for Chelsea, and other plays
In a suburb of Paris. Oscar Wilde's Salomé. 1 act
In Revealing moment, and other plays
In the small hours. Psychological. 1 act
In Two passengers for Chelsea, and other plays
King's vigil. Samuel Pepys. 1 act
In Bride of quietness, and other plays
Last meeting. Character. 1 act
In Two passengers for Chelsea, and other plays
Looking-glass. Social. 1 act
In Two passengers for Chelsea, and Drama 16:171
Odd entanglement. Comedy. 1 act
In Two passengers for Chelsea, and other plays
Reference. Social. 1 act
In Two passengers for Chelsea, and other plays
Drama 14:215
Reticent convict. Character. 1 act
In Drama. v. 18. no. 5:141
Revealing moment. Anton Chekhov. 1 act
In Revealing moment, and other plays
Rim of the desert. Social. 1 act
In Two passengers for Chelsea, and other plays
Strange visitor. Cyrus Northrop. 1 act
In Minnesota Daily. N. 16, 1929

Tulip and camellia. The two Dumas. 1 act
In Revealing moment, and other plays Cornhill 68:233
Turnpikes in Arcady. The Brownings. 1 act
In Bride of quietness, and other plays
Two great men, and one small boy. Ibsen and Björnson. 1 act
In Revealing moment, and other plays
Two passengers for Chelsea. Carlyle comedy. 1 act
In Two passengers for Chelsea, and other plays
Shay, F. ed. Fifty more one-act plays
Cornhill 60:163
Golden Bk 11:95
Unbidden guest. Fantasy. 1 act
In Two passengers for Chelsea, and other plays
Poet Lore 35:276
Undying prince. Hamlet. 1 act
In Two passengers for Chelsea, and other plays
Cornhill 64:231 (condensed)
Unknown woman. Prosper Merimée. 1 act
In Revealing moment, and other plays
Wave and the flame. René de Chateaubriand. 1 act
In Revealing moment, and other plays

Fisher, Mrs. Dorothea Frances Canfield, 1879-
Tourists accommodated. N.Y. Harcourt. 1934. 12°. 90p. Summer life in Vermont

Fitch, Clyde, i.e. **William Clyde,** 1865-1909
Climbers. Social. 4 acts
In Cordell, R. A. ed. Representative modern plays
Nathan Hale (Act 3) Historical
In Johnson, T. ed. Washington anniversary plays

Fitzhugh, Carroll
Cough. Comedy. 1 act
In Mon ami Pierrot, and other plays
Margaret in Naxos. Triangle. 1 act
In Mon ami Pierrot, and other plays
May and December. Comedy. 1 act
In Mon ami Pierrot, and other plays
Mon ami Pierrot. Old and new generation. 1 act
In Mon ami Pierrot, and other plays
Mountains of Bether. Comedy. 1 act
In Mon ami Pierrot, and other plays
Snake. Comedy. 1 act
In Mon ami Pierrot, and other plays

Fitzmaurice, George
Dandy dolls. Comedy. 1 act
In Canfield, C. ed. Plays of the Irish renaissance
Green stone. Comedy. 1 act
In Dublin M n. s. 1:33

Flavin, Martin A. 1883-
Amaco. . . . N.Y. French. 1933. 12°. 141p.
Broken dishes; a comedy in three acts. N.Y. French. c1930. 12°. 125p.
Criminal code. N.Y. Liveright. 1929. 12°. 200p. Tragedy. Prologue and three acts
In Mantle, B. ed. Best plays of 1929-30 (abridged)

Flavin, Martin A.—*Continued*
Cross roads, a play in three acts. N.Y.
French. c1930. 12°. 107p. [Copyrighted
1929 under title of "Grist to the
mill"]
Service for two; a comedy in three acts.
N.Y. French. c1927. 12°. 92p.

Flournoy, Richard
Enter the prodigal; a comedy in three
acts. Boston. Baker. [c1933] 131p.

Floyd, John
Wooden kimono; a melodramatic mystery play in three acts. N.Y. French.
c1933. 112p.

Folmsbee, Beulah
Gift of love
In Guki the moon boy, and other plays
Guki the moon boy
In Guki the moon boy, and other plays
Jacquenetta and the queen's gown
In Guki the moon boy, and other plays
King's cobbler
In Guki the moon boy, and other plays
Princess and the crystal pipe
In Guki the moon boy, and other plays

Fool, Tom, pseud.
School, or Thou shalt not commit.
Marionette. 1 act
In McPharlin, P. ed. Repertory of
marionette plays
Three men of Gotham. A motion for
marionettes. Being an interlude by
Tom Fool of Europe. Florence. 1919.
12°. 6p.

Ford, Harriet, 1868-
Are men superior? a farce-comedy in
one act. N.Y. French. 1933. 16p.
Same in One-act plays for stage and
study. ser. 7
Divine afflatus, a comedy in one act. N.Y.
French. c1931. 12°. 22p.
Heroic treatment; a comedy in one act.
N.Y. French. c1933. 12°. 28p.
In-laws. Comedy. 1 act
In One-act plays for stage and study.
ser. 4
Mr. Susan Peters, comedy in one act.
N.Y. French. [c1928] 12°. 21p.
Mysterious money, a comedy in three
acts. N.Y. French. c1929. 12°. 81p.
What are parents for? A play in one
act. N.Y. French. c1930. 12°. 21p.
What imagination will do; comedy in one
act. N.Y. French. [c1928] 12°. 19p.

Ford, Harriet, 1868- and **Tucker, Althea
Sprague**
Happy hoboes; a comedy in one act.
N.Y. French. c1928. 12°. 24p.
Wanted—money; a comedy in one act.
N.Y. French. c1928. 12°. 20p.

Ford, Harriet, *joint author. See* O'Higgins,
H. J. and Ford, Harriet

Ford, Julia Ellsworth
Snickerty Dick. Fairy. 2 scenes
In Moses, M. J. ed. Ring up the cur-
tain!

Fowler, Laura Andrews
Feather; a three-act ballet
In Player's M 9:20 Mr.-Ap. 1933

Francis, John Oswald, 1882-
Beaten track; a Welsh play in four acts.
London. French. [1927] 16°. 110p.
Birds of a feather; a Welsh wayside
comedy in one act. Newtown [Wales]
The "Welsh Outlook" press. [1927]
8°. 28p.
Same in Marriott, J. W. ed. One-act
plays of to-day. ser. 5
Cross currents; a play of Welsh politics
in three acts. Cardiff. Educ. pub. co.
[1922] 16°.
Crowning of peace; a short pageant of
the peace of nations. Cardiff. Educ.
pub. co. [1922] 16°.
Dark little people. A comedy of the
Welsh tribes. In three acts. Cardiff.
Educ. pub. co. 12°. 94p.
John Jones; an episode in the history
of Welsh letters. Newtown [Wales]
"Welsh Outlook" press. [1927] 8°.
28p.
Little village, a Welsh farce in three
acts. N.Y. French. c1930. 12°. 138p.
Perfect husband; a Welsh farce in one
act. Newtown [Wales] "Welsh Out-
look" press. [1927] 8°. 23p.
Poacher; comedy in one act
In Marriott, J. W. ed. One-act plays
of to-day. ser. 4

Francke, Caroline
Exceeding small; a play in three acts.
N.Y. French. c1930. 12°. 100p.

Frank, Bruno, 1887-
Twelve thousand; a play in three acts;
tr. from the German by William A.
Drake. N.Y. Knopf. 1928. 12°. 86p.

Frank, Mrs. Florence Kiper
Home for the friendly. Comedy. 1 act
In Shay, F. ed. Fifty more contem-
porary one-act plays
Over the hills and far away. Juvenile.
1 act
In Three plays for a children's theatre
Drama 2:80
Return of Proserpine. Juvenile. 1 act
In Three plays for a children's theatre
Three spinners. Juvenile. 1 act
In Three plays for a children's theatre
Visitors, a play to be acted by children,
in one act. Chicago. Dramatic pub.
co. [1916] 12°. 12p.

Frank, Leonhard, 1882-
Karl and Anna, a drama in three acts;
tr. by Ruth Langner. N.Y. Brentano's. 1929. 12°. 108p.

Frank, Maude Morrison, 1870-
Mistake at the manor. Oliver Goldsmith.
1 act
In Webber, J. P. and Webster, H. H.
eds. Typical plays for secondary
schools

Frank, Waldo David, 1889-
New Year's eve, a play. N.Y. Scribner.
1929. 12°. 156p. Social. 7 scenes

Franken, Rose L. (Mrs S. W. A. Franken)
Another language; a comedy drama in
three acts. N.Y. French. 1932. 12°.
163p.
Same in Mantle, B. ed. Best plays of
1931-32 (abridged)

Franklin, Pearl
Following father, a comedy in three acts.
N.Y. French. 1931. 12°. 110p.
Mountain wedding. . . N.Y. French.
1926. 12°. 26p. 1 act
Fredo, Alexander
Ladies and hussars: comedy in three acts.
tr. from the Polish by Florence
Noyes and George Rapall Noyes.
N.Y. French. c1925. 12°. 87p.
Frost, Robert, 1875-
Way out; a one act play. N.Y. Harbor
press. 1929. 8°. 19p. Crime
Fuller, Ethel K.
Dream canal boat; a fantasy in two
scenes. N.Y. French. 1928. 12°. 20p.
Fulton, Maud
Miss Baxter. 1 act
_In_ Nicholson, K. ed. Hollywood plays
Furniss, Grace Livingston
Father walks out; a comedy in three acts.
N.Y. French. c1928. 12°. 88p.
Second floor, Spoopendyke. A farce in
two acts. Boston. Baker. [1892] 12°.
27p.
Fussler, Irene
Ever' snitch. Comedy. 1 act
_In_ Koch, F. H. ed. Carolina folk com-
edies
Fyleman, Rose, 1877-
Cabbages and kings. Juvenile. 1 act
_In_ Eight little plays for children
Phillips, Le R. and Johnson, T. eds.
Types of modern dramatic com-
position
Darby and Joan. Juvenile. 1 act
_In_ Eight little plays for children
Fairy and the doll. Juvenile. 1 act
_In_ Eight little plays for children
Fairy riddle. Juvenile. 1 act
_In_ Eight little plays for children
Father Christmas. Juvenile. 1 act
_In_ Eight little plays for children
In Arcady. Juvenile. 1 act
_In_ Eight little plays for children
Johnson, T. ed. Ten fantasies for
stage and study
Noughts and crosses. Juvenile. 1 act
_In_ Eight little plays for children
Weather clerk. Juvenile. 1 act
_In_ Eight little plays for children
Gale, Zona, 1874-
Clouds. 1 act
_In_ New plays for women and girls
Neighbors. Comedy. 1 act
_In_ Eastman, F. ed. Modern religious
dramas
Uncle Jimmy. 1 act
_In_ Hughes, G. ed. Short plays for
modern players
Phillips, Le R. and Johnson, T. eds.
Types of modern dramatic com-
position
Galsworthy, John, 1867-1933
Bit o' love. Social. 3 acts
_In_ Plays (Scribner. 1928)
Defeat. World war. 1 act
_In_ Plays (Scribner. 1928)
Eldest son. Domestic. 3 acts
_In_ Plays (Scribner. 1928)

Escape. Ethical. Prologue and 9 epi-
sodes
_In_ Plays (Scribner. 1928)
Plays: seventh series
Mantle, B. ed. Best plays of 1927-
28 (abridged)
Exiled; an evolutionary comedy in three
acts. London. Duckworth. 1929. 12°.
118p.
Same in Plays (Duckworth. 1929)
Plays: seventh series
Family man. Marriage. 3 acts
_In_ Plays (Scribner. 1928)
First and the last. Tragedy. 3 scenes
_In_ Plays (Scribner. 1928)
Forest. African. 3 acts
_In_ Plays (Scribner. 1928)
Foundations. Sweatshop. 3 acts
_In_ Plays (Scribner. 1928)
Fugitive. Social. 4 acts
_In_ Plays (Scribner. 1928)
Hall-marked. Satire. 1 act
_In_ Plays (Scribner. 1928)
Joy. Social. 3 acts
_In_ Plays (Scribner. 1928)
Justice. Tragedy. 4 acts
_In_ Plays (Scribner. 1928)
Watson, E. B. and Pressey, B. eds.
Contemporary drama. English
and Irish plays. v. 1
Little dream. Allegory. 6 scenes
_In_ Plays (Scribner. 1928)
Little man. Satire. 3 scenes
_In_ Plays (Scribner. 1928)
Cohen, H. L. ed. One-act plays by
modern authors. 1934 edition
Hampden, J. ed. Nine modern
plays
Loyalties. Race prejudice. 3 acts
_In_ Plays (Scribner. 1928)
Pence, R. W. ed. Dramas by pres-
ent-day writers
Watson, E. B. and Pressey, B. eds.
Contemporary drama. English
and Irish plays
Mob. Social. 4 acts
_In_ Plays (Scribner. 1928)
Old English. Character. 3 acts
_In_ Plays (Scribner. 1928)
Pigeon. Fantasy. 3 acts
_In_ Plays (Scribner. 1928)
Punch and go. Comedy. 1 act
_In_ Plays (Scribner. 1928)
Roof, a play in seven scenes. N.Y. Scrib-
ner. 1931. 12°. 125p.
Same in Plays (Duckworth. 1929)
Plays: seventh series
Show. Criminals. 3 acts
_In_ Plays (Scribner. 1928)
Silver box. Comedy. 3 acts
_In_ Plays (Scribner. 1928)
Skin game. Tragi-comedy. 3 acts
_In_ Plays (Scribner. 1928)
Strife. Strike. 3 acts
_In_ Plays (Scribner. 1928)
Marriott, J. W. ed. Great modern
British plays
Whitman, C. H. ed. Seven con-
temporary plays

Galsworthy, John—*Continued*
Sun. Tragi-comedy. 1 act
In Plays (Scribner. 1928)
Windows. Comedy. 3 acts
In Plays (Scribner. 1928)

Gandy, Ida
Fairy fruit; a play for children. Boston. Baker. 1927. 12°. 38p.
Lardy cake; a comedy for village players. London. Deane. 1928. 12°. 12p.
Snowdrop and the dwarfs; a fairy play. Boston. Baker. 1925. 12°. 55p.
Stranger; a comedy in one act. London. Deane. 1929. 12°. 15p.

Gantillon, Simon
Maya; a play in a prologue, nine scenes and an epilogue. tr. from the French . . . by Ernest Gantillon. N.Y. McBride. 1928. 12°. 147p.

Garnett, Edward, 1868-
Breaking point
In Trial of Jeanne d'Arc, and other plays
Feud. Historical Icelandic
In Trial of Jeanne d'Arc, and other plays
Trial of Jeanne d'Arc; an historical play in five acts. London. Sidgwick. 1912. 12°. 79p.
Same in Trial of Jeanne d'Arc, and other plays

Gaw, Allison, 1877- and Gaw, Ethelean Tyson
Pharaoh's daughter; the winning biblical play of the 1927 contest. N.Y. Longmans. 1928. 8°. 146p. 3 acts
Same in Gaw, A. et al. Pharaoh's daughter, and other Biblical plays of the contest, 1927

Geddes, Virgil, 1897-
As the crow flies. Local color. 3 acts
In Native ground; a cycle of plays
Behind the night. Tragi-comedy. 3 acts
In Earth between and Behind the night
Drink is the body. Comedy
In Four comedies from the life of George Emery Blum
Earth between
In Earth between, and Behind the night
Frog; a play in five scenes. Paris. Titus. 1926. 16°. 93p.
I have seen myself. Comedy
In Four comedies from the life of George Emery Blum
In the tradition. Comedy
In Four comedies from the life of George Emery Blum
Native ground. Local color. 3 acts
In Native ground; a cycle of plays
Plowshare's gleam. Local color. 3 acts
In Native ground; a cycle of plays
Pocahontas and the elders, a folkpiece in four acts. Chapel Hill, N.C. Abernethy. 1933. 8°. 89p.
Soul you may bury. Comedy
In Four comedies from the life of George Emery Blum

George, Charles
Healthy, wealthy and wise . . . a farce comedy in three acts. N.Y. French. c1933. 12°. 89p.
Hope springs eternal, a comedy of romance and moonlight in three acts. N.Y. French. c1931. 12°. 91p.
Little Miss Fortune; a comedy of charm in three acts. N.Y. French. c1932. 12°. 93p.
Mama's baby boy; a riot of laughs in three acts. N.Y. French. c1933. 12°. 87p.
My China doll; a musical comedy in three acts. N.Y. French. c1926. 8°. 77p.
Pay as you enter; a light comedy in three acts. N.Y. Longmans. 1931. 12°. 108p.
Sentimental Sarah, a comedy of charm in three acts. N.Y. French. c1933. 12°. 84p.
Way down upon the Swanee river; a romance of the southland in three acts. N.Y. French. 1930. 12°. 110p.

George, Ernest
Down our street. East end, London. 3 acts
In Six plays

George, G. M.
Charms; a fairy play in two acts. N.Y. French. 12°. 35p.

Geraghty, Tom J.
Pound of flesh. 1 act
In Nicholson, K. ed. Hollywood plays

Géraldy, Paul, 1885-
Just boys (Les grands garçons). Father and son. 1 act
In Vernon, V. and F. eds. Modern one-act plays from the French

Gerstenberg, Alice
At the club. Comedy. 1 act
In Comedies all, short plays
Facing facts. Comedy. 1 act
In Comedies all, short plays
Latch-keys. Comedy. 1 act
In Comedies all, short plays
Menu. Comedy. 1 act
In Comedies all, short plays
Mere man. Comedy. 1 act
In Comedies all, short plays
Opera matinée; a social satire in one act, for fourteen women. Summit, N.J. Swartout. 1925. 12°. 27p.
Same in Comedies all, short plays
Puppeteer. Comedy. 1 act
In Comedies all, short plays
Rhythm. Comedy. 1 act
In Comedies all, short plays
Sentience; a one-act comedy. N.Y. French. c1933. 12°. 25p.
Setback. Comedy. 1 act
In Comedies all, short plays
Trap. 1 act
In Twelve one-act plays
Unseen. Comedy. 1 act
In Goldstone, G. A. ed. One-act plays
Upstage. Comedy. 1 act
In Comedies all, short plays

Water babies, a dramatization of Charles Kingsley's classic story. N.Y. Longmans. 1930. 12°. 78p.

Gerstenberg, Alice and Howard, Lorin
Overtones, a play in three acts . . . (Based on an original one-act play by Alice Gerstenberg). N.Y. French. c1929. 12°. 78p.

Geyer, Siegfried
By candlelight; a little comedy in three acts. Adapted by Harry Graham from the German. N.Y. French. c1930. 8°. 76p.

Gibbs, Arthur Hamilton, 1888-
Meredew's right hand; a farce in one act. Boston. Baker. c1907. 12°. ₁235₁-247p.
In Phillips, LeR. and Johnson, T. eds. Types of modern dramatic composition

Gibney, Sheridan
Merry madness, a farce-comedy in three acts. N.Y. French. 1931. 12°. 97p.

Gibson, Lawrence
Bumbo the clown. Fantasy. 1 act
In Shay, F. ed. Fifty more contemporary one-act plays

Gibson, Wilfrid Wilson, 1878-
Between fairs; a comedy. N.Y. Macmillan. 1928. 12°. 92p. Gipsies

Gielgud, Val
Chinese white. 3 acts
In Five three-act plays

Gilbert, Bernard, 1882-
Eldorado. Rural. 1 act
In Hampden, J. Eight modern plays
Modern short plays. ser. 2
Old bull. Comedy. 1 act
In Hampden, J. ed. Nine modern plays
Prodigal's return; a play in one act. N.Y. French. c1927. 12°. 32p.

Gilbert, Bonnie
May madness. 1 act
In Sanford, A. P. ed. Plays for graduation days

Gilbert, Christie
Stocking. 1 act
In Marriott, J. W. ed. Best one-act plays of 1932

Gilbert, Helen
Good Sainte Anne
In Poet Lore 35:576
Spot on the porch. 1 act
In Poet Lore 42:81

Gilbert, Sir William Schwenck, 1836-1911
Colossal idea; an original farce. London. Putnam. ₁1932₁ 12°. 62p.
Dulcamara; or, The little duck and the great quack. Extravaganza. 5 scenes
In New and original extravaganzas
Gondoliers; or, The king of Barataria. Comic opera. 2 acts
In Plays and poems [with Sullivan]
Savoy operas
Grand duke; or, The statutory duel. Comic opera. 2 acts
In Plays and poems
Savoy operas

H. M. S. Pinafore; or, The lass that loved a sailor. Comic opera. 2 acts
In Best known works of W. S. Gilbert
Mikado, and other operas
Plays and poems [with Sullivan]
Savoy operas
Happy land. *See* Gilbert, W. S. Wicked world
His Excellency; a comic opera. 2 acts
In Plays and poems
Iolanthe. Comic opera. 2 acts
In Mikado, and other operas
Plays and poems [with Sullivan]
Savoy operas
Merry Zingara; or, The tipsy Gipsy and the pipsy wipsy. Extravaganza
In New and original extravaganzas
Mikado; or, The town of Titipu. Japanese opera. 2 acts
In Best known works of W. S. Gilbert
Mikado, and other operas
Plays and poems [with Sullivan]
Savoy operas
Mountebanks. Comic opera. 2 acts
In Plays and poems
Ne'er do well. A comedy drama in three acts. The property of E. A. Sothern, comedian. ₁N.Y.? 1877₁ 8°. 80p.
Palace of truth; a comedy in three acts
In Plays and poems
Pirates of Penzance; or, The slave of duty. Comic opera. 2 acts
In Best known works of W. S. Gilbert
Mikado, and other operas
Plays and poems [with Sullivan]
Savoy operas
Pretty Druidess; or, The mother, the maid, and the mistletoe bough. Extravaganza. 3 scenes
In New and original extravaganzas
Princess Ida, or, Castle Adamant. Comic opera. 3 acts
In Plays and poems [with Sullivan]
Savoy operas
Pygmalion and Galatea. Comedy. 3 acts
In Marriott, J. W. ed. Great modern British plays
Robert the devil; or, The nun, the dun, and the son of a gun. Extravaganza. 6 scenes
In New and original extravaganzas
Ruddigore; or, The witch's curse. Comic opera. 2 acts
In Plays and poems [with Sullivan]
Savoy operas
Sorcerer. Comic opera. 2 acts
In Plays and poems
Savoy operas
Sweethearts. Comedy. 2 acts
In Cordell, R. A. ed. Representative modern plays
Webber, J. P. and Webster, H. H. eds. Typical plays for secondary schools
Thespis; or, The gods grown old. 2 acts
In Plays and poems [with Sullivan]
Trial by jury. Comic opera. 1 scene
In Plays and poems [with Sullivan]
Savoy operas

Gilbert, W. S.—*Continued*
Utopia, limited; or, The flowers of progress. Comic opera. 2 acts
 In Plays and poems
   Savoy operas
Vivandière; or, True to the corps. Extravaganza. 5 scenes
 In New and original extravaganzas
Yeoman of the guards; or, The merryman and his maid. Comic opera. 1 scene
 In Plays and poems [with Sullivan]
   Savoy operas

Giorloff, Ruth
Circumstances alter cases. Comedy in one act. N.Y. French. [1930] 12°. 27p.
Highness; a one-act drama. N.Y. Longmans. 1931. 12°. 33p.
Jazz and minuet, a comedy in one act. N.Y. Longmans. 1928. 12°. 30p. St. Valentine's day. 1 act
 Same in Schauffler, R. H. and Sanford, A. P. eds. Plays for our American holidays. v. 1
Lavender and red pepper; a comedy in one act for eight women
 In [New plays for women and girls]
Maizie. Domestic tragedy. 1 act
 In One-act plays for stage and study

Giraudoux, Jean, 1882-
Siegfried, a play in four acts. English version by Philip Carr. N.Y. Longmans. 1930. 8°. 167p. Amnesia

Girette, Marcel, 1849-
Weaver of dreams. Comedy. 1 act
 In Vernon, V. and F. eds. Modern one-act plays from the French

Glaspell, Susan, 1882-
Alison's house; a play in three acts. N.Y. French. 1930. 12°. 155p.
 Same in Mantle, B. ed. Best plays of 1930-31 (abridged)
   Six plays
Outside. Sea. 1 act
 In Trifles, and six other short plays
People. Journalism. 1 act
 In Trifles, and six other short plays
Trifles. Tragedy. 1 act
 In Trifles, and six other short plays
   Clark, B. H. and Nicholson, K. eds. American scene
   Pence, R. W. ed. Dramas by present-day writers
   Phillips, Le R. and Johnson, T. eds. Types of modern dramatic composition
Woman's honor. Comedy. 1 act
 In Trifles, and six other short plays

Glaspell, Susan, 1882- and Cook, George Cram, 1873-1894
Suppressed desires. Freud. 1 act
 In Trifles, and six other short plays
Tickless time. Comedy. 1 act
 In Trifles, and six other short plays
   Hampden, J. ed. Ten modern plays

Glaspell, Susan, 1882- and Matson, Norman Häghjem, 1893-
Comic artist; a play in three acts. N.Y. Stokes. 1927. 12°. 87p.

Glassie, Ada Boyd
Meadowgold. Hallowe'en. 1 act
 In Schauffler, R. H. and Sanford, A. P. eds. Plays for our American holidays. v. 1

Gleason, James
Shannons of Broadway; a comedy in three acts. N.Y. French. 1928. 12°. 117p.

Gleason, James and Taber, Richard
Is zat so? a comedy in three acts. N.Y. French. 1928. 12°. 141p.

Gleason, James, *joint author. See* Abott, George and Gleason, James

Glick, Carl
Fourth Mrs. Phillips. 1 act
 In One-act plays for stage and study. ser. 4
It isn't done; a play in one act. N.Y. French [c1928] 12°. 16p.
Outclassed; a melodramatic comedy in one act. N.Y. French. [1928] 12°. 21p.
Sun-cold; a play in one act. N.Y. French. [1928] 12°. 22p.
Ten days later; a comedy in one act. N.Y. French. c1928. 12°. 34p.

Glover, Halcott
Bellairs; a comedy in three acts. London. Routledge. 1928. 12°. 84p.
 Same in Three comedies
God's amateur; a comedy in three acts. London. Routledge. 1928. 12°. 87-174p.
 Same in Three comedies
Hail Caesar! Comedy. Ireland. 3 acts
 In Wat Tyler, and other plays
King's Jewry; a play. London. Bloomsbury press. [c1921] 8°. 77p. 1 act and prologue
 Same in Wat Tyler, and other plays
   Tucker, S. M. Modern American and British plays
Second round; a play. London. Routledge. 1923. 12°. 73p. Suicide. 3 acts
Wat Tyler. Historical. 4 acts
 In Wat Tyler, and other plays
Wills and ways; a comedy in three acts. London. Routledge. 1928. 12°. 177-256p.
 Same in Three comedies

Gnesin, Maurice
Mistress. 1 act
 In Baker, G. P. ed. Yale one-act plays

Goes, Bertha
Dowry of Columbine. 1 act
 In Jagendorf, M. A. ed. Nine short plays

Goethe, Johann Wolfgang von, 1749-1832
Junkdump fair. Puppet. 1 act
 In McPharlin, P. ed. Repertory of marionette plays

Gogol', Nikolaï Vasil'evich, 1809-1852
Gamblers. Fraud
 In Gamblers, and Marriage
   Government inspector, and other plays
Government inspector. (Inspectorgeneral) Comedy. 5 acts
 In Government inspector, and other plays

Lawsuit. Sketch
  In Government inspector, and other
    plays
    Slavonic R 4:587
Marriage. Satire. 2 acts
  In Gamblers, and Marriage
    Government inspector, and other
      plays
Official's morning. Sketch
  In Government inspector, and other
    plays
Servant's hall. Sketch
  In Government inspector, and other
    plays
Going, C. B.
Twilight of the moon. 1 act
  In Johnson, T. ed.   Ten fantasies for
    stage and study
Gold, Michael, 1894-
Money; a play in one act. N.Y. French
  c1930. 8°. 30p.
  Same in Clark, B. H. and Cook, T. R.
    eds.   One-act plays
    Clark, B. H. and Nicholson, K.
      eds.   American scene
Golden, Israel J.
Precedent, a play about justice.   N.Y.
  Farrar. 1931. 12°. 148p. 3 acts
Golden, John, 1874-
Vanishing princess. 1 act
  In Shay, F. ed.   Fifty more contem-
    porary one-act plays
Golden, John, 1874- **and Jarrett, Dan**
Salt water, a fresh play. N.Y. French.
  1930. 12°. 115p. 3 acts
Goldoni, Carlo
La locandiera. Comedy. 3 acts
  In Le Gallienne, E. ed.   Eva Le Gal-
    lienne's civic repertory plays
Goodman, Jules Eckert, 1876-
Back to your knitting; a mystery farce
  in one act. N.Y. French. c1931. 12°.
  29p.
Treasure Island; a play in four acts and
  ten scenes; dramatized from the story
  of Robert Louis Stevenson. N.Y.
  French. 1933. 102p.
Goodman, Kenneth Sawyer
Back of the yards. 1 act
  In Tucker, S. M. ed.   Twelve one-act
    plays for study and production
Dust of the road. Religious. 1 act
  In Eastman, F. ed.   Modern religious
    dramas
    Goldstone, G. A. ed.   One-act plays
    Shay, F. ed.   Appleton book of
      Christmas plays
Goodrich, Arthur Frederick
Mr. Grant; a play in three acts. N.Y.
  McBride. 1934. 12°. 184p. Historical
Goodrich, Arthur Frederick, 1878- **and
Palmer, Rose Amelia**
Caponsacchi; a play in three acts, pro-
  logue and epilogue. N.Y. Appleton.
  1927. 12°. 185p. Tragedy
Goold, Marshall Newton, 1881-
Paul and Thekla, a religious drama in
  four acts. N.Y. Century. c1930. 12°.
  72p.

Gordin, Jacob
Captain Dreyfus. 1 act
  In White, B. F. trans.   Nine one-act
    plays from the Yiddish
Gordon, Leon and Palmer, R. A.
Piker. . . Boston. Four Seas. 1928. 8°.
Gore-Browne, R. F. *joint author. See* Har-
  wood, Harold Marsh and Gore-Browne,
  R. F.
**Gorki, Maxim, pseud. (Pieshkov, Aleksei
Maksimovich)** 1868-
Lower depths. (Night's lodging) Trag-
  edy. 4 acts
  In Moses, M. J. ed.   Dramas of mod-
    ernism and their forerunners
    Tucker, S. M. ed.   Modern conti-
      nental plays
Gorman, Herbert Sherman, 1893-
Death of Nero.   Historical. 1 act
  In Shay, F. ed.   Fifty more contempo-
    rary one-act plays
Gow, Ronald
Gallows glorious; a play in three acts.
  London. Gollancz. 1933. 96p.
Golden west; a farce on the instalment
  plan. London. Gowans. 1932. 29p.
Miracle of Watling street
  In Bourne, J. ed.   Eight new plays for
    boys and girls
Vengeance of the gang; a play for boys,
  in six scenes. London. Gowans.
  1933. 64p.
Graham, David, 1854-
Pompilia; a play (founded on "The ring
  and the book") London. Nash. 1928.
  8°. 124p.
Graham, Manta S.
Call it a day. Comedy
  In Snook, L. O. ed.   Comedies seven
Grant, Neil Forkes, 1882-
Hat trick. 1 act
  In Bourne, J. ed.   8 new one-act plays
    for 1934
On Dartmoor. 1 act
  In Marriott, J. W. ed.   Best one-act
    plays of 1932
Granville, Edward
Moonbeam; a play of the little people
  in one act. N.Y. French. 1929. 12°.
  34p.
Granville-Barker, Harley Granville, 1877-
His Majesty; a play in four acts. Lon-
  don. Sidgwick. 1928. 12°. 131p. King-
  ship
Waste. Politics. 4 acts
  In Tucker, S. M. ed.   Modern Amer-
    ican and British plays
Grattan, Lawrence
Gossipy sex; a comedy in three acts.
  N.Y. [c1927] 12°. 97p.
Shorn lamb, a comedy drama in four
  acts.   no pub. 1906. 8°. 56p.
Gray, David, 1870- **and Hopwood, Avery,**
1884-
Best people; a comedy in three acts.
  N.Y. French. c1928. 12°. 111p.
Green, Cara Mae
Jumpin' the broom. Comedy. 1 act
  In One-act plays for stage and study.
    ser. 5

Green, Paul, 1894-
Blue thunder; or, The man who married a snake. 1 act
In One-act plays for stage and study. ser. 4
Field god. Negro. 3 acts
In Tucker, S. M. ed. Twenty-five modern plays
Goodbye. Negro. 1 act
In In the valley, and other Carolina plays
House of Connelly. Negro. 2 acts
In House of Connelly and other plays
Mantle, B. ed. Best plays of 1931-32
In Abraham's bosom: biography of a Negro. London. Allen. 1929. 12°. 152p. 7 scenes
Same in Dickinson, T. H. ed. Chief contemporary dramatists. ser. 3
Locke, A. Le R. and Gregory, M. eds. Plays of Negro life
Mantle, B. ed. Best plays of 1926-27 (abridged)
In Aunt Mahaly's cabin; a Negro melodrama in one act
In In the valley, and other Carolina plays
In the valley. Negro. 1 act
In In the valley, and other Carolina plays
Last of the Lowries; a play of the Croatan outlaws of Robeson county, N.C. N.Y. French. 1933. 31p.
Lord's will; tragedy of a country preacher; play in one act. N.Y. French. 1934. 12°. 5-45p.
Man on the house. Negro. 1 act
In In the valley, and other Carolina plays
Man who died at twelve o'clock. N.Y. French. 1927. 12°. 18p. Negro comedy. 1 act
Same in In the valley, and other Carolina plays
Church, V. W. ed. Curtain!
No 'count boy; a play in one act. N.Y. French. 1933. 25p. Negro
Same in In the valley, and other Carolina plays
Clark, B. H. and Cook, T. R. eds. One-act plays
Isaacs, E. J. ed. Plays of American life and fantasy
Locke, A. Le R. and Gregory, M. eds. Plays of Negro life
Picnic. Negro. 1 act
In In the valley, and other Carolina plays
Potter's field. A symphonic play of the Negro people. 1 act
In House of Connelly and other plays
Quare medicine. Comedy. 1 act
In In the valley, and other Carolina plays
Koch, F. H. ed. Carolina folk-plays. ser. 3
Shay, F. ed. Fifty more contemporary one-act plays

Saturday night. Negro. 1 act
In In the valley, and other Carolina plays
Supper for the dead. Negro. 1 act
In In the valley, and other Carolina plays
Tread the green grass. Folk fantasy. 2 pts.
In House of Connelly and other plays
Unto such glory. Negro. 1 act
In In the valley, and other Carolina plays
White dresses; a tragedy of Negro life. 1 act
In Locke, A. Le R. and Gregory, M. eds. Plays of Negro life

Green, Paul and Green, Erma
Fixin's; the tragedy of a tenant farm woman. 1 act
In Koch, F. H. ed. Carolina folk-plays
Schauffler, R. H. and Sanford, A. P. eds. Plays for our American holidays. v. 4

Gregory, Lady Isabella Augusta, 1859-1932
Bogie men. Ireland. 1 act
In Schauffler, R. H. and Sanford, A. P. eds. Plays for our American holidays. v. 1
Colman and Guaire. 1 act
In One-act plays for stage and study. ser. 6
Dave. Peasant life. 1 act
In Three last plays
Dragon. Comedy. 3 acts
In Moses, M. J. ed. Ring up the curtain!
Webber, J. P. and Webster, H. H. eds. Typical plays for secondary schools
Hyacinth Halvey. Comedy. 1 act
In Canfield, C. ed. Plays of the Irish renaissance
Watson, E. B. and Pressey, B. eds. Contemporary drama: English and Irish plays. v. 1
On the racecourse; a play in one act. N.Y. Putnam. [1926] 27p. [A rewriting of the author's first play which was called Twenty-five]
Rising of the moon. Comedy. 1 act
In Webber, J. P. and Webster, H. H. eds. One-act plays for secondary schools
Sancho's master. Comedy. 3 acts
In Three last plays
Spreading the news. Gossip. 1 act
In Cohen, H. L. ed. One-act plays by modern authors. 1934 edition
Pence, R. W. ed. Dramas by present-day writers
Talking dragon. Juvenile
In Moses, M. J. ed. Ring up the curtain!
Travelling man. Miracle play. 1 act
In Modern short plays. ser. 1
Twenty-five. *See* Gregory, I. A. On the racecourse

Workhouse ward. Comedy. 1 act
In Goldstone, G. A. ed. One-act plays
Tucker, S. M. ed. Twelve one-act
plays for study and production
Would-be-gentleman. tr. and adapted
from the French of Molière. Com-
edy. 1 act
In Three last plays

Gregson, James Richard, 1889-
Democrat from Debrett; a farcical com-
edy in three acts. London. [1931]
12°. 90p.
Devil a saint; a comedy in three acts.
London. Gay and Hancock. 1928. 12°.
81p.
Liddy. Yorkshire. 1 act
In Way of an angel, and other plays
Melchisedek. Yorkshire. 1 act
In Way of an angel, and other plays
Sar' Alice. London. Hodder. 1930. 12°.
155p. 4 acts
Way of an angel
In Way of an angel, and other plays
Youth disposes. Yorkshire. 1 act
In Way of an angel, and other plays

Gribble, Harry Wagstaff
Juliet and Romeo. Romantic. 1 act
In Shay, F. ed. Fifty more contempo-
rary one-act plays
Message. Unknown dead. 1 act
In Schauffler, R. H. and Sanford, A. P.
eds. Plays for our American
holidays. v. 3

Griffith, Eleanor Glendower
House the children built. Health. 1 act
In Schauffler, R. H. and Sanford, A. P.
eds. Plays for our American
holidays. v. 4
Little vegetable men. Health. 1 act
In Schauffler, R. H. and Sanford, A. P.
eds. Plays for our American
holidays. v. 4

Griffith, Hubert Freeling, 1896-
Red Sunday; a play in three acts. London. Richards. 1929. 12°. 89p.
Tender passion; a play in three acts and
seven scenes. N.Y. Brentano's. 1927.
12°. 85p. (British drama league library of modern British drama. no.
14)
Tragic muse, a play in three acts.
Adapted from the novel of Henry
James. London. Unwin. 1927. 12°.
93p.
Tunnel trench; a play in three acts and
seven scenes. London. Allen. [1924]
12°. 73p.

Grimball, Elizabeth B.
Snow queen. Fairy. 2 acts
In Schauffler, R. H. and Sanford, A. P.
eds. Plays for our American
holidays. v. 2
Waif; a Christmas morality of the twentieth century. N.Y. c1923. 16°.

Gropper, Milton Herbert
It won't be long now, a farce in three
acts. Acting edition. N.Y. Longmans. 1930. 12°. 116p

**Gropper, Milton Herbert and Hammer-
stein, Oscar, 2nd**
Gypsy Jim; a play in three acts. N.Y.
French. c1927. 12°. 94p.
New toys; a comedy in three acts. N.Y.
French. c1927. 12°. 125p.

Gropper, Milton Herbert and Siegel, Max
We Americans; a new play. N.Y.
French. c1928. 12°. 99p. 3 acts

Grover, Harry Greenwood
Summer holiday; a comedy in one act.
N.Y. French. c1933. 12°. 19p.

Grover, P. L.
Mariot and Mariette. Comedy. 1 act
In Johnson, T. ed. Diminutive com-
edies

Gue, Belle Willey
Washington, the statesman; a drama.
San Diego, Cal. The Canterbury
Company. 1928. 8°. 108p. Historical

Guinan, John
Black Oliver. Ireland. 1 act
In One-act plays for stage and study.
ser. 5
Dublin M 2:32
Cuckoo's nest; a comedy in three acts.
Dublin. Gill. [c1933] 8°. 66p.

Guinn, Dorothy C.
Out of the dark. Negro pageant. 1 act
In Richardson, W. ed. Plays and
pageants from the life of the
Negro

Guiterman, Arthur, 1871- **and Langner,
Lawrence**
School for husbands; adapted . . . from
Molière's comedy "L'Ecole des
maris." N.Y. French. 1933. 12°. 161p.
Comedy

Guitry, Sacha, 1885
Villa for sale. Comedy. 1 act
In Vernon, V. and F. eds. Modern
one-act plays from the French

Gunn, John Alexander, 1896-
Spinoza, the maker of lenses; a play in
three acts. London. Allen. [c1932]
12°. 99p.

Gunn, Neil M.
Back home. 1 act
In Marriott, J. W. ed. Best one-act
plays of 1931

Gunner, Frances
Light of the women. Negro pageant.
1 act
In Richardson, W. ed. Plays and pageants from the life of the Negro

**Guthrie, Thomas Anstey (F. Anstey,
pseud.)**
Game of adverbs. 1 act
In Golden Bk 10:99
Salted almonds. 1 act
In Golden Bk 14:372

Hackett, Albert and Goodrich, Frances
Up pops the devil; a comedy in three
acts. N.Y. French. 117p.

Hackett, Walter, 1876-
Barton mystery, a play in four acts. N.Y.
French. c1930. 8°. 63p.
Captain Applejack; an Arabian night's ad-
venture, in three acts. N.Y. French.
c1925. 12°. 121p.

Hackett, Walter—*Continued*
Freedom of the seas, a play in three acts. N.Y. French. 1929. 12°. 104p.
Other men's wives, a play in three acts. N.Y. French. 1929. 8°. 104p.
77, Park lane, an adventure in three acts. N.Y. French. c1929. 8°. 92p.
Sorry you've been troubled! A play in three acts. N.Y. French. c1931. 8°. 91p.
Way to treat a woman. N.Y. French. c1930. 8°. 95p.
Hackett, Walter, *joint author. See* Arlen, M. and Hackett, W.

Hagan, James
One Sunday afternoon
In Mantle, B. ed. Best plays of 1932-33 (abridged)

Hall, Holworthy, pseud. (Porter, Harold Everett, 1887- and Middlemass, Robert)
Valiant. Religious. 1 act
In Eastman, F. ed. Modern religious dramas
Twelve one-act plays

Halman, Doris Friend, 1895-
Closet. Domestic tragedy. 1 act
In Phillips, LeR. and Johnson, T. eds. Types of modern dramatic composition
Famine and the ghost. 1 scene
In Johnson, T. ed. More plays in miniature
Lenna looks down. 1 act
In One-act plays for stage and study. ser. 4

Halvey, P.
Wanderlust. 1 act
In Clark, B. H. and Nicholson, K. eds. American scene

Hamilton, Cicely Mary, 1875-
Jack and Jill and a friend. Comedy. 1 act
In Shay, F. ed. Fifty more contemporary one-act plays
Just to get married; a comedy in three acts. N.Y. French. c1914. 12°. 87p.
Old Adam, a fantastic comedy . . . Oxford. Blackwell. 1926. 12°. 99p.

Hamilton, Harry Lacy
Fingerbowls and Araminta; a comedy in one act for five women. Summit, N.J. Swartout. 1926. 12°. 28p.
Going straight; a comedy in three acts. Chicago. Denison. 1927. 12°. 173p.

Hamilton, Henry
Harvest; an original modern play, in a prologue and three acts. London. French. [1893] 67p.
Our regiment; a farcical comedy in three acts, adapted from the German of von Moser. N.Y. French. [188-?] 55p.
Three musketeers, a play in four acts, adapted from the novel of Alexander Dumas. N.Y. French. c1930. 12°. 122p.

Hamilton, Patrick, 1904-
Rope (Rope's end); a play in three acts. N.Y. French. 1933. 86p.

Hamlin, Mary P.
Burnt offering; a play about Jephthah's wife, in one act. N.Y. French. c1933. 12°. 26p.
He came seeing; a one-act play. N.Y. French. c1928. 8°. 35p.
Trouble with the Christmas presents; comedy in prologue and one act. N.Y. French. [1931] 12°. 36p.

Hamlin, Mary P. and Arliss, George
Hamilton, a play in four acts. Boston. Baker. 1918. 12°. 160p.

Hammerstein, Oscar, 2nd, *joint author. See* Gropper, M. H. and Hammerstein, O. 2nd

Hankin, St. John, 1869-1909
Alcestis. 1 scene
In Dramatic sequels
Caesar and Cleopatra. 1 scene
In Dramatic sequels
Caste. 1 scene
In Dramatic sequels
Charity that began at home; a comedy in four acts. N.Y. French. 1907. 12°. 112p.
Constant lover. Comedy. 1 act
In Marriott, J. W. ed. One-act plays. ser. 4
Critic. 1 scene
In Dramatic sequels
Dramatic version of Omar Khayyam. 1 scene
In Dramatic sequels
Hamlet. 1 scene
In Dramatic sequels
Lady from the sea. 1 scene
In Dramatic sequels
Lady of Lyons. 1 scene
In Dramatic sequels
Last of the De Mullins. Sociological. 3 acts
In Chandler, F. W. and Cordell, R. A. eds. Twentieth century plays
Much ado about nothing. 1 scene
In Dramatic sequels
New wing at Elsinore. 1 scene
In Hampden, J. ed. Ten modern plays
Patience. 1 scene
In Dramatic sequels
Return of the prodigal; a comedy in four acts. N.Y. French. c1907. 12°. 101p.
Same in Marriott, J. W. ed. Great modern British plays
School for scandal. 1 scene
In Dramatic sequels
Second Mrs. Tanqueray. 1 scene
In Dramatic sequels
She stoops to conquer. 1 scene
In Dramatic sequels
Two Mr. Wetherbys; a middle-class comedy in three acts. N.Y. French. 1907. 12°. 90p.

Hanlon, Daniel E. 1877-
Wolf at the door. 1 act
In One-act plays for stage and study. ser. 6

Hardy, Thomas, 1840-1928
Three wayfarers, a play in one act; dramatized from his story "The three strangers." N.Y. Fountain press. 1930. 4°. 34p.

Hare, Walter Ben

Aboard a slow train in Mizzoury, a farcical entertainment in three acts. Boston. Baker. 1920. 12°. 52p.

Adventures of grandpa; a wholesome farce in three acts. Boston. Baker. 1918. 70p.

Alabama bound, a dramatic comedy of youth triumphant, in three acts. Boston. Baker. [1929] 12°. 71p.

And Billy disappeared, a clean comedy of mystery in four acts. Boston. Baker. 1920. 12°. 148p.

And home came Ted, a comedy of mystery in three acts. Chicago. Denison. [1917] 12°. 156p.

Backwoods school in '49, an entertainment in one act. Boston. Baker. 1925. 12°. 28p.

Beantown baby show, a mirthquake of fun in one laughing shock. Boston. Baker. 1926. 12°. 15p.

Boy scouts; a play for boys in three acts. Boston. Baker. [1913] 51p.

Bride and groom, a farce in three acts. N.Y. Dick. c1916. 12°. 59p.

Camp-fire girls; a comedy for girls in four acts. Boston. Baker. [c1915] 46p.

Cheer-up; a comedy in three acts. Boston. Baker. 1925. 12°. 104p.

Civil service, an American drama in three acts; a play with a punch. Chicago. Denison. [1915] 12°. 68p.

College town; a college farce comedy in three acts. Chicago. Denison. [1910] 12°. 64p.

Colonial garden party. [From A pageant of history]
In Johnson, T. ed. Washington anniversary plays

Couple of million, an American comedy in four acts. Boston. Baker. 1917. 12°. 72p.

Cowpunchers, a play in one act. Boston. Baker. 1926. 12°. 38p.

Dutch detective, a farce in three acts. Boston. Baker. 1914. 12°. 53p.

Early bird, a comedy in three acts. Chicago. Denison. [1918] 12°. 88p.

Fascinations; a musical burlesque entertainment in one act. Chicago. Denison. [1913] 12°. 19p.

Grandma Gibbs of the Red Cross, a patriotic comedy drama in four acts. Boston. Baker. 1918. 12°. 62p.

Has anyone seen Jean? A melodramatic mystery comedy in three acts. Boston. Baker. c1927. 12°. 116p.

Heiress hunters, a comedy in three acts. Boston. Baker. 1915. 12°. 60p.

Hoodoo, a farce in three acts. Boston. Baker. 1913. 12°. 83p.

Isosceles, a play in one act. Boston. Baker. 1917. 12°. 13p.

Kicked out of college; a college farce in three acts; a companion play to "A college town." Chicago. Denison. [1916] 12°. 72p.

Macbeth à la mode, a school burletta in three acts. Chicago. Denison. [1914] 12°. 35p.

Old days in Dixie; a comedy-drama in three acts. Boston. Baker. 1920. 12°. 73p.

Old fashioned mother, a dramatic parable of a mother's love, in three acts. Chicago. Denison. [1917] 12°. 68p.

Parlor matches, an engaging comedy of society in two acts. Chicago. Denison. [1915] 12°. 40p.

Poor married man; a farce comedy in three acts. Chicago. Denison. [1915] 12°. 55p.

Professor Pepp, a farcical comedy with a college flavor, in three acts. Boston. Baker. 1915. 12°. 64p.

Rustic Romeo, a musical comedy in two acts. Chicago. Denison. [c1912] 12°. 87p.

Sewing for the heathen, a refined comedy in one act. Chicago. Denison. [1915] 12°. 20p.

Southern Cinderella, a comedy-drama in three acts. Chicago. Denison. [c1913] 12°. 51p.

Teddy; or, The runaways, a comedy in three acts. Boston. Baker. 1913. 12°. 64p.

Hargrave, Roy, *joint author. See* Britton, Kenneth Phillips and Hargrave, Roy

Harlan, Walter, 1867-
Nüremburg egg. Invention. 4 acts
In Katzin, W. ed. Eight European plays

Harnwell, Anna J.
Her name was Anne
In Sanford, A. P. ed. Lincoln plays

Harnwell, Anna J. *joint author. See* Meaker, Isabelle J. and Harnwell, Anna J.

Harper, H.
Christmas tale (based on the French of M. Bouchor)
In Shay, F. ed. Appleton book of Christmas plays

Harris, Edna May 1900-
Windblown; a fantasy in one act
In Poet Lore 38:426

Harris, Frank, 1856-1931
Joan la Romée, a drama. [N.Y. Harris. 1926] 8°. 91p. Joan of Arc

Harris, Hazel Harper
When a man wanders; a one-act play for women
In Poet Lore 40:602

Harris, Lillian
Marriage is so difficult. Farce. 1 act
In Poet Lore 38:452
Publicity. 1 act
In Poet Lore 38:590

Harris, May Pashley
Pageant of inauguration. Historical
In Johnson, T. ed. Washington anniversary plays

Harrison, Constance Cary (Mrs. Burton Harrison) 1846-1920
Tea at four o'clock. A drawing-room comedy, in one act. N.Y. DeWitt. c1892. 12°. 29p.

Hart, Moss, *joint author.* *See* Kaufman,
G. S. and Hart, Moss

Hartleben, Otto Erich, 1864-1905
Demands of society. Comedy. 1 act
In Shay, F. ed. Fifty more contem-
porary one-act plays

Hartley, Roland English
Other side of the door. 1 act
In Poet Lore 41:223

**Hartley, Roland English and Power, Caro-
line Marguerite**
Ambitious guest (N. Hawthorne)
In Short plays from great stories
Madame Delphine (G. W. Cable)
In Short plays from great stories
Mateo Falcone (P. Mérimée)
In Short plays from great stories
My double and how he undid me (E. E.
Hale)
In Short plays from great stories
Necklace (G. de Maupassant)
In Short plays from great stories
Outcasts from Poker Flat (B. Harte)
In Short plays from great stories
Purloined letter (E. A. Poe)
In Short plays from great stories
Rip Van Winkle (W. Irving)
In Short plays from great stories
Rose of the Alhambra (W. Irving)
In Short plays from great stories
Shot (A. Pushkin)
In Short plays from great stories
Siege of Berlin (Alphonse Daudet)
In Short plays from great stories
Sire de Malétroit's door (R. L. Steven-
son)
In Short plays from great stories
Sisterly scheme (H. C. Bunner)
In Short plays from great stories
Substitute (F. Coppée)
In Short plays from great stories
Three strangers (T. Hardy)
In Short plays from great stories
Two of them (J. M. Barrie)
In Short plays from great stories
Wee Willie Winkie (R. Kipling)
In Short plays from great stories
Young man with the cream tarts (R. L.
Stevenson)
In Short plays from great stories

Harwood, Harold Marsh, 1874-
Girl's best friend, a play in three acts.
London. Benn. 1929. 12°. 69p.
Man in possession; a play in three acts
and an epilogue. London. Benn. 1930.
12°. 89p.
So far and no father; a play in four
scenes. London. Benn. 1932. 12°. 85p.
Transit of Venus; a play in four acts.
London. Benn. 1927. 12°. 93p.

Harwood, Harold Marsh, 1874- **and Gore-
Browne, Robert**
Cynara: a play in a prologue, three acts
and an epilogue, adapted from "An
imperfect lover," a novel by R. Gore-
Browne. London. Benn. 1930. 12°.
114p.
Same in Mantle, B. ed. Best plays of
1931-32 (abridged)

King, queen, knave; a play in three acts.
London. Benn. 1932. 12°. 97p.

Hatch, Mrs. Mary R. (Platt) 1848-
Mademoiselle Vivine; a one-act play.
Boston. Four Seas. 1927. 12° 22p.
Mrs. Bright's visitor; a comedy in one
act. Boston. Four Seas. 1927. 12°.
22p.

Hatton, Fannie, *joint author.* *See* Hatton,
Frederic and Hatton, Fannie

Hatton, Frederic, 1879- **and Hatton, Fannie**
Lombardi, ltd.; a comedy in three acts.
N.Y. French. c1928. 12°. 172p.

Hauptmann, Gerhart, 1862-
Beaver coat [Der Bilberpelz]. Comedy.
4 acts
In Watson, E. B. and Pressey, B. eds.
Contemporary drama. European
plays. v. 1
Rats. Social. 5 acts
In Tucker, S. M. ed. Modern con-
tinental plays
Tucker, S. M. ed. Twenty-five mod-
ern plays
Sunken bell. Symbolic. 5 acts
In Whitman, C. H. ed. Seven contem-
porary plays

Haworth, Edith
Emperor's new clothes; a play in five
acts
In Players M 10:22 N.-D. 1933

Hayward, Grace
Graustark; or, Love behind a throne;
a modern romantic comedy . . .
dramatized from the novel of George
Barr McCutcheon. N.Y. French.
c1926. 12°. 74p.
Some girl; a comedy in three acts. N.Y.
French. 1928. 12°. 107p.

Head, Cloyd
Grotesques; a decoration in black and
white. Chicago. Dramatic pub. co.
1933. 12°. 62p.

Heal, Edith
Into the everywhere; a play for the
mind's eye. 1 act
In Poet Lore 38:466

Healey, Frances
Copper pot. 2 scenes
In Webber, J. P. and Webster, H. H.
eds. Typical plays for secondary
schools
Creeds. Religious conflict. 1 act
In Shay, F. ed. Fifty more contem-
porary one-act plays

Heath, Crosby
Unruly member. Comedy. 1 act
In Shay, F. ed. Fifty more contem-
porary one-act plays

Heath, E. P.
Bird in the hand. 1 act
In Nicholson, K. ed. Hollywood plays

Hecht, Ben, 1893- **and Fowler, Gene**
Great Magoo; a love-sick charade in
three acts and something like eight
scenes. N.Y. Covici. [1933] 8°. 208p.

Hecht, Ben and MacArthur, Charles
Front page. . . . N.Y. Covici. 1928. 12°.
189p. Melodrama. 3 acts
In Mantle, B. ed. Best plays of 1928-
29 (abridged)

Heckscher, Maurice, jr.
Tragic fugue; a play in three episodes.
Glen Head, N.Y. Ashlar press. 1933.
8°. 57p.

Heijermans, Herman, 1864-1924
Ahasverus. tr. from the Dutch by Caro-
line Heijermans-Houwink and Dr.
J. J. Houwink. 1 act
In Drama 19:145
Good Hope; a drama of the sea in four
acts; only authorized translation by
William Saunders and Caroline
Heijermans-Houwink. N.Y. French.
1928. 8°. 145p. Dutch shipping laws
Links. 4 acts
In Poet Lore 38:1
Rising sun (De opgaande zon) . . . a play
in four acts tr. by Christopher St.
John [pseud]. London. Labour pub.
co. [1926] 12°. 86p.

Hellman, Lillian
Children's hour. N.Y. Knopf. 1934. 12°.
115p. Slander. 3 acts

Hemingway, Ernest, 1898
To-day is Friday. 1 act
In Men without women

Hepworth, F. A.
Queen Dick; an episode founded upon the
novel of Alfred Tressider Sheppard
and dramatized by F. A. Hepworth.
1 act
In Bourne, J. ed. 8 new one-act plays

Herbert, Alan Patrick, 1890-
Derby day, a comic opera in three acts;
the words by A. P. Herbert. Lon-
don. Methuen. [1931] 12°. 126p.
Double demon. 1 act
In Mayor, B. ed. Four one-act plays
Helen, a comic opera in three acts, based
upon "La belle Hélène" by Henri
Meilhac and Ludovic Halevy; the
English version by A. P. Herbert.
London. Methuen. 1932. 12°. 112p.
Tantivy towers, a light opera in three
acts. . . . London. Methuen. [1931]
12°. 78p.
Two gentlemen of Soho. N.Y. French.
c1927. 12°. 28p. 1 act
Same in London Merc 16:490

Herbert, Alan Patrick, 1890- and Davies-
Adams, A.
La vie parisienne. A comic opera in
three acts. London. Benn. 1929. 12°.
76p.

Herne, James A. 1839-1901
Hearts of oak. Melodrama. 6 acts
In Shore Acres, and other plays
Sag Harbor; an old story. 4 acts
In Shore Acres, and other plays
Shore Acres. Comedy. 4 acts
In Shore Acres, and other plays

Heyward, Dorothy Hartzell (Kuhns)
Nancy Ann; a comedy in three acts.
N.Y. French c1927. 12°. 141p.

Heyward, Mrs. Dorothy Hartzell (Kuhns)
and De Jagers, Dorothy
Little girl blue, a romantic comedy in a
prologue and three acts. N.Y.
French. c1931. 12°. 80p.

Heyward, Mrs. Dorothy Hartzell (Kuhns)
and Heyward, Du Bose, 1885-
Porgy; a play in four acts . . . from the
novel of Du Bose Heyward. Garden
City, N.Y. Doubleday. 1928. 8°.
203p. Negro.
Same in Mantle, B. ed. Best plays of
1927-28 (abridged)

Heyward, Du Bose, 1885-
Brass ankle, a play in three acts. N.Y.
Farrar. c1931. 12°. 133p. Negro
problem

Hickenlooper, Margaret
Saint Anselm only carved one soul; a
Christmas fantasy
In Johnson, T. ed. Ten fantasies for
stage and study
Troll and the toll bridge. Comedy.
In Johnson, T. ed. Diminutive com-
edies

Hickerson, Harold, *joint author. See*
Anderson, Maxwell and Hickerson,
Harold

Hickson, Leslie M.
Leap year bride. Comedy. 1 act
In Shay, F. ed. Fifty more con-
temporary one-act plays
Whose money? *See* Dickson, L. and
Hickson, L. M. Whose money?

Hill, Leslie Pinckney, 1880-
Toussaint L'Ouverture; a dramatic history. Boston. Christopher. 1928.
12°. 137p. 5 acts

Hillyer, Robert, 1895-
Engagement ring; a comedy. [Hartford,
Conn. Haylofters. 1927] 12°. 31p.
1 act
Masquerade; a comedy. Hartford, Conn.
Haylofters. 1928. 12°. 31p.

Hilton, Charles
Broken pines. 1 act
In Poet Lore 40:461

Hines, Leonard J. and King, Frank
Vindication. Execution. 1 act
In Marriott, J. W. ed. Best one-act
plays of 1931

Hirschbein, Perez, 1880-
Bebele. Idyll. 1 act
In Block, E. ed. One-act plays from
the Yiddish. ser. 2.
Lone worlds! 1 act
In Block, E. ed. One-act plays from
the Yiddish. ser. 2

Hirschfeld, Georg, 1873-
Second life. 1 act
In Poet Lore 39:475

Hodge, Merton
Wind and the rain. A play in three acts.
London. Gollancz. 1934. 12°. 115p.
Same in Famous plays of 1933-34

Hodge, William Thomas, 1874-
Beware of dogs; a satirical tale in three
ways. 3 acts
In Plays. v. 2

Hodge, W. T.—*Continued*
Fixing sister. Comedy. 4 acts
In Plays. v. 1
For all of us. Melodrama. 3 acts
In Plays. v. 1
Guest of honor. Comedy. 3 acts
In Plays. v. 2
Judge's husband. Romance. 3 acts
In Plays. v. 1
Road to happiness. Comedy. 4 acts
In Plays. v. 2
Straight through the door; a mystery
comedy in three acts. N.Y. French.
1929. 12°. 123p.

Hodson, James Lansdale
Back way; a comedy in one act. Lon-
don. Gowans. 1927. 16°. 32p.
George proposes; a comedy in one act.
London. Gowans. 1927. 16°. 32p.
Harvest, a play in one act. London.
Gowans. 1931. 12°. 29p.
Proof; a play in one act. London.
Gowans. 1927. 24°. 32p.
Red night, a war play in a prologue
and four acts. . . . mainly adapted
from "Grey dawn—red night" by the
same author. London. Gollancz.
1930. 12°. 111p.
These fathers! A comedy in three acts.
London. Gowans. 1930. 12°. 148p.

**Hoffe, Monckton (Reaney Monckton
Hoffe-Miles) 1881-**
Faithful heart; an original play. Lon-
don. Heinemann. 1922. 12°. 80p. 2
acts
Little damozel; a comedy in three acts.
N.Y. French. 1912
Many waters. London. Gollancz. 1928.
12°. 126p. Satire. 4 acts
Same in Famous plays of to-day 1930
Plays of a half-decade
Stolen rolls. N.Y. French. c1926. 12°.
23p. 1 act

Hoffman, Phoebe, 1894-
About face, a comedy in one act, for
three women. Summit, N.J. Swart-
out. 1924. 12°. 18p.
Advantages of being shy, comedy in one
act. N.Y. French. c1927. 12°. 24p.
Lady of destiny, a comedy in one act
(for a number of women). N.Y.
French. c1925. 12°. 29p.
Man of ideas, a phantasy in one act.
Boston. Baker. [1927] 12°. 20p.
Man of the moment. Fantasy. 1 act
In Johnson, T. ed. Ten fantasies for
stage and study
Martha's mourning, a play in one act.
Boston. Baker. 1923. 12°. 14p.
Mrs. Leicester's school. 1 act
In New plays for women and girls
Triumph of Mary; a play in one act.
Boston. Baker. [1927] 12°. 20p.
Turn of a hair; a farce in one act. Phila-
delphia. Penn. 1929. 12°. 22p.
Undertones; a comedy in one act. N.Y.
French. c1925. 12°. 18p.

Hofmannsthal, Hugo von, 1874-
Electra. Tragedy. 1 act
In Dickinson, T. H. ed. Chief con-
temporary dramatists. ser. 3

Holbrook, Marion
All's vanity. 1 act
In Sanford, A. P. ed. One-act plays
for women
Backwoods. 1 act
In Johnson, T. ed. Washington anni-
versary plays
Better mouse trap. 1 act
In Sanford, A. P. ed. Plays for gradu-
ation days
Brandywine. Historical. 1 act
In Johnson, T. ed. Washington an-
niversary plays
Kid gloves. 1 act
In Sanford, A. P. ed. One-act plays
for women
Little general. 1 act
In Johnson, T. ed. Washington an-
niversary plays
Mount Vernon. Historical. 1 act
In Johnson, T. ed. Washington an-
niversary plays
Stitch in time. 1 act
In Johnson, T. ed. Plays about George
Washington

Holland, Harold
Dad, a play in three acts and an epilogue. London. Benn. 1928. 12°.
113p.

Holme, Constance
Home of vision. 1 act
In Marriott, J. W. ed. Best one-act
plays of 1932
"I want!" Fantasy. 3 acts
In Five three-act plays

Holmes, E. D.
Capture of Major André. 1 act
In Johnson, T. ed. Plays about George
Washington
Capture of the British sentinel at Stony
Point. 1 act
In Johnson, T. ed. Plays about George
Washington

Holmes, L. T. *joint author.* See Donahue,
Von and Holmes, L. T.

Hopkins, Arthur
Moonshine. North Carolina. 1 act
In Hampden, J. ed. Ten modern plays
Isaacs, E. J. ed. Plays of American
life and fantasy
Tucker, S. M. ed. Twelve one-act
plays for study and production

Hopkins, Arthur, *joint author. See* Watters, George Manker and Hopkins,
Arthur

Hopwood, Avery, 1884-
Alarm clock; a comedy in three acts.
N.Y. French. c1930. 12°. 112p.

Hopwood, Avery, *joint author. See* Gray,
David and Hopwood, Avery

Hopwood, Avery, *joint author. See* Rinehart, Mary Roberts and Hopwood,
Avery

Hornsey, Evelyn Grant
Denial. Boston. Baker. [c1927] 12°. 26p.
1 act

Some of us are like that. Comedy. 1
act
In Johnson, T. ed. Diminutive com-
edies
Hornthal, Larry, *joint author. See* Strode,
Hudson and Hornthal, Larry
Horowitz, Nathan, 1888-
Souls in exile; a play in four acts. Lon-
don. Narodiczky. 1928. 8°. 52p.
Houghton, Stanley, 1881-1913
Dear departed; a comedy in one act.
N.Y. French. c1910. 12°. 26p.
Hindle wakes. 3 acts
In Plays of to-day. v. 1
Tucker, S. M. ed. Modern Ameri-
can and British plays
Master of the house. Domestic. 1 act
In Marriott, J. W. ed. One-act plays
of to-day. ser. 3
Housman, Laurence, 1865-
Amende honorable (1846). 1 act
In Victoria and Albert
Bereavement (1861). 1 act
In Victoria and Albert
Bethlehem. Nativity play. 2 acts
In Phillips, Le R. and Johnson, T. eds.
Types of modern dramatic com-
position
Blue ribbon (1887). Queen Victoria
In Queen's progress
Brother Ass. St. Francis of Assisi. 1
act
In Comments of Juniper
Brother Wolf. St. Francis of Assisi.
1 act
In Hampden, J. ed. Ten modern plays
Shairp, A. M. ed. Modern plays in
one act
Called and the chosen. Village life.
1 act
In Ways and means
Charles! Charles! Comedy. 1 act
In 19th Cent 105:127
Consider your verdict. 1 act
In Ye fearful saints!
Death and the doctors (14th December
1861). 1 act
In Victoria and Albert
Enter prince (1840). 1 act
In Victoria and Albert
Fall from power (1842). 1 act
In Victoria and Albert
Go-between (December 1851). 1 act
In Victoria and Albert
Gods whom men love die old. 1 act
In Ye fearful saints!
"Good lesson!" (1842). 1 act
In Victoria and Albert
Great relief (1894). Queen Victoria.
1 act
In Queen's progress
Happy and glorious (1897). Queen Vic-
toria. 1 act
In Queen's progress
In this sign conquer. 1 act
In Ye fearful saints!
Intervention (30th November). 1 act
In Victoria and Albert
Intruder (1845). Queen Victoria. 1 act
In Queen's progress

Last comment. St. Francis of Assisi.
1 act
In Comments of Juniper
Leading-strings (1841). Queen Victoria.
1 act
In Queen's progress
Likely story. Village life. 1 act
In Ways and means
Makers of miracle. St. Francis of Assisi.
1 act
In Comments of Juniper
Mess of pottage. St. Francis of Assisi.
1 act
In Comments of Juniper
Mint o' money. Village life. 1 act
In Ways and means
Morning glory. (11th February, 1840).
1 act
In Victoria and Albert
New hangman, a play in one act. N.Y.
Putnam. 1930. 12°. 23p.
Old bottles. 1 act
In Ye fearful saints!
Order of release. St. Francis of Assisi.
1 act
In Comments of Juniper
Fortn 126:289
Painful necessity (1898). 1 act
In Victoria and Albert
Peace-makers. St. Francis of Assisi.
1 act
In Comments of Juniper
"Poor mama!" (1837) Queen Victoria.
1 act
In Queen's progress
Prize pigeon. Village life. 1 act
In Ways and means
Promotion cometh (1891). Queen Vic-
toria. 1 act
In Queen's progress
Religious difficulties (1879). 1 act
In Victoria and Albert
Revolting daughter. Queen Victoria. 1 act
In Palace plays
Royal favour (1859). Queen Victoria.
1 act
In Queen's progress
She-ass and the tied colt. 1 act
In Ye fearful saints!
Snow man. Village life. 1 act
In Ways and means
Clark, B. H. ed. Representative
one-act plays by British and Irish
authors
Time-servers. 1 act
In Ye fearful saints
Under fire (30th May 1842). 1 act
In Victoria and Albert
Waiting-room. 1 act
In Ye fearful saints!
We are not amused (1885). 1 act
In Victoria and Albert
Wicked uncles; or, Victorious virtue.
1 act
In Palace plays
Woman proposes (1839). Queen Victoria.
1 act
In Queen's progress
Wrong door. 1 act
In Ye fearful saints!

Howard, Francis Morton

Black sheep, a comedy in one act. N.Y. French. 1928. 12°. 24p.

Future arrangements, a comedy in one act. N.Y. French. c1929

Money for nothing! A rural conspiracy in one act. N.Y. French. c1932. 12°. 38p.

Person responsible, a village drama in one act. N.Y. French. c1932. 12°. 20p.

Poor old Sam, a pastoral farce in one act. N.Y. French. c1928. 12°. 23p.

Howard, Lorin, joint author. See Gerstenberg, Alice and Howard, Lorin

Howard, Sidney Coe, 1891-

Alien corn. N.Y. Scribner. c1931. 12°. 189p. Artistic temperament. 3 acts
Same in Famous plays of 1933
        Mantle, B. ed. Best plays of 1932-33 (abridged)

Dodsworth. *See* Howard, S. C. Sinclair Lewis's Dodsworth

Half gods. N.Y. Scribner. 1930. 12°. 202p. Comedy. 9 scenes

Late Christopher Bean, founded upon Prenez garde à la peinture, by René Fauchois. N.Y. French. 1933. 12°. 187p. 3 acts
Same in Mantle, B. ed. Best plays of 1932-33 (abridged)

Silver cord. Maternal tyranny. 3 acts
In Dickinson, T. H. ed. Chief contemporary dramatists. ser. 3
    Mantle, B. ed. Best plays of 1926-27 (condensed)
    Moses, M. J. ed. Dramas of modernism and their forerunners
    Tucker, S. M. ed. Twenty-five modern plays
    Watson, E. B. and Pressey, B. eds. Contemporary drama. American plays. v. 1

Sinclair Lewis's Dodsworth. N.Y. Harcourt. 1934. 12°. 162p.
Same in Mantle, B. ed. Best plays of 1933-34 (abridged)

They knew what they wanted. Comedy. 3 acts
In McDermott, J. F. ed. Modern plays

Yellow jack; a history. N.Y. Harcourt. 1934. 12°. 152p. Yellow fever

Howard de Walden, Thomas Evelyn Scott-Ellis, 8th baron, 1880-

Beauties and the beast. Pantomime. 4 scenes
In Five pantomimes

Bluebeard. Pantomime. 6 scenes
In Five pantomimes

Puss and brutes. Pantomime. 3 acts
In Five pantomimes

Reluctant dragon. Pantomime. 8 scenes.
In Five pantomimes

Sleeping beauty. Pantomime. 4 scenes
In Five pantomimes

Howell, Lois

New bride; a comedy in one act. N.Y. French. c1933. 12°. 33p.

Hsiung, S. I.

Mencius was a bad boy
In Bourne, J. ed. Eight new plays for boys and girls

Hubbard, Elbert, 1859-1915

Some sonnets; year 1588. Shakespeare. 1 act
In Philistine 11:74

Hubbard, Philip

Crumbs that fall
In Phillips, LeR. and Johnson, T. eds. Types of modern dramatic composition

Hubbard, Philip E. joint author. See Jacobs, William Wymark and Hubbard, Philip E.

Hudson, Eric

Unfair sex; a farcical comedy in three acts. N.Y. French. c1927. 8°. 92p.

Hudson, Holland

Pottery. Beauty. 1 act
In Shay, F. ed. Fifty more contemporary one-act plays

Hughes, Babette, 1906-

Backstage. 1 act
In Clark, B. H. and Cook, T. R. eds. One-act plays

Calf that laid the golden eggs. 1 act
In Hughes, G. ed. Short plays for modern players

First white woman. 1 act
In New plays for women and girls

Liar and the unicorn. Comedy. 1 act
In Shay, F. ed. Fifty more contemporary one-act plays

March heir; a comedy in one act
In One-act plays for stage and study. ser. 7

Murder! murder! murder! 1 act
In One-act plays for stage and study. ser. 6

No more Americans. Comedy. 1 act
In One-act plays for stage and study. ser. 5

Please do not pick the flowers. 1 act
In Yearbook of short plays. ser. 1

Three players, a fop and a duchess. 1 act
In One-act plays for stage and study. ser. 4

Hughes, Glenn, 1894-

Art and Mrs. Palmer. Farce-comedy. 1 act
In One-act plays for stage and study. ser. 5

Babbitt's boy; a comedy in one act. N.Y. French. 1933. 12°. 14p.
Same in One-act plays for stage and study. ser. 6

Cloaks, a fantasy in one act. Boston. Baker. 1932. 12°. 25p.

Eve in Evelyn. Comedy. 1 act
In Shay, F. ed. Fifty more contemporary one-act plays

For the love of Michael. Farce. 1 act
In New plays for women and girls

Funny business; a frivolous fantasy. 1 act
In One-act plays for stage and study. ser. 7

Happiness for six; a comedy in four acts. Evanston, Ill. Row

Harlequinade in green and orange; a sketch in one act. N.Y. French. 1925. 12°. 18p.

Heart of old Kentucky. Folk-play. 1 act
In New plays for mummers

Heaven will protect the working girl; a comedy in one act. Boston. Baker. 1931. 12°.

Killing of Aaron Kale. Mystery. 1 act
In New plays for mummers

Komachi, a romantic drama in three acts. N.Y. Longmans. 1929. 12°. 86p.

Lace (a Maeterlinckian play). 1 act
In Yearbook of short plays. ser. 1

Lady fingers; a comedy in one act. N.Y. French. c1925. 12°. 24p.

Life on the steppes. Russian tragedy. 1 act
In New plays for mummers

Lucy, the farmer's daughter. Melodrama. 1 act
In New plays for mummers

Manners and manors. Comedy. 1 act
In New plays for mummers

Nell of the golden West. Frontier. 1 act
In New plays for mummers

None too good for Dodo; a comedy of bad manners. N.Y. Appleton. 1929. 12°. 32p. 1 act

Pierrot's mother; a fantastic play in one act. 12°. 31p. [c1923] Cincinnati. Stewart Kidd

Pretty little Plum-Pit. Romance. 1 act
In New plays for mummers

Real Gloria; a comedy in one act. Evanston, Ill. Row

Red carnations; a comedy in one act. N.Y. French. 12p.

Showing up Mabel; a farce in one act. N.Y. French. 1926. 12°. 17p.

Suspicious drummer. Farce. 1 act
In New plays for mummers

Vengeance of Hello-Hello. South seas. 1 act
In New plays for mummers

Whittle. Character. 1 act
In New plays for mummers

Hughes, Hatcher
Hell bent for heaven. Blue Ridge Mts. 3 acts
In Cordell, R. A. ed. Representative modern plays
  McDermott, J. F. ed. Modern plays
  Tucker, S. M. ed. Modern plays

Hughes, Hatcher and Rice Elmer, L. 1892-
Wake up, Jonathan; a comedy in a prologue and three acts. N.Y. French. c1928. 12°. 98p.

Hughes, Joseph H.
Unbeliever; a comedy drama in three acts. N.Y. French. c1927. 12°. 69p.

Hughes, Richard Arthur Warren
Comedy of danger. Broadcasting. 1 act
In Shay, F. ed. Fifty more contemporary one-act plays

Comedy of good and evil; a play. London. Chatto. [1928] 12°. 40-141p. 3 acts
Same in Sisters' tragedy, and three other plays

Man born to be hanged. Tragedy. 1 act
In Sisters' tragedy, and three other plays

Sisters' tragedy. 1 act
In Sisters' tragedy, and three other plays

Hughes, Rupert, 1872-
Ambush. 1 act
In Hughes, G. ed. Short plays for modern players

On the razor edge. Tragi-comedy. 1 act
In Nicholson, K. ed. Hollywood plays

Hugo, Victor
Amy Robsart, a drama in five acts; tr. by Ethel Turner Blair and Evelyn Blair. Boston. Christopher. [c1933] 8°. 141p.

Hulley, Lincoln, 1865-
Abelard and Heloise. Tragedy. 5 acts
In Dramas. v. 3

Adam and Eve. Farce. 3 acts
In Dramas. v. 18

Agnes. Farce-comedy. 1 act
In Dramas. v. 2

Ananias and Sapphira; or, Is it ever right to lie? 3 acts
In Dramas. v. 9

Apollo and the muses. 5 acts
In Dramas. v. 19

Aristocrats of Charles Town, S. C. Historical. 4 acts
In Dramas. v. 8

Artist's colony; or, It's spring! Comedy. 3 acts
In Dramas. v. 3

Asa Steelman. Tragedy. 5 acts
In Dramas. v. 4

Bandolero. Comedy. 5 acts
In Dramas. v. 5

Bells of St. Mary's. Tragedy. 3 acts
In Dramas. v. 2

Beloved bachelor. 5 acts
In Dramas. v. 5

Beyond their means. Tragedy. 5 acts
In Dramas. v. 5

Boca Raton's mystery. 5 acts
In Dramas. v. 20

Bride and bridegroom. Tragedy. 5 acts.
In Dramas. v. 4

Brighteyes the witch. 5 acts
In Dramas. v. 6

Carlota Santolina of Socorro. Tragedy. 5 acts
In Dramas. v. 3

Cavalier and lady. Comedy. 5 acts
In Dramas. v. 6

Cherry cobbler; or, What was wrong with Cyrus Winfield? Tragedy. 5 acts
In Dramas. v. 1

Chester [Penn.] mill folk. Tragedy. 5 acts
In Dramas. v. 20

Christopher the peddler. 4 acts
In Dramas. v. 10

Robin Hood, gentleman outlaw. Comedy.
5 acts
In Dramas. v. 2
Rose o' my heart. 4 acts
In Dramas. v. 11
Saint Mary Magdalen. 5 acts
In Dramas. v. 17
San Gabriel's sun-dial. Tragedy. 5 acts
In Dramas. v. 12
Santa Claus and Mother Goose. Comedy.
5 acts
In Dramas. v. 15
Sister Felicity. 5 acts
In Dramas. v. 3
Splendor of God. Tragedy. 5 acts
In Dramas. v. 19
Sport of the gods. Tragedy. 5 acts
In Dramas. v. 17
Spread eagle. Tragedy. 5 acts
In Dramas. v. 5
Squire William; or, The fall of the
house of Munson. 5 acts
In Dramas. v. 10
Suwanee river Jim. Comedy. 5 acts
In Dramas. v. 7
Tomorrow. 3 acts
In Dramas. v. 14
Valley Forge. Historical. 5 acts
In Dramas. v. 1
Widow's third. Comedy. 3 acts
In Dramas. v. 1
Wise fool. Morality play. 4 acts
In Dramas. v. 12
Woman at the well. 5 acts
In Dramas. v. 11
Humphrey, Maude, 1868-
Immersion. 1 act
In Baker, G. P. ed. Yale one-act plays
Hunting, Ema Suckow
Double dummy; a comedietta in one act.
Boston. Baker. 1917. 12°. 13p.
In Johnson, T. ed. More plays in
miniature
Hurrie, Jane, *joint author. See* Andreas,
Eulalie and Hurrie, Jane
Huston, John
Frankie and Johnny. N.Y. Boni. c1929.
8°. 160p. 3 scenes, prologue and
epilogue. Melodrama
Hutchins, Will, *joint author. See* Warren,
Prescott and Hutchins, Will
Hutchinson, Harold and Williams, Margery
Out of the night, a mystery comedy in
three acts. N.Y. French. c1929. 12°.
131p.
Huxley, Aldous Leonard, 1894-
Albert: Prince Consort. Historical. 1
act
In Golden Hind 1. No. 4:13
Ambassador of Capripedia. 1 act
In Golden Hind 2. No. 3:9
Among the nightingales. [A one-act
play]
In Smart Set 63:71
World of light, a comedy in three acts.
Garden City, N.Y. Doubleday. 1931.
12°. 104p.
Hyakuzo, Kurata, 1891-
Priest and his disciples; a play; tr. from
the Japanese by Glenn W. Shaw.
N.Y. Benn. 1927. 12°. 246p.

Hyde, Douglas
Lost saint. Irish folklore. 1 act
In Johnson, T. ed. Miniature plays for
stage and study
Twisting of the rope. Comedy. 1 act
In Canfield, C. ed. Plays of the Irish
renaissance
Hyde, F. Austin
Wireless and sich-like. 1 act
In Hampden, J. ed. Seven modern
plays for younger players
Hymer, John B. and Clemens, LeRoy
Alias the deacon; a comedy in a prologue
and three acts. N.Y. French. c1928.
12°. 119p.
Ibbotson, Machon
Black dogs, a play in one act. London.
Deane. 1929. 12°. 23p.
Ibsen, Henrik, 1828-1906
Doll's house. Social. 3 acts
In McDermott, J. F. ed. Modern plays
Watson, E. B. and Pressey, B. eds.
Contemporary drama. European
plays. v. 1
Enemy of the people. Social. 5 acts
In Whitman, C. H. ed. Seven contem-
porary plays
Ghosts. Eugenics. 3 acts
In Steeves, H. R. ed. Plays from the
modern theatre
Hedda Gabler. Social
In LeGallienne, E. ed. Eva LeGal-
lienne's civic repertory plays
Ilsley, Samuel Marshall, 1863-
Feast of the Holy Innocents, a play in
one act. N.Y. French. [1930] 12°.
28p.
In Clark, B. H. and Nicholson, K. eds.
American scene
Teacher; a play in three acts. Santa
Barbara, Cal. Pacific coast pub. co.
1928. 12°. 105p.
Ingersoll, Patsy Grey
Troupers. Actors. 1 act
In Nicholson, K. ed. Hollywood plays
Ingram, Kenneth, 1882-
Out of darkness; a drama of Flanders.
London. Chatto. 1927. 12°. 312p.
Ireland, D. L. *joint author. See* Smith, E.
E. and Ireland, D. L.
Isaacs, E. S. and Albert, Rose
Release. 3 acts
In Hughes, H. et al. eds. Copy, 1928
Jacobs, William Wymark, 1863-
Distant relative, a comedy in one act.
N.Y. French. c1930. 12°. 21p.
Dixon's return, a comedy in one act.
N.Y. French. c1932. 12°. 22p.
Master mariners, a comedy in one act.
N.Y. French. c1930. 12°. 22p.
Matrimonial openings, a comedy in one
act. N.Y. French. c1931. 12°. 22p.
Warming pan, a comedy in one act.
N.Y. French. 1929. 12°. 23p.
**Jacobs, William Wymark and Hubbard,
Philip E.**
Love passage, a comedy in one act
In Pence, R. W. ed. Dramas by
present-day writers

Jagendorf, Moritz Adolf, 1888-
Dick Whittington. Juvenile
In Pantomimes for the children's
theatre
Gilone and Gillette. Juvenile
In Pantomimes for the children's
theatre
Gnomes' workshop. Juvenile
In Pantomimes for the children's
theatre
Merry Tyll. 1 act
In Jagendorf, M. A. ed. Nine short
plays
Pie and the tart. 1 act
In One-act plays for stage and study.
ser. 6
Pierrot and Columbine on Little West
Jones street. Juvenile
In Pantomimes for the children's
theatre

James, Grace
Cucumber king; a Chinese play for juvenile performers. N.Y. French.
c1924. 12°. 41p.
Jellyfish, a play in one act. N.Y. French.
c1931. 12°. 46p.
Pork pie hat; a Victorian play in two
acts for girls. N.Y. French. c1922.
8°. 30p.

Janney, Sam [Samuel MacPherson Janney]
1892-
Amateur detective; a play. Boston.
c1933. 12°.
Black flamingo; a play in three acts. N.Y.
French. c1930. 12°. 96p.
Expense no object, a play in three acts.
Boston. Baker. 1918. 12°. 84p.
Loose ankles; a comedy in three acts.
N.Y. Longmans. 1928. 12°. 117p.
Mr. Kelley from Kalamazoo, a farce in
three acts. Boston. Baker. 1912. 12°.
71p.
Picking a winner, a farce in three acts.
Boston. Baker. 1914. 12°. 45p.
This is so sudden! A farce in one act.
Boston. Baker. 1915. 12°. 15p.

Janney, Samuel MacPherson. *See* Janney,
Sam

Jennings, Gertrude E.
Between the soup and the savoury. 1
act
In Marriott, J. W. ed. One-act plays
of to-day. ser. 3
Bride. 1 act
In Marriott, J. W. ed. Best one-act
plays of 1931
Five birds in a cage. 1 act
In Marriot, J. W. ed. One-act plays
of to-day. ser. 4
Helping hands, a farce in one act. N.Y.
French c1930. 12°. 33p.
Pearly gates, a comedy in one act. N.Y.
French. c1932. 12°. 30p.
Spot; a comedy for two people. N.Y.
French. c1927. 12°. 22p. 1 act
These pretty things, a farcical comedy
in three acts. N.Y. French. c1930.
8°. 74p.

Job, Thomas
Giants in the earth, a tragedy [drama-
tization of Rølvaag's novel]. N.Y.
Harper. 1929. 12°. 155p. 3 acts and
prologue

Johnson, Georgia Douglas
Blue blood. Negro. 1 act
In Shay, F. ed. Fifty more contem-
porary one-act plays
Plumes. Negro. 1 act
In Locke, A. Le R. and Gregory, M.
eds. Plays of Negro life

Johnson, Mabel P.
Fashion show; a play in one act. N.Y.
French. 1927. 12°. 25p.

Johnson, Philip
Afternoon; a play in one act. Oxford.
Blackwell. 1928. 12°. 40p. Also
French. N.Y.
April shower; a further incident in the
lives of the spinsters of Lushe. 1 act
In Hampden, J. ed. Four new plays
for women and girls
Cage
In Four plays
Good and the bad
In Four plays
Legend; a play in one act. Oxford.
Blackwell. 1928. 12°. 36p.
Long shadows
In Four plays
Lovely miracle. 1 act
In Four plays
Marriott, J. W. ed. One-act plays
of to-day. ser. 5
Queer cattle, a play in three acts. Lon-
don. Benn. 1931. 12°. 112p.
Sad about Europe; a comedy in one act.
N.Y. French. 1932. 12°. 34p.
Send her victorious! A farcical study in
one act. N.Y. French. c1933. 12°. 41p.
Spinsters of Lushe; a comedy in one act
In Hampden, J. ed. Four modern plays

Johnston, Denis
Moon in the Yellow river; a play in
three acts. N.Y. French. [c1931] 12°.
154p. Problem
Same in Moon in the Yellow river and
The old lady says "No!"
Old lady says "No!"
In Moon in the Yellow river, and The
old lady says "No!"

Johnston, G. W.
Grill
In Twelve one-act plays

Jones, Henry Arthur, 1851-1929
Dolly reforming herself. Comedy. 4
acts
In Chandler, F. W. and Cordell, R. A.
eds. Twentieth century plays
Goal. Death. 1 act
In Clark, B. H. ed. Representative
one-act plays by British and Irish
authors
Pence, R. W. ed. Dramas by present-day writers

Knife; a drama in one act. N.Y. French. 18p.

Liars. Comedy. 4 acts
In Marriott, J. W. ed. Great modern British plays

Michael and his lost angel. Social. 5 acts
In Dickinson, T. H. ed. Chief contemporary dramatists. ser. 3

Mrs. Dane's defence. Social. 4 acts
In Cordell, R. A. ed. Representative modern plays

Jordan, Ethel Blair
What becomes of it. Red Cross. 2 acts
In Schauffler, R. H. and Sanford, A. P. eds. Plays for our American holidays. v. 4

Joseph, Mrs. Helen (Haiman)
Ali Baba and the forty thieves. Juvenile
In Ali Baba, and other plays

Beauty and the beast. Juvenile
In Ali Baba, and other plays

Coat of many colors. Juvenile
In Ali Baba, and other plays

Little Mr. Clown; the adventures of a marionette. N.Y. Harcourt. [c1932] 12°. 190p.

Princesses; a symbolic drama for marionettes. Cincinnati. Stewart Kidd. [c1923] 12°. 34p.

Judge, James P.
Square crooks; a comedy mystery play. N.Y. Longmans. 1927. 12°. 126p.

Kaiser, Georg, 1878-
Coral. Expressionistic. 5 acts
In Tucker, S. M. ed. Modern continental plays
Tucker, S. M. ed. Twenty-five modern plays

Fire in the opera house
In Katzin, W. ed. Eight European plays

From morn to midnight. Mystery. 7 scenes
In Dickinson, T. H. ed. Chief contemporary dramatists. ser. 3
Moses, M. J. ed. Dramas of modernism and their forerunners

Gas I-II. Expressionistic. 5 acts
In Tucker, S. M. ed. Modern continental plays

Kallas, A.
Bath-sheba of Saaremaa. 1 act
In Bourne, J. ed. 8 new one-act plays for 1934

Phantom lover, a play in three acts. tr. by Herman Bernstein and Adolph Meyer. N.Y. Brentano's. 1928. 12°. 110p. Sex

Kauffmann, Stanley
Red-handkerchief man; a play in three acts. N.Y. French. c1933. 12°. 56p.

Kaufman, George S. 1889-
Still alarm. Comedy. 1 act
In One-act plays for stage and study. ser. 6

Kaufman, George S. 1889- **and Connelly, Marc C.** 1890-
Beggar on horseback. Satire. 2 pts.
In Cordell, R. A. ed. Representative modern plays
Watson, E. B. and Pressey, B. eds. Contemporary drama. American plays. v. 1

Merton of the movies. Comedy. 4 acts
In Pence, R. W. ed. Dramas by present-day writers

To the ladies. Comedy. 3 acts
In Tucker, S. M. ed. Modern American and British plays

Kaufman, George S. 1889- **and Ferber, Edna,** 1887-
Dinner at eight. Garden City, N.Y. Doubleday. 1932. 12°. 259p. Social comedy. 3 acts
Same in Mantle, B. ed. Best plays of 1932-33 (abridged)

Royal family; a comedy in three acts. Garden City, N.Y. Doubleday. 1928. 12°. 280p. Also French. N.Y. (acting edition)
Same in Mantle, B. ed. Best plays of 1927-28 (abridged)

Kaufman, George S. 1889- **and Hart, Moss**
Merrily we roll along; a play. N.Y. Random House. 1914. 8°. 211p. 3 acts

Once in a lifetime; a comedy. N.Y. Farrar. [c1930] 12°. 236p. 3 acts
Same in Famous plays of 1932
Mantle, B. ed. Best plays of 1930-31 (abridged)

Kaufman, George S. 1889- **and Mankiewicz, Herman J.**
Good fellow; a play in three acts. N.Y. French. 1931. 12°. 111p.

Kaufman, George S. 1889- **and Ryskind, Morrie**
Let 'em eat cake; a sequel to "Of thee I sing"; a musical play. N.Y. Knopf. [1933] 12°. 241p. 2 acts

Of thee I sing; a musical play . . . with a foreword by George Jean Nathan. N.Y. Knopf. 1932. 12°. 214p. Satire. 3 acts
Same in Famous plays of 1933
Mantle, B. ed. Best plays of 1931-32 (abridged)

Kaufman, Hazel Sharrard
Little black Sambo. Juvenile. 3 scenes
In Moses, M. J. ed. Ring up the curtain!

Kaye-Smith, Sheila (Mrs. Theodore Penrose Fry)
Child born at the plough. Nativity play. 1 act
In Saints in Sussex

Shepherd of Lattenden. Passion play. 1 act
In Saints in Sussex

Kaye-Smith, Sheila and Hampden, John
Mrs. Adis. (Founded on short story of same name) Tragedy. 1 act
In Mrs. Adis . . . with the mockbeggar Hampden, J. ed. Ten modern plays
One-act plays for stage and study. ser. 5

Keener, Sara
Gray switch. Psychological. 1 act
In Lewis, B. R. ed. University of Utah
plays
Kelly, George [Edward] 1887-
Behold the bridegroom. Boston. Little.
1928. 12°. 172p. 3 acts
Same in Mantle, B. ed. Best plays of
1927-28 (abridged)
Craig's wife. Marriage. 3 acts
In Moses, M. J. ed. Dramas of mod-
ernism and their forerunners
Daisy Mayme. Comedy. 3 acts
In Mantle, B. ed. Best plays of 1926-
27 (abridged)
Flattering word. Satire. 1 act
In Cohen, H. L. ed. One-act plays by
modern authors. 1934 edition
Philip goes forth, a play in three acts.
N.Y. French. 1931. 12°. 211p. Comedy
Kelly, Mary
Spell. Playlet for 2 women. 1 act
In Hampden, J. ed. Three modern
plays and a mime
Kemp, Harry, 1883-
Boccaccio's untold tale. 1 act
In Eight one-act plays
Don Juan's Christmas eve. Miracle. 1
act
In Shay, F. ed. Fifty more contem-
porary one-act plays
Dramatic art [A Viennese fantasy]. 1 act
In Smart Set 74:41
Prodigal son. Comedy. 1 act
In Smart Set 52:83
White hawk. 1 act
In Goldstone, G. A. ed. One-act plays
Kemp, Thomas C.
Supremacy; a play in three acts. Lon-
don. Allen. [1932] 12°. 91p. Henry
VIII
Kennedy, Aubrey, *joint author. See* Ours-
ler, Fulton and Kennedy, Aubrey
Kennedy, Charles O'Brien
Man with the iron jaw. 1 act
In Hughes, G. ed. Short plays for
modern players
Men, women and goats. 1 act
In One-act plays for stage and study.
ser. 6
Kennedy, Charles Rann, 1871-
Admiral. Columbus
In Repertory of plays for a company
of three players. v. 1
Army with banners. Peace. 5 acts
In Repertory of plays for a company
of seven players
Chastening. Jesus Christ
In Repertory of plays for a company
of three players. v. 1
Crumbs. Resurrection. 5 acts
In Repertory of plays for a company
of three players. v. 2
Flaming ministers. The depression. 5
acts
In Repertory of plays for a company
of three players. v. 2
Fool from the hills. Fantasy. 5 acts
In Repertory of plays for a company
of seven players

Francis Beaumont; a tragedy. Birming-
ham. J. Guest [18-] 72p.
Idol breaker. Freedom. 5 acts
In Repertory of plays for a company
of seven players
Necessary evil. Prostitution. 1 act
In Repertory of plays for a company
of seven players
Old nobody. War. 5 acts
In Repertory of plays for a company
of three players. v. 2
Rib of the man. War. 5 acts
In Repertory of plays for a company
of seven players
Salutation. Dante
In Repertory of plays for a company
of three players. v. 1
Servant in the house. Jesus Christ. 5
acts
In Repertory of plays for a company
of seven players
Terrible meek. Jesus Christ. 1 act
In Repertory of plays for a company
of seven players
Winterfeast. Symbolic. 5 acts
In Repertory of plays for a company
of seven players
Kester, Katharine
Bargains. 1 act
In Johnson, T. ed. Miniature plays
for stage or study
Christmas child comes in: a play in two
acts. Boston. Baker. 1925. 12°. 49p.
[Dramatization of Zona Gale's story,
Christmas]
Love and lather. 1 act
In Johnson, T. ed. Miniature plays
for stage or study
Kester, Paul, 1870-
Beverly's balance, a comedy in three acts.
N.Y. Longmans. 1928. 12°. 93p.
Don Quixote, a dramatization of Cer-
vantes' novel. N.Y. French. c1930.
12°. 133p.
Dorothy Vernon of Haddon Hall; a ro-
mantic drama in four acts; adapted
from the novel by Charles Major.
N.Y. French. c1929. 12°. 102p.
Friend Hannah; a comedy in four acts.
N.Y. French. c1928. 12°. 91p.
Sweet Nell of old Drury; a comedy in
four acts. N.Y. French. c1928. 12°.
82p.
Tom Sawyer; a play in four acts, founded
on the story by S. L. Clemens. N.Y.
French. c1932. 106p.
When knighthood was in flower; a play
in four acts; dramatized from the
novel by Charles Major. N.Y. French.
c1931. 12°. 101p.
Kester, Paul, 1870- and Lewers, William
Course of true love; a comedy in four
acts. N.Y. French. c1930. 12° 97p.
Kidder, Edward E. 1849?-1927
Peaceful valley, the famous play in three
acts, precisely as given by the late
Sol Smith Russell. N.Y. French.
1911. 12°. 83p.

Run for her money, a comedy in three acts. Chicago. Denison. [c1927] 12°. 90p.

Kidder, Edward E. 1849?-1927 and Kidder, Augusta Raymond

Bridge party, a kindly social satire in one act. N.Y. French. c1927. 12°. 25p.

Bungalow bride; a one-act comedy with dramatic comments. N.Y. French c1926. 12°. 24p.

College Cinderella, an original three act play. N.Y. French. c1915. 12°. 65p.

Hollyhock house; the tale of a pretty typist; a one-act playlet. N.Y. French. 1928. 12°. 23p.

Stage struck, a breezy comedietta of these times in one act. N.Y. French. c1926. 12°. 27p.

Kilpatrick, Florence A.

Camilla in a caravan; a comedy of the open road. London. Nash. [1925] 12°. 254p.

Virginia's husband, a farcical comedy in three acts. N.Y. French. c1931. 12°. 92p.

King, Frank, *joint author. See* Hines, Leonard J. and King, Frank

Kingsbury, Sara R.

Our Christ liveth; an Easter play in three acts. N.Y. Abingdon Press. [c1930] 8°. 24p.

Voice of Montezuma
In Dickon goes to the fair, and other plays

Kingsley, Sidney

Men in white; a play in three acts. N.Y. Covici. [c1933] 12°. 137p. Hospital
Same in Mantle, B. ed. Best plays of 1933-34 (abridged)

Kirchon, V. *See* Kirshon, Vladimir Mikhailovich

Kirkland, John.

Tobacco road; a three act play from the novel by Erskine Caldwell. N.Y. Viking. 1934. 12°. 176p. Poor whites

Kirkpatrick, John Alexander, 1895-

Ada beats the drum, a comedy in three acts. N.Y. French. c1930. 12°. 101p.

"Charm"; a comedy in three acts. N.Y. French. c1926. 12°. 103p.

Green eyes from Romany; a comedy in one act
In New plays for women and girls

Love expert, a comedy in three acts. N.Y. French. c1930. 12°. 98p.

Romance is a racket, a farce comedy in one act. N.Y. French. [c1932] 12°. 48p.

Tea-pot on the rocks; a comedy in one act
In One-act plays for stage and study. ser. 7

Theme song for the married; a farce in one act. N.Y. French. [1932] 12°. 51p.

Wedding. 1 act
In One-act plays for stage and study. ser. 4

Woman who understood men. 1 act
In One-act plays for stage and study. ser. 6

Women-folks; a comedy in one act. N.Y. French. c1928. 12°. 35p.

Kirshon, Vladimir Mikhailovich and Uspenskii, Andrei Vasil'evich

Red rust; adapted from the Russian by Virginia and Frank Vernon. N.Y. Brentano's. 1930. 12°. 182p. Soviet Russia

Knoblock, Edward, 1874-

My lady's lace (one scene from My lady's dress). Comedy. 1 act
In Webber, J. P. and Webster, H. H. eds. One-act plays for secondary schools

Knoblock, Edward, 1874- and Nichols, Beverly, 1889-

Evensong, a play in three acts, adapted from the novel of Beverly Nichols. N.Y. French. c1932. 8°. 90p.

Knoblock, Edward, *joint author. See* Bennett, Arnold and Knoblock, Edward

Knox, Ethel Louise

Twelfth night festivities. Twelfth night. 1 act
In Schauffler, R. H. and Sanford, A. P. eds. Plays for our American holidays. v. 2

Knox, Florence Clay

For distinguished service. Comedy. 1 act
In Johnson, T. ed. Miniature plays for stage or study

Many happy returns of the day; a comedy in one act. N.Y. Longmans. c1929. 12°. 29p.

Matrimonial fog, a comedy in one act. Boston. Baker. 1918. 19p.

Kosor, Josip

Passion's furnace. 4 acts
In Poet Lore 41:459

Woman. 3 acts
In Poet Lore 41:317

Kotzebue, August Friedrich Ferdinand von, 1761-1819

Dead nephew (Der tote Neffe). Comedy 1 act
In Poet Lore 38:160

Man who couldn't talk; a comedy in one act
In Poet Lore 40:223

Nightcap of the prophet Elias. Farce. 1 act
In Poet Lore 40:391

Old love affair. (Die alte Liebeschaften) Comedy. 1 act
In Poet Lore 38:220

Our Frank (Unser Fritz). Foster-child. 1 act
In Poet Lore 38:206

Pharaoh's daughter. 1 act
In Webber, J. P. and Webster, H. H. eds. Typical plays for secondary schools

Quakers. Historical. 1 act
In Poet Lore 38:177

Seven one act dramas
In Poet Lore 38:159

Kotzebue, A. F. F. von—*Continued*
Turkish ambassador. (Turkische Ge-
sandte). 1 act
In Poet Lore 38:192
Walled-up window (Das zugemauerte
Fenster). Comedy. 1 act
In Poet Lore 38:246
Watch and the almond tart (Die Uhr
und die Mandeltorte). 1 act
In Poet Lore 38:240

Krasna, Norman
Louder, please, a play in three acts.
N.Y. French. c1932. 12°. 113p.

Kreymborg, Alfred, 1883-
Brother Bill. A little play from Har-
lem. 1 act
In Isaacs, E. J. ed. Plays of Ameri-
can life and fantasy
One-act plays for stage and study.
ser. 4
Theatre Arts M 11:299
I'm not complaining; a Kaffeeklatsch.
1 act
In New plays for women and girls
Lima beans, a scherzo-play in one act.
N.Y. French. 1925. 12°. 21p.
Limping along. Patriotic duo. 1 act
In One-act plays for stage and study.
ser. 5
Manikin and Minikin, a bisque play in
one act. N.Y. French. 1925. 12°.
20p.
In Webber, J. P. and Webster, H. H.
eds. One-act plays for secondary
schools
Trap doors. Travesty. 1 act
In Isaacs, E. J. ed. Plays of American
life and fantasy

Kummer, Mrs. Clare (Beecher)
"Good gracious, Annabelle." Farce-
comedy. 3 acts
In Mantle, B. and Sherman, G. P. eds.
Best plays of 1909-1919
Her master's voice. Comedy. 3 acts
In Mantle, B. ed. Best plays of 1933-
34 (abridged)
Pomeroy's past; a comedy in three acts.
N.Y. French. c1926. 12°. 103p.
So's your old antique, a comedy in one
act. N.Y. French. c1928. 12°. 29p.
Same in One-act plays for stage and
study. ser. 4

**Landman, Isaac, 1880- and Landman,
Michael Lewis, 1883-**
Man of honor; a drama in three acts.
N.Y. French. c1928. 12°. 111p.

**Langner, Lawrence and Langner, Armina
(Marshall)**
Pursuit of happiness. N.Y. French. 1934.
12°. 191p. Comedy

**Lardner, Ring W. 1885-1933 and Kaufman,
George S. 1889-**
June moon; a comedy in a prologue and
three acts. N.Y. French. 1930.
8°. 187p. Also Scribner
Same in Mantle, B. ed. Best plays of
1929-30 (abridged)

Larkin, Margaret
El Cristo. Religious. 1 act
In Eastman, F. ed. Modern religious
dramas

**Larrimore, Lida, pseud. (Lida Larrimore
Turner)**
Cousin Julia's jade ear-ring, a comedy in
two acts. Philadelphia. Penn. 1923.
16°
Third floor front. Philadelphia. Penn.
1928. 12°
In Prize plays of 1928
Yesterday's roses; a comedy in three
acts and a prologue. Philadelphia.
Penn. 1927. 12°. 88p.
Same in Prize plays of 1927

Lavedan, Henri [Leon Emile] 1859-
King's pet (La chienne du roi). Madame
du Barry. 1 act
In Vernon, V. and F. eds. Modern
one-act plays from the French

Laverack, Belle Radcliffe
Bells of the Madonna [a play in three
acts]. Boston. Beacon press. 1934.
12°. 55p.

Lawrence, R. B.
Decision at dawn, a one-act George
Washington play. N.Y. Longmans.
1932. 12°. 32p.

Lawson, John Howard
Gentlewoman
In With a reckless preface
International, a New playwright's theatre
production. N.Y. Macauley. 1928.
12°. 276p.
Processional. American life. 4 acts
In Watson, E. B. and Pressey, B. eds.
Contemporary drama. American
plays. v. 1
Pure in heart
In With a reckless preface
Success story. N.Y. Farrar. 1932. 12°.
245p. 3 acts. Character

**Lay, Ellen, *joint author. See* Stout, N. and
Lay, Ellen**

Lecocq, Alexandre Charles, 1832-1911
Daughter of Madame Angot. Directory.
3 acts
In Plays of the Moscow art theatre
musical studio

Lee, Charles James, 1870-
Banns of marriage; a play in one act.
N.Y. French. 1927. 12°. 46p.
Mr. Sampson; a play in one act. N.Y.
French. 1927. 12°. 46p.

LeGallienne, Eva and Friebus, Florida
Alice in Wonderland. Adapted from
Lewis Carroll's Alice in Wonderland.
N.Y. French. c1932. 12°. 137p. 2pts.

Leighton, George Ross
Solemn pride. Civil war. 1 act
In Webber, J. P. and Webster, H. H.
eds. One-act plays for secondary
schools

Leivick, H.
Golem. 1 act
In White, B. F. trans. Nine one-act
plays from the Yiddish

Lenormand, Henri René, 1882-
Coward. (Le lâche.) Espionage. 4 acts
In Three plays
Chandler, F. W. and Cordell, R. A.
Twentieth century plays
Dream doctor. (Le mangeur de rêves)
Tragedy. 3 acts
In Three plays
Moses, M. J. ed. Dramas of mod-
ernism and their forerunners
Man and his phantoms (L'homme et ses
fantomes). Dissolute life. 4 acts
In Three plays
Time is a dream. Relativity. 6 scenes
In Dickinson, T. H. ed. Chief con-
temporary dramatists. ser. 3
Leonard, Martia
Immortal beloved, a fantastic possibility
in one act. N.Y. French. c1927.
12°. 19p.
Lester, Elliott
Take my advice; or, A helping hand; an
American comedy in three acts. N.Y.
French. c1928. 12°. 116p.
Levin, Z.
Doctor's first operation. 1 act
In White, B. F. trans. Nine one-act
plays from the Yiddish
Levinger, Mrs. Elma Ehrlich, 1887-
Burden; a play in one act. Boston.
Baker. 1918. 12°. 32p.
Cow with wings. Domestic comedy. 1
act
In Clark, B. H. and Nicholson, K. eds.
American scene, 1930
Great hope. Modern play
In Stratford J 5:231
Return of the prodigal; a one-act play
based on a certain parable in Luke
. . . Boston. Pilgrim press. [c1927]
12°. 27p. [Awarded first prize in
the 1925 religious drama contest held
by the Drama league of America]
Tenth man. A play in one act. Bos-
ton. Baker. [1913] 12°. 32p.
Levy, Benn Wolf, 1900-
Art and Mrs. Bottle. Comedy
In Art and Mrs. Bottle; and Mrs.
Moonlight
Devil passes; a religious comedy in three
acts and a prologue. N.Y. French.
1932. 12°. 116p. [Pub. in England un-
der title "The devil"]
Same in Mantle, B. ed. Best plays of
1931-32 (abridged)
Mrs. Moonlight, a piece of pastiche. 3
acts
In Art and Mrs. Bottle; and Mrs.
Moonlight
Famous plays of to-day
Mud & treacle; or, The course of true
love; a shameless tract in three acts
and a post-dated prologue. London.
Gollancz. 1928. 12°. 128p.
Springtime for Henry; a farce in three
acts. N.Y. French. 1932. 12°.
110p.
This woman business; a play. London.
Benn. 1932. 128p.

Levy, Benn Wolf, 1900- **and Van Druten,
John,** 1902-
Hollywood holiday; an extravagant com-
edy. London. Secker. 1931. 12°. 139p.
Lewis, D. Bevan Wyndham
At the mule. Villon. 1 act
In Schauffler, R. H. and Sanford, A. P.
eds. Plays for our American holi-
days. v. 4
Lewisohn, Ludwig, 1882-
Adam; a dramatic history. N.Y. Har-
per. 1929. 12°. 99p. Prologue, seven
scenes and epilogue
**Lezama, Antonio de and Meneses, Enrique
de**
Wasted lives; a comedy in four acts
In Poet Lore 41:159
Libin, Z.
Colleagues. 1 act
In White, B. F. trans. Nine one-act
plays from the Yiddish
Lindsay, Howard and Robinson, Bertrand
Tommy; a comedy in three acts. N.Y.
French. 1928. 12°. 140p.
Your Uncle Dudley. N.Y. French.
c1930. 12°. 135p.
Lines, Leonard J. and King, Frank
Arrow by day, a play in one act. N.Y.
French. c1931. 12°. 23p.
Lipscomb, W. P. and Minney, J. R.
Clive of India. Historical
In Famous plays of 1933-34
Lipskeroff, Constantin, 1899-
Carmencita and the soldier. Lyric trag-
edy. 4 acts
In Plays by the Moscow Art Theatre
musical studio (1925)
Lloyd, Harold Clayton, 1894-
American comedy. N.Y. Longmans.
1928. 8°. 204p. 3 acts
Lloyd, Richard Ernest, 1875-
Beyond the road. African
In Two African plays
Up the road. African
In Two African plays
Longnecker, E. B.
References
In Prize plays of 1928
Lonsdale, Frederick, 1881-
Canaries sometimes sing; a comedy in
three acts. N.Y. French. c1931.
8°. 68p.
Fake, a play in three acts. N.Y. French.
1931. 8°. 59p.
High road. London. Collins. [c1927] 12°.
158p.
Last of Mrs. Cheyney; a comedy in three
acts. N.Y. French. 1929. 8°. 91p.
On approval, a comedy. London. Col-
lins. [1927] 12°. 136p.
Spring cleaning. London. Gollancz.
[1925] 12°. 168p. Comedy. 3 acts
Street singer, a musical play in three
acts. London. French. c1929. 75p
Lord, Daniel Aloysius, 1888-
Fantasy of the passion. St. Louis.
Queen's work press. c1929. 12°. 80p.
Loring, E.
Where's Peter?
In Prize plays of 1928

Loving, Boyce
Gay; a comedy in three acts. N.Y. French. c1933. 12°. 93p.
Pedagogue; a comedy in three acts. Evanston. Row. [c1930] 12°. 121p.
Worm, a comedy in three acts. Evanston. Row. [c1930] 12°. 134p.

Lowndes, Marie Adelaide (Belloc) (Mrs. Frederic Sawrey Archibald Lowndes) 1868-
Key, a love drama in three acts. London. Benn. 1931. 12°. 95p.
What really happened; a play in a prologue, two acts and an epilogue. London. Benn. 1932. 12°. 89p. Also N.Y. Grosset. 1929. 12°. 317p.
With all John's love; a play in three acts. London. Benn. 1931. 12°. 87p.

Lowndes, Marie Adelaide (Belloc) 1868- **and Lowndes, Frederic Sawrey Archbald**
Why be lonely? A comedy in three acts. London. Benn. 1931. 12°. 128p.

Ludwig, Emil, 1881-
Bismarck; the trilogy of a fighter; three plays. N.Y. Putnam. 1927 12°. 405p. I. King and people; II. Union; III. Dismissal
Versailles; a play in five acts. London. Putnam. [1932] 12°. 173p.

Lyon, Elbridge S.
Shamrock. St. Patrick's Day. 1 act
In Schauffler, R. H. and Sanford, A. P. eds. Plays for our American holidays. v. 1
Synthetic Santa. Christmas. 1 act
In Schauffler, R. H. and Sanford, A. P. eds. Plays for our American holidays. v. 1

MacArthur, Charles, *joint author. See* Hecht, Ben and MacArthur, Charles

McCarthy, Myles
Crooked money; a comedy in three acts. N.Y. French. 1928. 12°. 101p.

McCauley, Clarice Vallette
Threshold. Psychic. 1 act
In Shay, F. ed. Fifty more contemporary one-act plays

McCauley, Mary Weaver, *joint author. See* Cuddy, Lucy A. and others

McCoo, Edward J.
Ethiopia at the bar of justice. Negro pageant. 1 act
In Richardson, W. ed. Plays and pageants from the life of the Negro

McDermott, John Francis, 1902-
'Twas well done and quickly.
In Poet Lore 39:415

MacDonagh, Thomas, 1817-1916
Metempsychosis; or, A mad world. A play in one act.
In Irish R 1:585
Pagans; a modern play in two conversations. Dublin. Talbot. 1920. 12°. 40p.
When the dawn is come, a tragedy in three acts. Dublin. Maunsel. 1908. 12°. 48p.

Macdonald, H. C.
Meeker and Meeker
In Hughes, H. et al. eds. Copy, 1928

MacDonald, Murray, *joint author. See* Massingham, Dorothy and MacDonald, Murray

McEvoy, Charles, 1879-
Likes of her. Comedy. 3 acts
In Marriott, J. W. ed. Great modern British plays

McFadden, Elizabeth Apthorp, 1875-
Boy who discovered Easter; a play in three scenes. N.Y. French. [c1926] 8°. 57p.
Same in Why the chimes rang and other plays
Knights of the silver shield; a play in one act . . . adapted from the story of the same name by Raymond MacDonald Alden. N.Y. French. 1929. 8°. 42p.
Same in Why the chimes rang and other plays
Product of the mill; a play in four acts. N.Y. French c1927. 12°. 117p.
Tidings of joy; a Christmas play in one act. N.Y. French. c1933. 8°. 40p.
Why the chimes rang. 1 act
In Why the chimes rang and other plays

McFadden, Elizabeth and Crimmins, Agnes
Man without a country. Patriotism. 1 act
In Schauffler, R. H. and Sanford, A. P. eds. Plays for our American holidays. v. 3

McGuire, Harry
When the ship goes down; a play in three acts. N.Y. French. 1928. 12°. 75p.
Yella. Melodrama. 1 act
In Baker, G. P. ed. Yale one-act plays

McGuire, William Anthony
Divorce question; a play in three acts. N.Y. French. c1928. 12°. 76p.

MacHugh, Augustin, 1877-
Meanest man in the world, a comedy-drama. N.Y. French. 1928. 12°. 107p.

MacIntyre, John (John Brandane, pseud.) 1869-
Change-house, a play in one act. London. Gowans. 1921. 12°. 50p. Tragedy
Same in Cohen, H. L. ed. More one-act plays by modern authors
Happy war. 1 act
In Treasure ship
Heather gentry; a comedy in three acts. London. Constable. 1932. 12°. 127p.
Inn of adventure; a comedy in three acts. London. Constable. 1932. 12°. 98p.
Rory aforesaid. 1 act
In Treasure ship
Marriott, J. W. ed. One-act plays of to-day. ser. 3
Treasure ship. Comedy. 4 acts
In Treasure ship

MacIntyre, John, 1869- **and Yuill, A. W.**
Spanish galleon; a play in one act. London. Gowans. 1932. 12°. 44p.

Mack, Orin
Last day for grouse. 1 act
In Clark, B. H. and Nicholson, K. eds. American scene
[University of Washington plays. ser. 2]

Mackay, Constance D'Arcy (Mrs. Roland Holt)
Abraham Lincoln, rail splitter. Historical. 1 act
In Schauffler, R. H. and Sanford, A. B. eds. Plays for our American holidays. v. 3
America triumphant; a pageant of patriotism. N.Y. Appleton. 1926. 12°. 65p.
Beau of Bath. Fantasy. 1 act
In Webber, J. P. and Webster, H. H. eds. One-act plays for secondary schools
Benjamin Franklin: journeyman. Historical. 1 act
In Webber, J. P. and Webster, H. H. eds. Short plays for young people
Boston tea-party. Historical. 1 act
In Webber, J. R. and Webster, H. H. eds. Short plays for young people
Calendar of joyful saints. Pageant of holidays
In Youth's highway, and other plays for young people
Counsel retained. 18th century. 1 act
In Pence, R. W. ed. Dramas by present-day writers
First Noel. Christmas
In Youth's highway, and other plays for young people
In the days of Piers Ploughman
In Youth's highway, and other plays for young people
Midsummer eve, an outdoor fantasy in three scenes. N.Y. French. 1932
Nimble-wit and fingerkin, a morality play. 1 act
In Moses, M. J. ed. Ring up the curtain!
On Christmas eve; a play for children. N.Y. French. c1909. 12°. p. 143-68. 1 act
Pageant of sunshine and shadow
In Youth's highway, and other plays for young people
Prince of court painters. George Romney. 1 act
In Webber, J. P. and Webster, H. H. eds. Typical plays for secondary schools
Silver thread. Cornish folk-play. 3 acts
In Moses, M. J. ed. Treasury of plays for children
Youth's highway. Michael Angelo
In Youth's highway, and other plays for young people

Mackay, Isabel Ecclestone, 1875-1928
Goblin gold; comedy drama in three acts. N.Y. French. c1933. 12°. 89p.

Last cache; a play in one act. N.Y. French. 1927. 8°. 31p.
Last chance; a play in one act. N.Y. c1927. 12°.
Second lie. 1 act
In Massey, V. ed. Canadian plays from Hart House theatre. v. 1
Treasure; a play in one act. N.Y. French c1927. 12°. 25p.
Two too many. A comedy in three acts. Philadelphia. Penn. 1927. 12°. 78p.

MacKay, Louis Alexander
Freedom of Jean Guichet. 3 acts
In Massey, V. ed. Canadian plays from Hart House theatre. v. 2

Mackay, William Gayer and Ord, Robert [pseud.] (Mrs. William Gayer Mayer)
Dr. Wake's patient; a comedy in four acts. London. French. c1909
Paddy the next best thing; a play in four acts . . . adapted from the novel . . . by Gertrude Page. N.Y. French. c1927. 8°. 91p.

MacKaye, Percy, 1875-
Chuck. New Hampshire. 1 act
In Clark, B. H. and Nicholson, K. eds. American scene
Funeralizing of Crickneck. Kentucky. 1 act
In Kentucky mountain fantasies
George Washington at the Delaware. Historical. 1 act
In Johnson, T. ed. Washington anniversary plays
Schauffler, R. H. and Sanford, A. P. eds. Plays for our American holidays. v. 3
Jeanne d'Arc [a drama]. N.Y. Macmillan. 1906. 12°. 163p. 5 acts
Kinfolk of Robin Hood, a play in four acts. N.Y. French. [1926] 8°. 42p.
Maid of France. Jeanne D'Arc. 1 act
In Cohen, H. L. ed. One-act plays by modern authors. 1934 edition
Napoleon crossing the Rockies. Folk life. 1 act
In Kentucky mountain fantasies
Church, V. W. ed. Curtain!
Scarecrow. Tragedy. 4 acts
In Dickinson, T. H. Chief contemporary dramatists
Timber. Folk life. 2 pts.
In Kentucky mountain fantasies
Wakefield, a folk-masque of America; being a mid-winter night's dream of the birth of Washington. Washington bicentennial commission. c1932. 4°. 22p.
Washington and Betsy Ross; a dramatic action in two scenes; an arrangement from the three act play entitled Washington, the man who made us. N.Y. French. 1927. 8°. 34p.
Same in Schauffler, R. H. and Sanford, A. P. eds. Plays for our American holidays. v. 3

MacKaye, Percy—*Continued*
Young Washington at Mt. Vernon. A dramatic action in three scenes and a prologue. Selected from the three act play entitled Washington, the man who made us. N.Y. French. [1927] 8°. 62p.

MacKaye, Robert Keith
Honey Holler, a play in three acts, with an introduction by Oliver M. Sayler. N.Y. Brentano's. 1930. 8°. 201p.

Mackenzie, Ronald
Musical chairs. 3 acts
In Famous plays of 1932
Plays of a half-decade

McKinnel, Norman
Bishop's candlesticks; a play in one act. N.Y. French. 1908. 12°. 20p.
Same in Hampden, J. ed. Nine modern plays
Marriott, J. W. ed. One-act plays of to-day. ser. 3
Dick's sister [a play in one act]. London. French. c1911. 12°. 11p.

Mackintosh, Elizabeth. *See* Daviot, Gordon, pseud.

McMeekin, Mrs. Isabella (McLennan) 1895-
Goblin and the princess; a play in two acts. N.Y. French. c1929. 12°. 15p.
Thanks to Johnny Appleseed, a play in three acts. N.Y. French. 1929. 12°. 26p.

MacMillan, C. M.
His father's boots
In Hughes, H. et al. eds. Copy, 1928

MacMillan, Mary Louise, 1870-
Her doll; a play in one act. N.Y. French. c1927. 12°. 38p.
Plenty of time; a comedy in one act. N.Y. Appleton. 1928. 12°. 37p.

McMullen, Joseph Carl, 1882-
Antoinette comes to town. 1 act
In Evening of plays for men
Arnold goes into business; a play in three acts. Boston. 1926. 12°.
Back stage, a play in three acts. Boston. Baker. [c1930] 12°. 129p.
Boob; a comedy of business life in one act. Boston. Baker. 1921. 22p.
Conjurer's stone. 1 act
In Evening of plays for men
Little things; a play in three acts. Boston. Baker. [c1928] 12°. 96p.
Nicked. 1 act
In Evening of plays for men
Peculiar old duffer. 1 act
In Evening of plays for men
Rebellion of youth, in a prologue, two acts and an epilogue. N.Y. French. c1926. 12°. 77p.
Redemption play; a play in three acts depicting Christ's redemption of man. Boston. Baker. [c1933] 12°. 133p.

MacNair, Irene Taylor
Color line. Religious. 1 act
In Eastman, F. ed. Modern religious dramas

Macnamara, Margaret
Elizabeth refuses; a miniature comedy from Jane Austen's Pride and Prejudice
In Hampden, J. ed. Ten modern plays
Hat and stick. Comedy. 1 act
In Hampden, J. ed. Four new plays for women and girls
Penny for a guy! A play in one act. Oxford. Blackwell. 1928. 12°. 28p.
Yesterday; an historical comedy in four acts. London. Benn. 1926. 12°. 128p.

McOwen, Bernard J.
Why the bachelor? A comedy in three acts. N.Y. French. c1933. 12°. 99p.

McOwen, Bernard J. and Riewarts, J. P.
Blue ghost, a mystery melodrama in three acts. N.Y. French. c1932. 12°. 92p.

Maeterlinck, Maurice, 1862-
Death of Tintagiles. Tragedy. 5 acts
In McPharlin, P. ed. Repertory of marionette plays
Intruder. Death. 1 act
In Cohen, H. L. ed. One-act plays by modern authors. 1934 edition
Pélléas and Mélisande. Tragedy. 5 acts
In Tucker, S. M. ed. Modern continental plays
Tucker, S. M. ed. Twenty-five modern plays

Magre, Maurice, 1877-
Tin soldier and the paper dancer (Soldat de plomb et la danseuse de papier). Comedy. 1 act
In Vernon, V. and F. eds. Modern one-act plays from the French

Malleson, Miles, 1888-
Four people, a comedy in three acts. N.Y. Payson. 1928. 12°. 111p.
Love at second sight, a light comedy in three acts (from the novel "Safety first" by Margot Neville.) N.Y. French. c1929. 12°. 90p.
Man of ideas. Comedy. 1 act
In Hampden, J. ed. Four modern plays
Johnson, T. ed. Diminutive comedies
Modern short plays. ser. 3
Maurice's own idea. Dream-play. 1 act
In Phillips, LeR. and Johnson, T. Types of modern dramatic composition
Michael. Russian peasants. 1 act
In Hampden, J. ed. Eight modern plays
Paddy pools. Fairy. 3 scenes
In Marriott, J. W. ed. One-act plays of to-day. ser. 4
Yours unfaithfully, a comedy in three acts. London. Gollancz. 1933. 12°. 96p.

Maltz, Albert
Black pit. N.Y. Putnam. c1935. 12°. 108p. Coal camp. 3 acts

Maltz, Albert, *joint author.* *See* Sklar, George and Maltz, Albert

Mankiewicz, Herman J. *joint author.* *See* Kaufman, G. S. and Mankiewicz, H. J.

Mann, Heinrich, 1871-
Madame Legros. Historical. 3 acts
In Katzin, W. ed. Eight European
plays
Mansur, Frank L.
Dispatch goes home. 1 act
In Johnson, T. ed. Miniature plays for
stage or study
Marble, Annie Russell, 1864-
Faith of our fathers. Colonial pageant.
1 act
In Schauffler, R. H. and Sanford, A. P.
eds. Plays for our American holi-
days. v. 2
Drama. Pilgrim celebration no. 1920.
p. 373
Marble, Thomas Littlefield
Mistress Penelope. 1 act
In Johnson, T. ed. Plays about George
Washington
Marcin, Max, 1879- **and Bolton, Guy**
Nightcap, a mystery comedy in three acts.
N.Y. French. c1929. 12°. 100p.
Marion, Frances
Cup of life. 1 act
In Nicholson, K. ed. Hollywood plays
Mark, Francis
Tarakin. Soviet Russia. 1 act
In Marriott, J. W. ed. Best one-act
plays of 1932
Marks, Jeannette Augustus, 1875-
Deacon's hat. Comedy. 1 act
In Merry, merry cuckoo, and other
Welsh plays
Look to the end. 1 act
In Merry, merry cuckoo, and other
Welsh plays
Love letters. 1 act
In Merry, merry cuckoo, and other
Welsh plays
Merry, merry cuckoo. Character. 1 act
In Merry, merry cuckoo, and other
Welsh plays
Steppin' westward. 1 act
In Merry, merry cuckoo, and other
Welsh plays
Tress of hair. 1 act
In Merry, merry cuckoo, and other
Welsh plays
Welsh honeymoon. Comedy. 1 act
In Merry, merry cuckoo, and other
Welsh plays
Cohen, H. L. ed. One-act plays by
modern authors. 1934 edition
Marquis, Don, 1878-
Master of the revels; a comedy in four
acts. Garden City, N.Y. Doubleday.
1934. 12°. 202p. Henry VIII
Out of the sea; a play in four acts. Gar-
den City, N.Y. Doubleday. 1927.
12°. 133p.
Marschall, Phyllis
Grandpa tells about Lincoln
In Sanford, A. P. ed. Lincoln plays
Martínez Sierra, Gregorio, 1881-
Cradle song (Canción de cuna). Comedy.
2 acts
In Cradle song and other plays
Mantle, B. ed. Best plays of 1926-
27 (abridged)

Holy night, a miracle play in three
scenes: English version by Philip
Hereford. N.Y. Dutton. 1928. 8°.
55p.
Kingdom of God (El reino de Dios); a
play in three acts, in an English
version by Helen and Harley Gran-
ville Barker. London. Sidgwick.
1927. 12°. 105p.
Same in Kingdom of God and other
plays
Mantle, B. ed. Best plays of
1928-29 (abridged)
Love magic (Hechizo de amor). Comedy.
2 scenes
In Cradle song and other plays
Lover (El enamorado). Comedy. 1 act
In Cradle song and other plays
Madama Pepita. Comedy. 3 acts
In Cradle song and other plays
Poor John (El pobrecito Juan). Comedy.
1 act
In Cradle song and other plays
Romantic young lady (Sueño de una
noche de agosto) a comedy in three
acts. English version by Helen and
Harley Granville Barker. N.Y.
French. 1923. 12°. 297p.
In Kingdom of God and other plays
Take two from one; a farce in three acts,
in an English version by Helen and
Harley Granville Barker. London.
Sidgwick. 1931. 12°. 89p.
Two shepherds (Los pastores). Comedy.
2 acts
In Kingdom of God and other plays
Wife to a famous man (La mujer del
heróe). Comedy. 2 acts
In Kingdom of God and other plays
Martínez Sierra, Gregorio, 1881- **and
Martínez Sierra, Maria**
Lily among thorns. Comedy. 1 act
In Dickinson, T. H. ed. Chief contem-
porary dramatists. ser. 3
Martyn, Edward, 1859-1923
Maeve. Patriotism. 2 acts
In Canfield, C. ed. Plays of the Irish
renaissance
Masefield, John, 1878-
Coming of Christ. N.Y. Macmillan.
1928. 8°. 57p.
Easter; a play for singers. N.Y. Mac-
millan. 1929. 8°. 24p.
End and beginning. N.Y. Macmillan.
1933. 12°. 50p. Mary Stuart. 1 act
Sweeps of ninety-eight; a drama of the
Irish wars in one act.
In Golden Bk 17:550
Tristan and Isolt; a play in verse. Lon-
don. Heinemann. [1927] 12°. 135p.
Mason, Alfred Edward Woodley, 1865-
At the Villa Rosa, a play in four acts.
London. Hodder. 1928. 12°. 135p.
**Massingham, Dorothy and MacDonald,
Murray**
Lake; a play in three acts. N.Y. Double-
day. 1934. 12°. Tragedy. 3 acts
Masters, Edgar Lee, 1868-
Acoma. American Indians
In Gettysburg, Manila, Acoma

Masters, Edgar Lee—*Continued*
Eileen; a play in three acts. Chicago. Rooks press. 1910. 12°. 84p.
Gettysburg. Abraham Lincoln
In Gettysburg, Manila, Acoma
Godbey, a dramatic poem. N.Y. Dodd. 1931. 8°. 253p.
Jack Kelso. N.Y. Appleton. 1928. 12°. 264p. Historical
Lee; a dramatic poem. N.Y. Macmillan. 1926. 8°. 139p.
Manila. Philippines
In Gettysburg, Manila, Acoma

Mather, Charles Chambers
Dispatches for Washington; a play in one act. Boston. Baker. 1916. 12p.
Same in Johnson, T. ed. Plays about George Washington
Double-crossed; a comedy in one act. Boston. Baker. c1916. 14p.

Mathews, John
'Cruiter. Negro. 1 act
In Locke, A. Le R. and Gregory, M. eds. Plays of Negro life
Ti Yette. Negro. 1 act
In Richardson, W. ed. Plays and pageants from the life of the Negro

Matthews, Adelaide, 1886- and Nichols, Anne
Just married; a comedy in three acts. N.Y. French. 1929. 12°. 129p.

Matthews, Adelaide, 1886- and Sawyer, Lucille
Sunset glow; a comedy drama in three acts. Boston. Baker. c1929. 12°. 148p.

Matthews, Adelaide, *joint author. See* Stanley, Martha M. and Matthews, Adelaide

Maugham, William Somerset, 1874-
Breadwinner, a comedy. Garden City, N.Y. Doubleday. 1931. 8°. 184p.
Same in Chandler, F. W. and Cordell, R. A. eds. Twentieth century plays
Circle. Comedy. 3 acts
In Cordell, R. A. ed. Representative modern plays
McDermott, J. F. ed. Modern plays
Marriott, J. W. ed. Great modern British plays
Moses, M. J. ed. Dramas of modernism and their forerunners
Tucker, S. M. ed. Twenty-five modern plays
Watson, E. B. and Pressey, B. eds. Contemporary drama: English and Irish plays
Constant wife. Comedy. 3 acts
In Mantle, B. ed. Best plays of 1926-27 (condensed)
For services rendered; a play in three acts. Garden City, N.Y. Doubleday. 1933. 87p.
Jack Straw. Farce. 3 acts
In Plays. v. 1
Lady Frederick. Comedy. 3 acts
In Plays. v. 1

Land of promise. Comedy. 4 acts
In Plays. v. 2
Letter; a play in three acts. N.Y. Doran. c1925. 12°. 177p. Emotional
Mrs. Dot. Farce. 3 acts
In Plays. v. 1
Our betters. Comedy. 3 acts
In Moses, M. J. ed. Representative British dramas, Victorian and modern
Penelope. Comedy. 3 acts
In Plays. v. 2
Sacred flame; a play in three acts. N.Y. Doubleday. 1928. 12°. 187p. Problem
Sheppey; a play in three acts. 12°. 118p. 1933. London. Heinemann
Smith. Comedy. 1 act
In Plays. v. 2

Maurey, Max, 1868-
Rosalie; a comedy in one act. . . tr. by Barrett H. Clark. N.Y. French. c1913. 12°. 14p.

Mavor, Osborne Henry (James Bridie, pseud.) 1888-
Amazed evangelist; a nightmare. London. Constable. 1932. 8°. 12p. 1 act
Same in Anatomist and other plays Anatomist; Tobias and the angel; Amazed evangelist
Anatomist. London. Constable. 1931. 8°. Comedy. 1 act
Same in Anatomist and other plays Anatomist; Tobias and the angel; Amazed evangelist
Jonah and the whale; a morality in three acts and a prologue. London. Constable. 1932. 166p.
Mrs. Waterbury's millennium. 1 act
In Bourne, J. ed. Eight new one-act plays for 1934
Pardoner's tale. Morality
In Switchback; Pardoner's tale; Sunlight sonata
Sunlight sonata. Farce morality
In Switchback; Pardoner's tale; Sunlight sonata
Switchback. Comedy
In Switchback; Pardoner's tale; Sunlight sonata
Tobias and the angel. London. Constable. 1931. 8°. 162p. Comedy. 3 acts
Same in Anatomist and other plays Anatomist; Tobias and the angel; Amazed evangelist

Maxfield, Mina R.
Ruth of Moab. Biblical
In Gaw, A. and others. Pharaoh's daughter, and other Biblical plays of the contest, 1927

Mayer, Edwin Justus
Children of darkness; an original tragicomedy. N.Y. Liveright. 1929. 12°. 232p.

Mayo, Margaret, 1882-
Polly of the circus; a comedy-drama in three acts. N.Y. Longmans. 1933. 98p.

Mayo, Margaret, 1882- and **Field, Edward Salisbury,** 1878-
Twin beds, a farce in three acts. N.Y. French. 1931. 12°. 154p.

Mayor, Beatrice
In a shop. Juvenile. 1 act
In Four plays for children
In a street. Juvenile. 1 act
In Four plays for children
Musical box. Juvenile. 1 act
In Four plays for children
Old home. Juvenile. 1 act
In Four plays for children
Pleasure garden. Comedy. 4 acts
In Plays of to-day. ser. 3
Thirty minutes in a street. Comedy. 1 act
In Hampden, J. ed. Ten modern plays
Herbert, A. P. Four one-act plays
Mayor, B. ed. Four one-act plays

Meadon, Joseph
Pearls before swine. Comedy. 1 act
In Players book of one act plays. ser. 1
Vespers. Morality. 1 act
In Players book of one act plays. ser. 1

Meaker, Isabelle J. and **Harnwell, Anna J.**
Knife. World war. 1 act
In Schauffler, R. H. and Sanford, A. P. eds. Plays for our American holidays. v. 3
Sojourners. Puritans. 1 act
In Schauffler, R. H. and Sanford, A. P. eds. Plays for our American holidays. 1 act. v. 2

Meaker, Isabelle J. and **Perkins, Eleanor Ellis**
My lady's Yule-tide. Christmas. 1 act
In Schauffler, R. H. and Sanford, A. P. eds. Plays for our American holidays. v. 1

Mechem, Kirke
Who won the war? a play in three acts, written for the American legion. N.Y. French. c1928. 12°. 89p.

Medcraft, Russell Graham, 1900-
First dress-suit; a comedy in one act. N.Y. French. c1929. 8°. 26p.
Same in One-act plays for stage and study. ser. 5
Poetry and plaster. Comedy. 1 act
In One-act plays for stage and study. ser. 6
Queen's nose; a comedy in one act. N.Y. French. c1933. 12°. 21p.
Saucy goose; a comedy in one act. N.Y. French. c1931. 12°. 14p.

Medcraft, Russell G. and **Mitchell, Norma**
Cradle snatchers, a farce comedy in three acts. N.Y. French. [c1931] 12°. 85p.

Meigs, C. H.
Man of Uz; a drama in three acts. N.Y. London. Putnam. 1933. 25-285p.

Meirovitz, Joseph Moses, 1884-
New generation; a drama in three acts. Boston. Four Seas. 1928. 12°. 39p.

Mellon, Evelyn Emig
China pig. 1 act
In Two prize plays and four others
Love! love! love! 1 act
In Two prize plays and four others

Mother and son. 1 act
In Two prize plays and four others
Old order. 1 act
In Two prize plays and four others
Pen-and-ink. 1 act
In Two prize plays and four others
Trains. 1 act
In Two prize plays and four others
Poet Lore 41:424

Meneses, Enrique de
Glittering highway. World war. 4 acts
In Poet Lore 38:317

Merchant, Abby
New frock for Pierrette; dramatic revue and fashion show. N.Y. French. c1933. 12°. 61p.

Merivale, Philip, 1886-
Peace of Ferrara; a drama in three acts. Boston. Four Seas. 1927. 12°. 119p.

Merrill, Fenimore, d. 1919
Avenue. Comedy. 1 act
In Shay, F. ed. Fifty more contemporary one-act plays
Drama 10:53

Metcalf, Felicia
Auntie up, a three-act comedy. Franklin, Ohio. c1932. 12°.
Some easy, a comedy in three acts. N.Y. French. c1933. 12°. 99p.

Middleton, George, 1880-1916
Blood money; a melodrama in three acts; from a story of H. H. Van Loan. N.Y. French. c1929. 12°. 122p.
Hiss! Boom! Blah!!! a three-act American comedy in fifty scenes; being a cross section community chronicle of some mad years (1917-193-?). N.Y. French. 1933. 194p.

Middleton, George, 1880- and **Thomas, A. E.**
Big pond; a tran-Atlantic comedy in three acts. N.Y. French. c1930. 12°. 122p.

Millay, Edna St. Vincent (Mrs. E. J. Boissevain) 1892-
Aria da capo. Love. 1 act
In Church, V. W. ed. Curtain!
King's henchman. Anglo-Saxon legendary history. 3 acts
In Tucker, S. M. ed. Modern American and British plays
Princess marries the page; a play in one act. N.Y. Harper. 1932. 8°. 51p. Romantic

Miller, Mrs. Alice (Duer) 1874-
Springboard; a comedy in three acts. N.Y. French. c1928. 12°. 109p.

Miller, Ashley
Mr. Scrooge; a dramatic fantasy after Charles Dickens' "A Christmas carol." N.Y. Dodd. c1928. 12°. 129p. 3 acts

Miller, Louis, 1889-
Mr. Man; a play in four acts and eight scenes. tr. from the Yiddish by S. K. Padover and Chasye Cooperman
In Poet Lore 40:475

Miller, May
Graven images. Negro. 1 act
  In Richardson, W. ed. Plays and
    pageants from the life of the
    Negro
Riding the goat. Negro. 1 act
  In Richardson, W. ed. Plays and
    pageants from the life of the
    Negro
Mills, Mervyn
Nelson of the Nile; a play in four acts.
  N.Y. Putnam. c1933. 12°. 167p.
Milne, Alan Alexander, 1882-
Boy comes home. Comedy. 1 act
  In Webber, J. P. and Webster, H. H.
    eds. One-act plays for secondary
    schools
Dover road. Comedy. 3 acts
  In Dickinson, T. H. ed. Chief contem-
    porary dramatists. ser. 3
Fourth wall. A detective story in three
  acts. N.Y. French. 1929. 8°. 82p.
  (Played in America under title "The
  perfect alibi")
Great Broxopp. Comedy. 4 acts
  In Church, V. W. ed. Curtain!
Ivory door; a legend in a prologue and
  three acts. N.Y. Putnam. 1928. 8°.
  221p.
  Same in Tucker, S. M. ed. Modern
    plays
Make-believe. Juvenile. 3 acts and
  prologue
  In Moses, M. J. ed. Another treasury
    of plays for children
Man in the bowler hat. Comedy. 1 act
  In Marriott, J. W. ed. One-act plays
    of to-day. ser. 4
Michael and Mary. London. Chatto.
  1930. 12°. 96p. Problem. 3 acts.
  Also N.Y. French. 1932. 8°.
  Same in Four plays (Putnam 1932)
      Mantle, B. ed. Best plays of
      1929-30 (abridged)
Mr. Pim passes by
  In McDermott, J. F. ed. Modern plays
    Watson, E. B. and Pressey, B. eds.
    Contemporary drama: English and
    Irish plays
Perfect alibi (English title: Fourth wall).
  Detective. 3 acts
  In Four plays (Putnam 1932)
  See also Fourth wall
Portrait of a gentleman in slippers.
  Fairy tale. 1 act
  In Four plays (Putnam 1932)
Princess and the woodcutter. Fairy. 1 act
  In Hampden, J. ed. Eight modern
    plays
Success. 3 acts
  In Cordell, R. A. ed. Representative
    modern plays
To meet the prince (English title: To
  have the honour). Comedy. 3 acts
  In Four plays (Putnam 1932)
Toad of Toad Hall. A play from Ken-
  neth Grahame's "The wind in the
  willows." N.Y. Scribner. 1929. 12°.
  168p. Fantasy

Truth about Blayds. Comedy. 3 acts
  In Moses, M. J. ed. Dramas of mod-
    ernism and their forerunners
    Tucker, S. M. ed. Twenty-five mod-
    ern plays
Wurzel-Flummery. Comedy. 1 act
  In Modern short plays. ser. 2
    Cohen, H. L. ed. One-act plays by
    modern authors. 1934 edition
Mitchell, Langdon Elwyn, 1862-
Becky Sharp, a play in four acts.
  Founded on Thackeray's "Vanity
  Fair." n. pub. c1899. 12°. 35p.
New York idea. Social comedy. 4 acts
  In Watson, E. B. and Pressey, B. eds.
    Contemporary drama. American
    plays
Mitchell, Norma, *joint author. See* Med-
  craft, Russell G. and Mitchell, Norma
Mitchell, Thomas, *joint author. See* Dell,
  Floyd and Mitchell, Thomas
Mitchison, Naomi
Nix-nought-nothing. Fairy. 1 act
  In Hampden, J. ed. Seven modern
    plays for younger players
Mitcoff, Elena Y.
Petroushka. Puppet. 1 act
  In McPharlin, P. ed. Repertory of
    marionette plays
Moeller, Phillip, 1880-
Madame Sand. Comedy. 3 acts
  In Tucker, S. M. ed. Modern Ameri-
    can and British plays
Molnár, Ferenc, 1878-
Cab. Dialogue. Comedy
  In Plays of Molnar (Jarrolds)
Carnival. Symbolic. 3 acts
  In Plays of Ferenc Molnár (Macy-
    Masius)
Curtain. Dialogue
  In Plays of Molnar (Jarrolds)
Devil. 3 acts
  In Plays of Ferenc Molnár (Macy-
    Masius)
Fashions for men. Comedy. 3 acts
  In Plays of Ferenc Molnár (Macy-
    Masius)
    Plays of Molnar (Jarrolds)
Fledglings. Dialogue
  In Plays of Molnar (Jarrolds)
Glass slipper. Comedy. 3 acts
  In Plays of Ferenc Molnár (Macy-
    Masius)
Good fairy, a new play; tr. and adapted
  by Jane Hinton. N.Y. Long. 1932.
  12°. 178p. Comedy
Guardsman. (Where ignorance is bliss)
  Comedy. 3 acts
  In Plays of Ferenc Molnár (Macy-
    Masius)
Heavenly and earthly love. Dialogue
  In Plays of Ferenc Molnár (Macy-
    Masius)
    Plays of Molnar (Jarrolds)
Husbands and lovers: nineteen dialogues
  In Plays of Molnar (Jarrolds)
Key. Dialogue
  In Plays of Molnar (Jarrolds)
Kiss. Dialogue
  In Plays of Molnar (Jarrolds)

Knight of the blue chin. Dialogue
In Plays of Molnar (Jarrolds)
Lawyer. Farce. 3 acts
In Plays of Ferenc Molnár (Macy-
Masius)
Leave-taking. Dialogue
In Plays of Molnar (Jarrolds)
Lies. Dialogue
In Plays of Molnar (Jarrolds)
Liliom. Symbolic. 7 scenes and pro-
logue
In Plays of Ferenc Molnár (Macy-
Masius)
Plays of Molnar (Jarrolds)
Dickinson, T. H. ed. Chief contem-
porary dramatists. ser. 3
Moses, M. J. ed. Dramas of
modernism and their forerunners
Steeves, H. R. ed. Plays from the
modern theatre
Tucker, S. M. ed. Modern conti-
nental plays
Tucker, S. M. ed. Twenty-five
modern plays
Man in the cab. Dialogue
In Plays of Molnar (Jarrolds)
Marshal. Stage life. 1 act
In Plays of Ferenc Molnár (Macy-
Masius)
Matter of husbands. Dialogue
In Plays of Molnar (Jarrolds)
Mima. (Redmill) Human life. 3 pts.
In Plays of Ferenc Molnár (Macy-
Masius)
Olympia, tr. by Sidney Howard. N.Y.
Brentano. 1928. 12°. 133p. Ro-
mantic comedy. 3 acts
Same in Plays of Ferenc Molnár
(Macy-Masius)
Phantom lover. *See* Molnár, F. Tale of
the wolf
Phosphorus. Dialogue
In Plays of Molnar (Jarrolds)
Play's the thing [adapted by P. G.
Wodehouse]. Comedy. 3 acts
In Plays of Ferenc Molnár (Macy-
Masius)
Mantle, B. ed. Best plays of 1926-
27 (condensed)
Preliminary skirmish. Dialogue
In Plays of Molnar (Jarrolds)
Prologue to "King Lear." Stage life.
1 act
In Plays of Ferenc Molnár (Macy-
Masius)
Putty club. Juvenile. 1 act
In Theatre Arts M 7:25 Jl. '23
Railroad adventure. Dialogue
In Plays of Molnar (Jarrolds)
Red mill. *See* Molnár, F. Mima
Riviera. Mannikins. 2 acts
In Plays of Ferenc Molnár (Macy-
Masius)
Sacred and profane art. Dialogue
In Plays of Molnar (Jarrolds)
Seven o'clock in the evening. Dialogue
In Plays of Molnar (Jarrolds)
Still life. 1 act
In Plays of Ferenc Molnár (Macy-
Masius)

Street and number. Dialogue
In Plays of Molnar (Jarrolds)
Swan; a romantic comedy in three acts;
tr. from the Hungarian by Melville
Baker. N.Y. Longmans. 1929. 12°.
122p.
Same in Plays of Ferenc Molnár (Macy-
Masius)
Plays of Molnar (Jarrolds)
Chandler, F. W. and Cordell,
R. A. eds. Twentieth cen-
tury plays
Tale of the wolf. (Phantom lover)
Comedy. 3 acts
In Plays of Ferenc Molnár (Macy-
Masius)
Two slaps in the face. Dialogue
In Plays of Molnar (Jarrolds)
Unpardonable sin. Dialogue
In Plays of Molnar (Jarrolds)
Violet. Stage life. 1 act
In Plays of Ferenc Molnár (Macy-
Masius)
Where ignorance is bliss. *See* Molnár, F.
Guardsman
White cloud. Miracle play. 5 scenes
In Plays of Ferenc Molnár (Macy-
Masius)
Witch. Comedy. 1 act
In Plays of Ferenc Molnár (Macy-
Masius)

Monkhouse, Allan Noble, 1858-
Cecilia, a play in four acts. London. Gol-
lancz. 1931. 12°. 79p.
Grand cham's diamond; a play in one act.
London. Gowans. 1924. 16°. 53p.
In Hampden, J. ed. Seven modern
plays for younger readers
Tucker, S. M. ed. Twelve one-act
plays for study and production
King of Barvender; a melodrama in one
act. London. Gowans. 1927. 16°. 42p.
Same in Marriott, J. W. ed. One-act
plays of to-day. ser. 5.
Night watches, a comedy in one act.
Boston. Baker. [c1930] 12°. 16p.
Nothing like leather; an indiscretion in
one act. London. Gowans. 1930. 24°.
48p.
Same in Manchester Playgoer N. 7,
1913
O death, where is thy sting? a play in
one act. London. Gowans. 1926. 12°.
31p.
Paul Felice, a play in four acts. London.
Gollancz. 1930. 12°. 96p.
Rag; an incident in three acts. London.
Sidgwick. [1928] 12°. 80p.
Wily one. 1 act
In One-act plays for stage and study.
ser. 4

Montague, Clifford M. 1907-
Tropics. 1 act
In Poet Lore 40:414

Moore, Bernard Francis
Government detective, a play in four acts.
Boston. Baker. 1910. 12°. 51p.

Moore, E. Hamilton
Dove uncaged, a play in one act. N.Y.
French. c1912. 12°. 24p.

Moore, Florence B.
Tale from India. 1 act
In Jagendorf, M. A. ed. Nine short plays

Moore, Frank Frankfort, 1855-
Jessamy bride. 1 act
In Kitty Clive, and other plays in one act
Kitty Clive. 1 act
In Kitty Clive, and other plays in one act
Poor actress. 1 act
In Kitty Clive, and other plays in one act
Sword of Damocles. 1 act
In Kitty Clive, and other plays in one act

Moore, George, 1852-1933
Making of an immortal; a play in one act. N.Y. Bowling Green press. 1927. 8°. 59p.
Passing of the Essenes; a drama in three acts. London. Heinemann. 1930. 8°. 96p.

Moore, Lidian Ruth
Mantuan, a Vergil play in three acts (with a prologue). N.Y. Longmans. 1930. 12°. 131p.

Moratin, José
Fanny's consent. Comedy. 12 scenes
In Poet Lore 40:159

Morax, René, 1873-
King David, a play in two parts, taken from the Bible. tr. by Dennis Arundell. Cambridge [Eng.] University Press. 1929. 12°. 132p.

Morbio, P.
Psychological moment. 1 act
In Johnson, T. ed. Diminutive comedies

Morley, Christopher Darlington, 1890-
Good theatre. Shakespeare. 1 act
In Church, V. W. ed. Curtain
"In modern dress," a one-act play. Larchmont, N.Y. Peter Pauper press. 1929. 8°. 19p.
On the shelf. Books. 1 act
In Schauffler, R. H. and Sanford, A. P. eds. Plays for our American holidays. v. 4
Really, my dear. . . . 1 act
In Hughes, G. ed. Short plays for modern players
Thursday evening. N.Y. Appleton. 1926. 12°. 34p. Comedy. 1 act
Same in Pence, R. W. ed. Dramas by present-day writers
Tucker, S. M. ed. Twelve one-act plays for study and production

Morris, Hilda
Book children's Christmas. 1 act
In Curtis, A. ed. Christmas plays for one and all

Morrison, Anne
Wild Westcotts; a comedy in three acts. N.Y. French. c1926. 12°. 109p.

Morrison, Anne and Toohey, John Peter, 1880-
Jonesy, a comedy in three acts. . . (based on a series of short stories by Mr. Toohey). N.Y. French. c1929. 12°. 123p.

Moseley, Katharine P.
Daggers and diamonds; a travesty in one act. Boston. Baker. 1921. 44p.
In Phillips, LeR. and Johnson, T. eds. Types of modern dramatic composition

Moses, Grace Celeste
Tree of memory. Armistice day pageant. 1 act
In Schauffler, R. H. and Sanford, A. P. eds. Plays for our American holidays. v. 3

Mourguet, Laurent
Coq brothers. Marionette. 1 act
In McPharlin, P. ed. Repertory of marionette plays

Muggeridge, Malcolm
Three flats, a play in three acts. N.Y. Putnam. [1931] 12°. 119p.

Mullally, Don
Camels are coming, a comedy in three acts. . . N.Y. French. c1932. 12°. 98p.
Laff that off; a comedy in three acts. N.Y. French. c1928. 12°. 105p. [copyright, 1921 under title "The ingrate"]

Munro, Charles Kirkpatrick, 1889-
At Mrs. Beams. Comedy. 3 acts
In Marriott, J. W. ed. Great modern British plays
Plays of today. ser. 3
Bluestone quarry; a play. London. Gollancz. 1931. 125p.
Three plays. London. Gollancz. 1932. 288p.

Munro, Hector Hugh (Saki, pseud.) 1870-1916
Death-trap. Comedy. 1 act
In Novels and plays
Square egg and other sketches
Modern short plays. ser. 1
Karl-Ludwig's window. Melodrama. 1 act
In Novels and plays
Square egg and other sketches
Modern short plays. ser. 3
Watched pot (The mistress of Briony). Comedy. 3 acts
In Novels and plays
Square egg and other sketches

Murfin, Jane
Prince Gabby. 1 act
In Nicholson, Kenyon, ed. Appleton book of short plays. ser. 2

Murphy, Rolph
Sure fire; a comedy in three acts. N.Y. French. c1927. 12°. 130p.

Murphy, Thomas Francis, 1867-
Mary Brice. Comedy. 1 act
In Players book of one act plays. ser. 1

Murray, Anne
Zee-Zee. A comedy in three acts. Philadelphia. Penn. 1927. 12°. 87p.
In Prize plays of 1927

Murray, Thomas C.
  Birthright. Tragedy. 2 acts
    In Canfield, C. ed. Plays of the Irish
      renaissance
  Michaelmas eve: a play in three acts.
    London. Allen. 1932. 8°. 88p.
  Pipe in the fields. Music. 1 act
    In One-act plays for stage and study.
      ser. 4
Muse, George A.
  Close call. First aid. 1 act
    In Schauffler, R. H. and Sanford, A. P.
      eds. Plays for our American holi-
      days. v. 4
Musset, Alfred de, 1810-1857
  Fantasis; a comedy in two acts; tr. by
    Maurice Baring. N.Y. Harper. 1929.
    12°. 57p.
Mussolini, Benito, 1883- and Giovacchino,
    Forzano, 1884-
  Napoleon: the hundred days; a play,
    adapted from the Italian for the Eng-
    lish stage by J. Drinkwater. London.
    Sidgwick. 1932. 96p.
Mygatt, Tracy Dickinson
  His son. 1 act
    In Poet Lore 39:605
  Noose. 1 act
    In Drama 20:42
Nagle, Brother Urban, 1905-
  Barter; a drama in four acts . . . the win-
    ning Biblical play of the 1928 Drama
    league. N.Y. Longmans. 1929. 12°.
    92p.
  Catherine the valiant; a religious drama
    in five acts. N.Y. Longmans. 1931. 8°.
    98p.
Nakamura, Kichizo, 1877-
  ·Death of Ii Tairo. tr. by Mock Joya.
    Tokyo. Japan Times [1927?]
  Razor. Jealousy. 1 act
    In Shay, F. ed. Fifty more contem-
      porary one-act plays
Neale, Ralph, *joint author. See* Chesterton,
    Ada E. and Neale, Ralph
Neebe, J. H.
  Fog. Melodrama. 1 act
    In Players book of one act plays.
      ser. 1
  Guts; alternate title: Who wouldn't? a
    melodrama. 1 act
    In Players book of one act plays. ser. 1
Neilson, Francis, 1867-
  Prince Ananias, as performed by "The
    Bostonians." N.Y. E. Schuberth.
    c1894. 8°. 72p. Comic opera. 2 acts
  Queen of Nectaria; a fantasy in four acts.
    N.Y. Viking press. 1924. 12°. 123p.
Nesbitt, Catharine May, 1884-
  Net. 1 act
    In Schofield, S. ed. Marble god, and
      other one-act plays
Neumann, Alfred, 1895-
  Patriot; a play in three acts; adapted by
    Ashley Dukes. N.Y. Boni. c1928. 12°.
    142p. Historical
  Such men are dangerous; a play in eight
    scenes, adapted by Ashley Dukes from
    "The Patriot." London. Gollancz.
    1928. 12°. 118p. American edition pub.
    under title: The patriot

Neuville, Lemercier de
  Mr. Goodman and Mrs. Gracious.
    Marionette. 1 act
    In McPharlin, P. ed. Repertory of
      marionette plays
Newman, Benjamin W.
  Underground. 1 act
    In Poet Lore 38:571
Newton, Alfred Edward, 1863-
  Mr. Strahan's dinner party; a comedy in
    one act, with prologue and
    epilogue. . . and a note by Edward
    F. O'Day. fol. San Francisco. J.
    H. Nash. Printed for the Book club
    of California. 1930. 43p.
Nichols, Beverly, *joint author. See* Knob-
    lock, Edward and Nichols, Beverly
Nichols, Robert Malise Bowyer, 1893- and
    Browne, Maurice
  Wings over Europe; a dramatic extrava-
    ganza on a pressing theme. N.Y.
    Covici. 1929. 12°. 172p. Universal
    peace
    Same in Church, W. W. ed. Curtain!
      Mantle, B. ed. Best plays of
        1928-29 (abridged)
      Moses, M. J. ed. Dramas of
        modernism and their fore-
        runners
Nichols, Robert Malise Bowyer, 1893- and
    Tully, Jim, 1888-
  Twenty below; being a drama of the
    road. London. Holden. 1927. 12°.
    91p.
Nicholson, Kenyon, 1894-
  Barker; a play of carnival life in three
    acts. N.Y. French. 1927. 12°. 150p.
  Hint to brides; a comedy in one act.
    N.Y. c1923. 12°.
  Man pays; a comedy in one act. Boston.
    Baker. c1927. 12°. 16p.
  Marriage of little Eva. Comedy. 1 act
    In Shay, F. ed. Fifty more contem-
      porary one-act plays
  Snake eater. Comedy. 1 act
    In One-act plays for stage and study.
      ser. 4
  Tell me your troubles; a farce-comedy in
    three acts. . . (based on a short story
    of the same name by Meredith
    Nicholson). N.Y. French. c1928.
    12°. 113p.
  Torch song, a play in prologue and three
    acts. N.Y. French. 1930. 12°. 194p.
    Melodrama
  Wanderlust, a play in one act. Boston.
    Baker. [1920] 12°. 43-60p.
    Same in Phillips, Le R. and Johnson,
      T. eds. Types of modern
        dramatic composition
  Woman forgives, a comedy in one act.
    Boston. Baker. c1927. 12°. 15p.
  Words and music. Comedy. 1 act
    In One-act plays for stage and study.
      ser. 5
Nicholson, Kenyon and Barrows, Thomas
  Two weeks off; a summertime comedy.
    N.Y. French. c1927. 12°. 102p.

Nicholson, Kenyon and Behrman, Samuel
Bedside manners; a comedy of convalescence. N.Y. French. c1924. 12°. 18p.

Nicholson, Kenyon and DeSola, Alis
Shame the devil; a drama in one act. N.Y. Appleton. 1928. 12°. 27p.

Nicholson, Kenyon, 1894- and Golden, John, 1874-
Eva the fifth, the odyssey of a Tom show in three acts. N.Y. French. 1928. 12°. 181p.

Nicholson, Kenyon and Knox, Charles
Here's to your health! an adventure of a medicine man in three acts. N.Y. French. 1927. 12°. 85p.

Nicholson, Kenyon and Pendray, G. E.
Organ. 1 act
In Clark, B. H. and Cook, T. R. eds. One-act plays

Nicholson, Kenyon, 1894- and Robinson, Charles
Sailor, beware! a play. Variations on a familiar theme in eight scenes. N.Y. Farrar. [1933] 259p.

Noël-Paton, M. H.
Hidden people; a short play. London. Allen. [1933] 12°. 64p. Based on the ballads of Tam Lin and Thomas the Rymer

Norris, Kathleen, 1880-
Victoria; a play in four acts and twelve scenes. Garden City, N.Y. Doubleday. 1934. 12°. 140p. Queen Victoria

Norris, Kathleen, 1880- and Totheroh, Dan
Kelly Kid. Comedy. 1 act
In Clark, B. H. and Cook, T. R. eds. One-act plays
Phillips, Le R. and Johnson, T. eds. Types of modern dramatic composition

Norton, Bert J.
Digging up the dirt, a comedy in three acts; adapted by William M. Sloane III. N.Y. Longmans. 1931. 12°. 129p.

Novello, Ivor, 1893-
Truth game; a light comedy in three acts. N.Y. French. c1929. 8°. 72p.

Noyes, Alfred, 1880-
Robin Hood. 1 act
In Hampden, J. ed. Eight modern plays

O'Brien, James Henry
Marching men; a play in one act. N.Y. French. 1927. 12°. 18p.

O'Brien, Seumas, 1880-
Birdcatcher. Elopement. 1 act
In Shay, F. ed. Fifty more contemporary one-act plays
Christmas eve. 1 act
In One-act plays for stage and study. ser. 4
Shay, F. ed. Appleton book of Christmas plays
Wild boar. Allegory of Ireland. 1 act
In Poet Lore 38:536

O'Casey, Sean
Juno and the paycock
In Canfield, C. ed. Plays of the Irish renaissance
Cordell, R. A. ed. Representative modern plays

Dickinson, T. H. ed. Chief contemporary dramatists. ser. 3
Watson, E. B. and Pressey, B. eds. Contemporary drama: English and Irish plays
Plough and the stars. Tragedy. 4 acts
In Mantle, B. ed. Best plays of 1927-28 (abridged)
Shadow of a gunman, a tragedy in two acts. N.Y. French. c1932. 12°. 48p.
Silver Tassie; a tragi-comedy in four acts. N.Y. Macmillan. 1928. 12°. 140p.
Within the gates; a play in four scenes in a London park. London. Macmillan. 1933. 12°. 203p.

O'Connell, Wilkeson
Lie. Revolutionary Carolina. 1 act
In Koch, F. H. ed. Carolina folk comedies

O'Connor, Patricia
My dear! Comedy. 1 act
In Johnson, T. ed. Diminutive comedies

O'Dea, Mark
Song of Solomon. Episode. 1 act
In Clark, B. H. and Cook, T. R. eds. One-act plays

Odets, Clifford
Awake and sing. N.Y. Random House. 1935. 3 acts
Same in Three plays
Till the day I die. Hitler's Germany. 7 scenes
In Three plays
Waiting for Lefty, and Till the day I die
Waiting for Lefty. 6 episodes
In Three plays
Waiting for Lefty, and Till the day I die

Offenbach, Jacques, 1819-1880
La Périchole. Melodrama. 3 acts
In Plays of the Moscow Art Theatre musical studio 1925

Oglesbee, Delle Houghton
Ten fingers of François. Christmas. 1 act
In Schauffler, R. H. and Sanford, A. P. eds. Plays for our American holidays. v. 1

O'Higgins, Harvey Jerrold, 1876- and Ford, Harriet, 1868-
Argyle case; a drama in four acts . . . with the co-operation of William J. Burns. N.Y. French. c1927. 12°. 128p.
Old P. G.; a play in three acts. N.Y. French. c1928. 12°. 81p.
Orphan Aggie; a romantic comedy. N.Y. French. c1927. 12°. 96p.

Okamoto, Kidō, 1872-
American envoy (Townsend Harris), a play; tr. by Masano Inouye. Kobe. J. L. Thompson. 1931. 12°. 56p.
Human pillar; a drama in one act; tr. from the Japanese by Zoë Kinkaid and Hanso Tarao. N.Y. French. c1928. 12°. 27p.
Lady Hosokawa, an historical drama in two acts; tr. from the Japanese by Asataro Miyameri.
In Poet Lore 37:[No. 1]:1

Mask-maker; a drama in three acts; adapted and prepared for stage production by Zoë Kinkaid, from the translation of Hanso Tarao. N.Y. French. 1928. 12°. 28p.

Olcott, Virginia
Alphabet tree. Juvenile
In Industrial plays for young people
April fool. Juvenile. 1 act
In Schauffler, R. H. and Sanford, A. P. eds. Plays for our American holidays. v. 2
Blue flower of home. Juvenile
In Household plays for young people
Cart-load of kettles. Juvenile
In Household plays for young people
Cave of the Fates. New Year. 1 act
In Schauffler, R. H. and Sanford, A. P. eds. Plays for our American holidays. v. 2
Crystal cave. Juvenile
In Industrial plays for young people
Fire of icicles. Juvenile
In Industrial plays for young people
Golden locket of darkness. Juvenile
In Household plays for young people
Jewel boy of Florence. Juvenile
In Industrial plays for young people
Mademoiselle Cocoon. Juvenile
In Industrial plays for young people
Magic cargoes. Juvenile
In Household plays for young people
Offering of mirrors. Juvenile
In Household plays for young people
Rainbow robe. Juvenile
In Household plays for young people
Runaway simnel cake. Juvenile
In Household plays for young people
Secret under the berry moon. Juvenile
In Household plays for young people
Seven spinning meisjes. Juvenile
In Industrial plays for young people
T'ien Jung and the eight immortals. China
In Industrial plays for young people
Wonder watch of the Jura. Juvenile
In Industrial plays for young people

O'Neill, Eugene, 1888-
Ah, Wilderness! N.Y. Random house. [c1933] 8°. 159p. Adolescence. 3 acts
Same in Mantle, B. ed. Best plays of 1933-34 (abridged)
All God's chillun's got wings. Race prejudice. 2 acts
In Nine plays
Beyond the horizon. Social. 3 acts
In Whitman, C. H. Seven contemporary plays
Bound east for Cardiff. Sea. 1 act
In Clark, B. H. and Nicholson, K. eds. American scene
Days without end. N.Y. Random house. 1934. 12°. Dual personality. 4 acts
Desire under the elms. Sex. 3 acts
In Nine plays
Moses, M. J. ed. Dramas of modernism and their forerunners
Diff'rent. Mistakes. 2 acts
In Cordell, R. A. ed. Representative modern plays

Dreamy kid. Negro. 1 act
In Isaacs, E. J. ed. Plays of American life and fantasy
Locke, A. Le R. and Gregory, M. eds. Plays of Negro life
Dynamo. N.Y. Liveright. 1929. 12°. 159p. Tragedy. 3 acts
Emperor Jones. Negro, tragedy. 8 scenes
In Nine plays
Church, V. W. ed. Curtain!
Dickinson, T. H. ed. Chief contemporary dramatists. ser. 3
Locke, A. Le R. and Gregory, M. eds. Plays of Negro life
McDermott, J. F. ed. Modern plays
Tucker, S. M. ed. Modern plays
Watson, E. B. and Pressey, B. eds. Contemporary drama. American plays
Great God Brown. Fantasy. 4 acts
In Nine plays
Steeves, H. R. ed. Plays from the modern theatre
Tucker, S. M. ed. Twenty-five modern plays
Hairy ape. Social. 8 scenes
In Nine plays
Ile. Obsession. 1 act
In Clark, B. H. and Cook, T. R. eds. One-act plays
Cohen, H. L. ed. One act plays by modern authors. 1934 edition
Goldstone, G. A. ed. One-act plays
Pence, R. W. ed. Dramas by present-day writers
Lazarus laughed; a play for an imaginative theatre. N.Y. Boni. 1927. 12°. 179p. Symbolic masque
Same in Nine plays
Long voyage home; a play in one act
In Smart Set anthology
Marco millions. Satire. **3 acts**
In Nine plays
Chandler, F. W. and Cordell, R. A. eds. Twentieth century plays
Moon of the Caribbees. Sea. 1 act
In Shay, F. ed. Fifty more contemporary one-act plays
Mourning becomes Electra. A trilogy. N.Y. Liveright. 1931. 12°. 256p. 14 scenes
Same in Nine plays
Mantle, B. ed. Best plays of 1931-32 (abridged)
Strange interlude. N.Y. Boni. 1928. 8°. 352p. Freudian. 9 acts
Same in Nine plays
Mantle, B. ed. Best plays of 1927-28 (abridged)
Where the cross is made. Sea. 1 act
In Tucker, S. M. ed. Twelve one-act plays for study and production

Openshaw, Charles Elton
All the king's horses; comedy in three acts. N.Y. French. c1927. 8°. 66p.

O'Ryan, Anne Wynne
Angel cake; a comedy in three acts. N.Y. French. 1928. 12°. 84p.
Things; a comedy in three acts. N.Y. French. 1923. 80p.

Osborn, Paul
Vinegar tree, a play. N.Y. Farrar. 1931.
12°. 180p. Comedy. 3 acts

Osborne, Hubert
Mary's lamb. Hartford, Conn. Haylofters co. 1927. 12°. 37p. 1 act

Osborne, Marian
Point of view. Comedy of manners. 1 act
In Massey, V. ed. Canadian plays
from Hart House theatre. v. 1
Sappho and Phaon, a lyrical drama. To-
ronto. Macmillan. 1926. 12°. 68p.

Osgood, Erastus
Affair at the "Sea Gull"; a comedy drama
in three acts. N.Y. French. 1928.
12°. 67p.
Cupid scores a touchdown; a comedy in
three acts. N.Y. French c1927. 12°.
68p.
Erastus; a farce comedy in two acts.
N.Y. French. 1927. 12°. 35p.

**Ostrovskiĭ, Aleksandr Nicolaevich, 1823-
1886**
Cat has not always carnival. Moscow.
4 acts
In Poet Lore 40:317
Fairy gold. Comedy. 5 acts
In Poet Lore 40:1
Forest; comedy in five acts. N.Y. French.
c1926. 12°. 126p.
Last sacrifice; a comedy in five acts
In Poet Lore 39:317
Poor bride. Comedy. 5 acts
In Noyes, G. R. ed. Masterpieces of
the Russian drama
Thunderstorm, drama in five acts. N.Y.
French. c1927. 12°. 83p.

Ould, Hermon, 1886-
Ada Wodderspoon, a play in four acts.
Boston. Baker. c1932. 80p. 78p.
Between sunset and dawn. A play in four
scenes. London. Sidgwick. 1914. 12°.
75p.
Black virgin; a play in four acts. Lon-
don. Palmer. 1922. 12°. 87p.
Discovery. Columbus. 1 act
In Hampden, J. ed. Eight modern
plays
Joan the maid. Historical. 1 act
In Modern short plays. ser. 2
Light comedian, a comedy in three acts.
London. Benn. 1928. 12°. 93p.
Miser of Rogafjord; a play in one act.
London. Deane. 1931. 12°. 19p.
Moon rides high; a play in three acts.
Oxford. Blackwell. 1927. 12°. 106p.
Pathfinder. David Livington. 1 act
In Marriott, J. W. ed. One-act plays
of to-day. ser. 5
Peter the pied piper. London. Oxford
Univ. press. 1924. 12°. 31p. 6 scenes
Piper laughs; a play in ten scenes. Lon-
don. Benn. 1927. 12°. 77p.
Princess Mirabelle and the swineherd;
a play for young people. N.Y.
French. 1929. 12°. 31p.
Shim Sham; or, Prepopterops the giant;
or, Betty's dream, a play for chil-
dren. N.Y. French. c1930. 12°. 22p.

Oursler, Fulton, 1893- and Brentano, Lowell
Spider; a mystery melodrama in three
acts. N.Y. French. c1932. 12°. 125p.

Oursler, Fulton, 1893- and Kennedy, Aubrey
Behold this dreamer; a play in four acts
(based on Fulton Oursler's novel of
same name). N.Y. French. c1930. 12°.
97p.

Page, Mann
House afire, a comedy in three acts. N.Y.
French. c1930. 12°. 83p.

Page, Mann, *joint author*. *See* Dickey, Paul
and Page, Mann

Pailleron, Édouard Jules Henri, 1834-1899
Spark. Comedy. 1 act
In Poet Lore 38:373

Pain, Mrs. Barry
Vicious circle. 1 scene
In Johnson, T. ed. More plays in
miniature

Pakington, Hon. Mary Augusta, 1875-
Black horseman; a play in one act. Ox-
ford. Blackwell. 1929. 12°. 40p.
Cats and kittens. Comedy. 1 act
In Hampden, J. ed. Four new plays
for women and girls
Doctor's engagements; comedetta in one
act. London. French. c1903. 12°. 16p.
Experiment; a play in one act. Lon-
don. Allen. 1932. 12°. 34p. Telepathy
Same in Marriott, J. W. ed. Best one-
act plays of 1932
House with the twisty windows. 1 act
In Hampden, J. ed. Ten modern plays
Schofield, S. ed. Marble gods, and
other one-act plays
Poet's corner. 1 act
In Marriott, J. W. ed. Best one-act
plays of 1931
Polar post, drama in one act. N.Y.
French. 1929. 12°. 20p.
Scarlet mantle; a play in one act. N.Y.
French. c1928. 12°. 24p.
Tear up the joker! a play in one act.
N.Y. French. c1931. 12°. 21p.
True likeness, a fantasy of the middle
ages in two acts and four scenes.
London. Benn. 1928. 12°. 77p.

Paradis, Mrs. Marjorie Bartholomew
New freedom, a comedy in three acts.
N.Y. French. [c1931] 12°. 167p.

Paramore, Edward E. jr.
Set a thief; a mystery melodrama in three
acts. N.Y. French. [c1927] 12°. 107p.

Parke, James Hambright, 1905-
Atonement; a tragedy in one act
In Poet Lore 41:59
It runs in the family; a mystery comedy
in three acts. Philadelphia. Penn. 12°.
Same in Prize plays of 1927-28. v. 2

**Parker, Mrs. Dorothy (Rothschild) 1893-
and Rice, Elmer L. 1892-**
Close harmony; or, The lady next door, a
play in three acts. N.Y. French. 1929.
12°. 91p.

Parker, Louis Napoleon, 1852-
Cardinal; a play in four acts. N.Y. French.
1923. 8°. 69p.
Change alley; a comedy. London. 1899.
84p. For private circulation

Disraeli. Historical. 4 acts
  In Mantle, B. and Sherman, G. P. eds.
    Best plays of 1909-1919
Happy life; a comedy in four acts. n. pub.
  [189-?] Printed for private circulation
  only
In Taunton vale; an original play in
  three acts. Sherbourne. J. C. Sawtell.
  1890
Love-knot; an original play in four acts.
  Sherbourne. J. C. Sawtell. 1899
Minuet. French Revolution. 1 act
  In Tucker, S. M. ed. Twelve one-act
    plays for study and production
Monkey's paw; a story in three scenes
  by W. W. Jacobs; dramatised by
  Louis N. Parker. N.Y. French.
  c1910. 12°. 35p.
  Same in Marriott, J. W. ed. One-act
    plays of to-day. ser. 2
On board the "Golden Hind," 1578; a play
  in one act
  In Hampden J ed. Seven modern plays
    for younger players
Rosemary, that's for remembrance; a
  comedy in four acts. N.Y. French.
  c1924. 8°. 73p.
St. George and the dragon; a farcical
  comedy. Sherbourne. J. C. Sawtell.
  1890. 35p.

Parr, E. P.
Nurse in charge of the case; a play in
  one act. N.Y. French. c1927. 12°. 28p.

Parsons, Margaret Colby (Getchell) 1891-
Elfin knight of the Hallowe'en. Hal-
  lowe'en. 1 act
  In Schauffler, R. H. and Sanford, A.
    P. eds. Plays for our American
    holidays. v. 1
Graduation gifts. 1 act
  In Sanford, A. P. ed. Plays for gradua-
    tion days
Hansel and Gretel. Fairy. 1 act
  In Schauffler, R. H. and Sanford, A. P.
    eds. Plays for our American
    holidays. v. 1
Massa Linkum's sojer
  In Sanford, A. P. ed. Lincoln plays
Mothers they forgot. Mother's Day. 1 act
  In Schauffler, R. H. and Sanford, A. P.
    eds. Plays for our American holi-
    days. v. 4
Prophecy. 1 act
  In Johnson, T. ed. Plays about George
    Washington
Sailing west to find the east. Columbus.
  1 act
  In Schauffler, R. H. and Sanford, A. P.
    eds. Plays for our American holi-
    days. v. 4

Passano, Leonard Magruder, 1866-
Family affair; a comedy. Boston. Four
  Seas. [c1927] 12°. 48p.

Paull, Harry Major, 1854-
Back to the college; a play in one act,
  for seven girls. N.Y. French. c1923.
  12°. 21p.
Gentleman whip. An original comedy in
  one act. London. French. 1895. 12°.
  20p.

In Nelson's days; a play in one act.
  London. French. 1896. 12°. 22p.
Merrifield's ghost. An original comedy
  in one act. London. French. 1896.
  12°. 16p.
Mrs. Larkin's lodger; a play for boys in
  one act. N.Y. French. c1927. 12°. 20p.
Unknown star. A Christmas mystery
  play in prose and verse
  In 19 Cent. 86:1065

Paulton, Edward Antonio, 1868-
Half the better half; a comedy in one
  act. N.Y. French. c1926. 12°. 19p.
Her temporary husband; a comedy in
  three acts. N.Y. French. c1927. 12°.
  117p.
Stone lady; a farcical comedy in three
  acts; an up-to-date version of the
  famous comedy "Niobe all Smiles."
  N.Y. French. c1926. 12°. 106p.
Your uncle Dudley; a farce in three acts.
  Based on "The noble Art," by Eille
  Norwood. N.Y. French. c1928. 12°.
  124p.

Paulton, Edward, *joint author*. See Dodge,
  Henry Irving, Marston, Laurence,
  and Paulton, Edward

**Peabody, Josephine Preston (Mrs. Lionel
  Simeon Marks) 1874-1922**
Fortune and men's eyes. Historical.
  Shakespeare's sonnets. 1 act
  In Collected plays
Marlowe. Historical. 5 acts
  In Collected plays
Piper. Symbolic. 4 acts
  In Collected plays
Portrait of Mrs. W. Mary Wollstone-
  craft. 3 acts
  In Collected plays
Wings. Northumbria. 1 act
  In Collected plays
Wolf of Gubbio. Comedy. 3 acts
  In Collected plays

Peacey, Howard
Island of destiny; a modern tragedy.
  London. Sidgwick. 1933. 12°. 111p.
  Ireland
Warren Hastings; a play in four acts.
  London. Cayme Press. 1928. 12°.
  131p.

Peach, L. duGarde
Cross calling. 1 act
  In Ever ready plays
Light and shade. 1 act
  In Ever ready plays
Matter of course. 1 act
  In Ever ready plays
Night of horror. 1 act
  In Ever ready plays
Parting
  In More ever ready plays
Reggie makes complaint
  In More ever ready plays
Sale by auction, a comedy in one act.
  Boston. Baker. 1926. 12°. 16p.
Stranger
  In More ever ready plays
Stung
  In More ever ready plays
Wave lengths
  In More ever ready plays

Peach, L. du Garde—*Continued*
While shepherds watch. 1 act
In Ever ready plays
Wind o' the moors. Derbyshire. 1 act.
In Shay, F. ed. Fifty more contemporary one-act plays

Pearmain, John
Old Moore's almanac. Farce. 1 act
In Hampden, J. ed. Three modern plays and a mime

Pearn, Violet A.
Invisible playmate, a play in three acts. N.Y. French. c1930. 8°. 65p.

Pearse, Padraic H. 1880-1916
Singer. Patriotism. 1 act
In Canfield, C. ed. Plays of the Irish renaissance

Peet, Telfair
New moon. Fantasy. 1 act
In Koch, F. H. ed. Carolina folk comedies

Pellerin, J.
Forgotten room
In Bourne, J. ed. Eight new plays for boys and girls

Peltret, Eduard, *joint author. See* Savage, George Milton and Peltret, Edouard

Pemberton, Anemone
Nelagony, or Good Water. Indian. 1 act
In Schauffler, R. H. and Sanford, A. P. eds. Plays for our American holidays. v. 4

Pendray, G. E.
Organ. Homesteaders. 1 act
In Clark, B. H. and Nicholson, K. eds. American scene

Pendray, G. E. *joint author. See* Nicholson, Kenyon and Pendray, G. E.

Peretz, Isaac Leibush L.
Sewing of the wedding gown. 1 act
In White, B. F. trans. Nine one-act plays from the Yiddish

Peretz, Isaac Loeb. *See* Perez, Isaac Loeb

Perez, Isaac Loeb, 1851-1915
After the funeral. Death. 1 act
In Block, E. ed. One act plays from the Yiddish. ser. 2
Of an early morning. 1 act
In Block, E. ed. One act plays from the Yiddish. ser. 2
Sisters. Comedy. 1 act
In Block, E. ed. One act plays from the Yiddish. ser. 2

Pérez Galdós, Benito, 1845-1920
Electra. Symbolic. 5 acts
In Tucker, S. M. ed. Modern continental plays

Perkins, Eleanor Ellis, *joint author. See* Meaker, Isabelle J. and Perkins, Eleanor Ellis

Pertwee, Roland, 1885-
Counsel's opinion. 1 act
In One-act plays for stage and study. ser. 7
Early birds; a sketch in one act. N.Y. French. c1927. 12°. 21p.
Heat wave. Oriental. 3 acts
In Five three-act plays
Honours easy, a play in three acts. N.Y. French. c1932. 8°. 71p.

Speaking terms. 1 act
In One-act plays for stage and study. ser. 6
Voice said "goodnight"; a play in one act. N.Y. French. c1928. 12°. 20p.

Pertwee, Roland and Dearden, Harold
Interference, a play in three acts. N.Y. French. c1929. 12°. 85p.

Peters, Paul and Sklar, George
Stevedore; a play in three acts. N.Y. Covici. c1934. 8°. 123p. Negro. 3 acts

Peterson, Agnes E.
Gilt-edged. 1 act
In Hughes, G. ed. Short plays for modern players

Phelps, George Harrison and Pitkin, Maxwell Irving
Pearl thief. Comedy. 1 act
In Players book of one act plays. ser. 1

Phelps, Pauline
Adolescent young; a satirical farce in one act. N.Y. French. c1927. 12°. 29p.
Blue ribbon hat; a play in one act. N.Y. French. c1930. 12°. 25p.
Cyclone for a cent, a farce in one act. Boston. Baker. 1894. 12°. 17p.
Home, sweet home; a comedy in one act. N.Y. French. 1929. 12°. 24p.
I know George Washington. 1 act
In New plays for women and girls
Moon and the moonstruck; a play in one act. N.Y. French. [1930] 12°. 19p.
Night club girl. 1 act
In New plays for women and girls
Pease and beans; a one-act satirical farce. N.Y. French. c1928. 12°. 37p.
Shakespearian conference [a drama]. N.Y. Werner. 1901. 12°. 15p.
Sister Sally, a farce comedy in three acts. Boston. Baker. [c1933] 12°. 118p.
Sprightly Widow Bartlett; a colonial play in one act. N.Y. French. c1930. 12°. 25p.

Phelps, Pauline and Short, Marion
Flour girl; a comedy in three acts. N.Y. French. c1927. 12°. 82p.
Impatience of Job, a character comedy in three acts. N.Y. French. c1932. 12°. 100p.
Jack's brother's sister; a sketch in one act. Boston. Baker. 1916
Ryerson mystery, a play in three acts. N.Y. French. c1933. 12°. 87p.
Shavings, a comedy in three acts . . . from J. C. Lincoln's story. N.Y. French. c1930. 12°. 102p.

Phillips, LeRoy, 1870-
Mother of Washington. Historical. 1 act
In Johnson, T. ed. Washington anniversary plays

Phillips, Marguerite Kreger
Boy who found the king; a Christmas play in three episodes . . . adapted from the story of the same name by Raymond McDonald Alden. N.Y. French. c1929. 8°. 32p.
Once in a palace; a comedy in three acts. Chicago. Dramatic pub. co. [1931] 8°. 73p.

Phillips, Stephen, 1868-1915
Harold; a chronicle play; with an introduction by Arthur Symons. 3 acts

Phillpotts, Adelaide Eden
Akhnaton; a play. London. Butterworth. [1926] 12°. 237p. Egypt
Arachne. London. Palmer. [c1920] 8°. 45p. 2 scenes
Camillus and the school-master; a play in one act. London. Gowans. 1923. 24°. 23p.
Savitri, the faithful; a play in one act. London. Gowans. 1923. 24°. 27p.

Phillpotts, Adelaide Eden, *joint author. See* Phillpotts, Eden and Phillpotts, Adelaide Eden

Phillpotts, Eden, 1862-
Bert; a play in one act. N.Y. French. c1932. 12°. 20p.
Blue comet; a comedy in three acts. N.Y. Macmillan. 1927. 12°. 281p. Also French
Buy a broom; a comedy in three acts. London. Duckworth. [1929] 16°. 143p.
Cup of happiness, a comedy in three acts. London. Duckworth. [1933] 12°. 127p.
Devonshire cream. English rural life. 3 acts
  In Devonshire cream
Farmer's wife, a comedy in three acts. N.Y. French. c1929. 8°. 102p.
  Same in Devonshire plays
Good old days, a comedy in three acts. N.Y. Duckworth. 1932. 12°. 124p.
Jane's legacy, a folk play in three acts. Duckworth. [1931] 12°. 133p.
Market-money. 1 act
  In Three short plays
Purple bedroom. 1 act
  In Three short plays
  Modern short plays. ser. 2
Runaways; a comedy in three acts. London. Duckworth. [1928] 12°. 122p.
Something to talk about. 1 act
  In Three short plays
  Modern short plays. ser. 1

Phillpotts, Eden, 1862- **and Groves, Charles**
Golden wedding; an original comedy in one act. London. French. c1899. 12°. 22p.

Phillpotts, Eden, 1862- **and Phillpotts, Adelaide Eden**
Yellow sands; a comedy in three acts. N.Y. French. 1927. 12°. 143p.
  Same in Phillpotts, E. Devonshire plays

Phipps, A. H.
More about apples; an old legend in modern dress. 1 act
  In Poet Lore 40:144

Pieratt, Alice
Day's end. 1 act
  In Clark, B. H. and Nicholson, K. eds. American scene

Pierce, Carl Webster [Adam Applebud, pseud.] 1898-
Guest retainer; a farce in three acts. Boston. Baker. 1920. 67p.
Oh, Kay! A comedy in three acts, interlarded with mystery and thrills. Boston. Baker. [c1927] 12°. 115p.

Who am I? a one-act comedy. Chicago. Denison. [1923] 12°. 10p.

Pike, Charles Sumner
Glorious martyr. Historical comedy. 1 act
  In Players book of one act plays. ser. 1
String of pearls. Domestic comedy. 1 act
  In Players book of one act plays. ser. 1

Pilcher, Velona, 1894-
Searcher, a war play. . . London. Heinemann. 1929. 8°. 84p. Impressionistic

Pinero, Sir Arthur Wing, 1855-1934
Child. man; a sedate farce in three acts. London. Chiswick press. 1928. 8°. 91p. (Printed for use in the theatre, not for circulation)
Hester's mystery; a comedy in one act. London. [1890] 24p.
Iris. Social. 5 acts
  In Cordell, R. A. ed. Representative modern plays
Mid-channel. Social. 4 acts
  In Watson, E. B. and Pressey, B, eds. Contemporary drama. English and Irish plays. v. 1
Second Mrs. Tanqueray. Social. 4 acts
  In Steeves, H. R. ed. Plays from the modern theatre
Thunderbolt. Provincial family. 4 acts
  In Chandler, F. W. and Cordell, R. A. eds. Twentieth century plays
  Tucker, S. M. ed. Twenty-five modern plays
Trelawny of the "Wells." Comedietta. 4 acts
  In Marriott, J. W. ed. Great modern British plays
Widow of Wasdale Head. Fantasy. 1 act
  In Clark, B. H. ed. Representative one-act plays by British and Irish authors

Pinski, David, 1872-
Cripples; a comedy in one act. tr. by I. Goldberg. N.Y. French. 1932. 12p.
Dollar; a comedy in one act; tr. by I. Goldberg. N.Y. French. 1932. 24p.
Forgotten souls; a drama in one act. N.Y. French. 1932. 20p.
Sorrows. 1 act
  In White, B. F. trans. Nine one-act plays from the Yiddish

Pirandello, Luigi, 1867-
As you desire me (Come tu mi vuoi) a play in three acts; tr. from the Italian by Samuel Putnam. N.Y. Putnam. [c1931] 12°. 221p.
At the gate (All'uscita); a profane mystery. 1 act
  In One-act plays
By judgment of court. Superstition. 1 act
  In One-act plays
Chee-chee (Cecè). Comedy. 1 act
  In One-act plays
Doctor's duty. (Il dovere del medico) Ethical. 1 act
  In One-act plays

Lantern light. Witchcraft. 3 acts
In Short plays from American history
and literature [v. 1]
Little Lady Dresden. Mount Vernon.
1 act
In Short plays from American history
and literature [v. 1]
Maytime in Plymouth. Historical. 3 acts
In Short plays from American history
and literature. v. 2
Memories. Commencement pageant. 1 act
In Short plays from American history
and literature [v. 1]
Red dusk. Indian fantasy. 1 act
In Short plays from American history
and literature. v. 2
Sandman's pack o' dreams. 1 act
In Johnson, T. ed. Washington an-
niversary plays
Washington marches on; a play on the
life of George Washington. N.Y.
French [c1931] 12°. 146p.
West o' the Alleghanies. Pioneers. 1 act
In Short plays from American history
and literature. v. 2
White asters. World war. 3 acts
In Short plays from American history
and literature [v. 1]
Young Hale of Connecticut. Historical.
2 acts
In Short plays from American history
and literature. v. 2

Pride, Leo Boyan, 1896-
Aftermath. Coal fields
In Shadow of the mine, and other plays
of the coal fields
Barbarians. Coal fields
In Shadow of the mine, and other plays
of the coal fields
Clark, B. H. and Nicholson, K. eds.
American scene
Devils. Coal fields
In Shadow of the mine, and other plays
of the coal fields
Fortune's hired man. Coal fields
In Shadow of the mine, and other plays
of the coal fields
Foursquare. Coal fields
In Shadow of the mine, and other plays
of the coal fields
Haunted coal mine. Superatural. 1 act
In One-act plays for stage and study.
ser. 5
On the way home. Coal fields
In Shadow of the mine, and other plays
of the coal fields
Shadow of the mine. Coal fields
In Shadow of the mine, and other plays
of the coal fields

Priestley, John Boynton, 1894-
Dangerous corner, a play in three acts.
London. Heinemann. [1932] 12°. 85p.
Comedy
Laburnum grove; an immoral comedy in
three acts. London. Heinemann.
[1934] 12°. 107p.
Roundabout, a comedy in three acts.
London. Heinemann. [1933] 12°. 114p.

Pryce, Richard, 1864-
Helen with the high hand; a play in three
acts. Adapted from Arnold Bennett's novel. N.Y. French. [1914] 12°.
103p.
Little Mrs. Cummin, a comedy in three
acts; adapted from "The Eglamore
portraits," by Mary E. Mann. N.Y.
French. c1910. 12°. 97p.
Visit, a play in one act . . . adapted from
"Freddy's ship," a story by Mary
E. Mann. N.Y. French. c1910. 12°.
24p.

Quintero. See Alvarez Quintero, Serafín
and Joaquín
Raisin, Abraham. *See* Reisen, Abraham
Raleigh, Sir Walter, 1861-1922
Riddle. Comedy. 1 act
In Modern short plays. ser. 2
Ranck, Edwin Carty
Night riders; a play in three acts. Cam-
bridge. Harvard Dram. club. [c1911]
8°. 65p.
Weakest link. Philadelphia. Penn. 1928.
12°. 3 acts
In Prize plays of 1927
Rappoport Solmon, 1863-1920 **(S. Ansky,
pseud.)**
Dybbuk. Spirit possession. 4 acts
In Dickinson, T. H. ed. Chief contem-
porary dramatists. ser. 3
Father and son. A play in one act. tr.
by Bessie White. Boston. Baker.
[1932] 12°. 28p.
Ratcliffe, Mrs. Dorothy Una (Clough)
Blind man of Hiltune. 1 act
In Blind man of Hiltune, and two other
plays
Courting of Margaret Ruth. Folk play.
1 act
In Blind man of Hiltune, and two other
plays
Desormais. Shepherd's play. 1 act
In Blind man of Hiltune, and two other
plays
Modern short plays. ser. 2
The gone away; a romance of the dales,
in three acts. London. Lane. 1930.
4°. 96p.
Gypsy Dorelia; a story-play in three
acts. London. Lane. [1932] 8°. 123p.
Mary of Scotland in Wensleydale. His-
torical. 2 pts.
In Modern short plays. ser. 3
Nathaniel Baddeley, bookman; a play for
the fireside in one act. Leeds. Swan
press. 1924. 8°. 50p.
Rath, Frederick
First night, a melodrama in three acts.
N.Y. French. c1931. 12°. 98p.
Raymond, Ernest, 1888-
Berg, a play in three acts. London. Benn.
1929. 12°. 78p.
Multabello road; a play in three acts.
London. Cassell. [1933] 12°. 126p.
Raymond, Sister Mary
Her mother's daughter
In Easy plays for amateurs
In the hall of statuary
In Easy plays for amateurs

Raymond, Sister Mary—*Continued*
Landing of Columbus
In Easy plays for amateurs
Learn to give by giving
In Easy plays for amateurs
Little deserter
In Easy plays for amateurs
Power of woman
In Easy plays for amateurs
Tangled threads
In Easy plays for amateurs
Raynal, Paul
Unknown warrior; a tragedy in three
acts; tr. by Cecil Lewis. N.Y. Cen-
tury. 1928. 12°. 289p.
Reed, Howard, 1885-
Boomer, a rural comedy in three acts.
N.Y. Longmans. 1928. 12°. 121p.
Buzzin' around; a comedy in three acts.
Boston. Baker. 1929. 12°. 158p.
Drums of death; a mystery play in three
acts. Chicago. Dramatic pub. co.
[c1930] 12°. 110p.
Sound your horn! a comedy in three acts.
Chicago. Dramatic pub. co. [c1931]
12°. 96p.
Town Hall—tonight; a comedy in one
act. N.Y. Longmans. 1928. 12°. 38p.
Reed, Mark White
Let's get rich, an American comedy in
three acts. N.Y. French. c1933. 12°.
94p.
Skyrocket; a three-act comedy. N.Y.
French. c1929. 12°. 95p.
Reely, Mary Katharine
Daily bread. Poverty. 1 act
In Schauffler, R. H. and Sanford, A. P.
eds. Plays for our American holi-
days. v. 4
Lean years. Economy. 1 act
In Phillips, Le R. and Johnson, T. eds.
Types of modern dramatic com-
position
Reid, Leslie
Trespasser. Comedy. 3 acts
In Massey, V. ed. Canadian plays from
Hart House theatre. v. 2
Reisen, Abraham
Brothers; a comedy. Poverty. 1 act
In Block, E. ed. One-act plays from
the Yiddish. ser. 2
Shay, F. ed. Fifty more contem-
porary one-act plays
Reisin, Abraham. *See* Reisen, Abraham
Remison, A.
Ding-a-ling (adapted by M. Relonde).
1 act
In Jagendorf, M. A. ed. Nine short
plays
Reznikoff, Charles
Abram in Egypt. 1 act
In Nine plays
Black death. 1 act
In Chatterton, Black death, and Meri-
wether Lewis
Nine plays
Captive Israel. 1 act
In Coral, and Captive Israel
Nine plays

Chatterton. Historical. 1 act
In Chatterton, Black death, and Meri-
wether Lewis
Nine plays
Coral. 1 act
In Coral, and Captive Israel
Nine plays
Genesis. 1 act
In Nine plays
Meriwether Lewis. 1 act
In Chatterton, Black death, and Meri-
wether Lewis
Nine plays
Rashi.
In Nine plays
Uriel Acosta: a play . . . N.Y. Cooper
press. [c1921]
Same in Nine plays
Rhodes, Harrison, *joint author. See* Benri-
mo, J. H. and Rhodes, Harrison Gar-
field
Rice, Cale Young, 1872-
Arduin. Alchemy. 1 act
In Selected plays and poems
Charles di Tocca. Historical. 4 acts
In Selected plays and poems
David. Biblical. 4 acts
In Selected plays and poems
Gerhard of Ryle. Cologne. 1 act
In Selected plays and poems
Giorgione. Renaissance. 1 act
In Selected plays and poems
Immortal lure. India. 1 act
In Selected plays and poems
Mihrima. Astrology. 1 act
In Selected plays and poems
Night in Avignon. Petrarch. 1 act
In Selected plays and poems
O'Ume's gods. Japanese. 1 act
In Selected plays and poems
Porzia. Betrayal. 3 acts
In Selected plays and poems
Swamp bird, a drama. N.Y. Century.
[c1931] 12°. 108p.
Yolanda of Cyprus. Historical. 4 acts
In Selected plays and poems
Rice, Elmer L. 1892-
Adding machine. Monotony. 7 scenes
In Plays of Elmer Rice
Counsellor-at-law, a play in three acts.
N.Y. French. 1931. 12°. 298p. Melo-
drama
Same in Plays of Elmer Rice
Famous plays of 1932-33
Diadem of snow. Romanoffs. 1 act
In One-act plays for stage and study.
ser. 5
House in blind alley, a comedy in three
acts. N.Y. French. 1932. 12°. 92p.
Judgment day: a melodrama in three acts.
N.Y. Coward. 1934. 12°. 201p. Politi-
cal
Left bank, a play in three acts. N.Y.
French. 1931. 12°. 225p. Social
Same in Mantle, B. ed. Best plays of
1931-32 (abridged)
On trial. Domestic. 4 acts
In Mantle, B. and Sherman, G. P. eds.
Best plays of 1909-1919
Passing of Chow-Chow; a comedy in one
act. N.Y. French. 1933. 19p.

See Naples and die, a comedy in three acts. N.Y. French. 1930. 12°. 182p.
Same in Plays of Elmer Rice
 Famous plays of 1932
Street scene, a play in three acts. N.Y. French. 1929. 12°. 239p. Street life
Same in Plays of Elmer Rice
 Chandler, F. W. and Cordell, R. A. eds. Twentieth century plays
 Mantle, B. ed. Best plays of 1928-29 (abridged)
 Six plays
Subway, a play in nine scenes. N.Y. French. 1929. 12°. 153p. Impressionistic
We, the people; a play in twenty scenes. N.Y. Coward-McCann. [c1933] 12°. 253p.
Same in Mantle, B. ed. Best plays of 1932-33 (abridged)

Rice, Elmer L. 1892- **and Barry, Philip,** 1896-
Cock Robin, a play in three acts. N.Y. French. 1929. 12°. 170p.

Rice, Elmer L. 1892- , *joint author*
See Hughes, Hatcher and Rice, Elmer L.; Parker, Dorothy and Rice, Elmer

Richardson, Frank Collins, 1870-1917
Bonnie Dundee, a play in one act. N.Y. French. c1910. 12°. 28p.

Richardson, Willis, 1889-
Black horseman. Negro. 1 act
In Richardson, W. ed. Plays and pageants from the life of the Negro
Broken banjo. Negro. 1 act
In Locke, A. LeR. and Gregory, M. eds. Plays of Negro life
Chip woman's fortune. Negro. 1 act
In Shay, F. ed. Fifty more contemporary one-act plays
Flight of the natives. Negro. 1 act
In Locke, A. LeR. and Gregory, M. eds. Plays of Negro life
House of sham. Negro. 1 act
In Richardson, W. ed. Plays and pageants from the life of the Negro
King's dilemma. Negro. 1 act
In Richardson, W. ed. Plays and pageants from the life of the Negro

Riddle, George
Come here. 1 scene
In Johnson, T. ed. More plays in miniature

Rideout, Ransom
Goin' home [a play in three acts] London. Longmans. 1928. 12°. 91p. Versailles treaty

Ridley, Arnold
Ghost train, a drama in three acts. N.Y. French. c1931. 8°. 71p.
Keepers of youth, a play in four acts. London. Benn. 1929. 12°. 92p.
Third time lucky; a comedy in three acts. N.Y. French. 1932. 8°. 70p.

Riewerts, J. P. *joint author. See* McOwen, Bernard J. and Riewarts, J. P.

Riggs, Lynn, 1899-
Big Lake; a tragedy in two parts, as produced by the American laboratory theatre, New York city. N.Y. French. 1927. 8°. 81p.
Green grow the lilacs, a play. N.Y. French. 1931. 8°. 106p. Comedy. 3 acts
Same in Mantle, B. ed. Best plays of 1930-31 (abridged)
Knives from Syria, a play in one act. N.Y. French. [c1928] 12°. 26p.
Same in Clark, B. H. and Cook, T. R. eds. One-act plays
Lantern to see by. Oklahoma
In Sump'n like wings, and A lantern to see by
Reckless. Texas. 1 act
In Clark, B. H. and Nicholson, K. eds. American scene
 One-act plays for stage and study. ser. 4
Roadside, a comedy . . . foreword by Arthur Hopkins. N.Y. French. 1930. 12°. 158p.
Sump'n like wings. Oklahoma
In Sump'n like wings, and A lantern to see by

Riley, Alice Cushing (Donaldson) 1867-
Little new moon, a fantasy in the Chinese manner. N.Y. French. c1929. 12°. 94p.
Taxi; a comedy in one act. N.Y. French. c1927. 12°. 21p.
Ten minutes by the clock. Comedy. 1 act
In Moses, M. J. ed. Ring up the curtain!
Uplifting Sadie. 1 act
In News plays for women and girls
Valentines; a fantasy in a prologue, a first playlet, an intermezzo, a second playlet and an epilogue. N.Y. French. [1927] 12°. 70p.

Riley, Laurence
Personal appearance; a new comedy in three acts. N.Y. French. 1935. 12°. 171p.

Rinehart, Mrs. Mary Roberts, 1876- **and Hopwood, Avery,** 1884-
Bat, a play of mystery in three acts. N.Y. French. c1932. 12°. 140p.
Seven days, a farce in three acts. N.Y. French. c1931. 12°. 138p.

Ring, Mrs. Lina Barbar (Taylor)
Are all men like that?
In Three plays under three flags
Bit o' dimocrasy
In Three plays under three flags
Monsieur Tytgat
In Three plays under three flags
$100,000 club paper, a comedy in one act. Boston. Baker. 1922. 12°. 34p.

Ritchey, Belle M.
They clean the attic. Comedy
In Snook, L. O. ed. Comedies seven

Roberts, Carl Eric Bechhofer, 1894- **and Forester, Cecil Scott,** 1899-
Nurse Cavell; a play in three acts. London. Lane. [c1933] 104p. World war

Roberts, Cyril
Exit. 1 act
In Marriott, J. W. ed. Best one-act
plays of 1931
Genuine antique, a play. N.Y. French.
c1928. 12°. 16p. 1 act
Last rib; a play in one act. N.Y. French.
c1933. 12°. 26p. Hypnotism
In Bourne, J. ed. 8 new one-act plays
of 1933
So good; a comedy in one act. N.Y.
French. 1929. 12°. 21p.
Village industries, a play. N.Y. French.
c1928. 12°. 21p. 1 act
Young love, a play. N.Y. French. c1928.
12°. 19p. 1 act

Robertson, Marjorie Freeland
When toys talk; a musical play in one
act. N.Y. French. [c1928] 12°. 16p.

Robertson, Thomas William, 1829-1871
Caste. Comedy. 3 acts
In Cordell, R. A. ed. Representative
modern plays
Marriott, J. W. ed. Great modern
British plays

Robertson, William Graham, 1867-
Archibald; a farce for ten girls. London.
French. c1919. 12°. 130p. 1 act
Masque of May morning. London. Lane.
1904. 4°. 61p.
Same in Moses, M. J. ed. Ring up the
curtain!
Pinkie and the fairies. Drama in three
acts and in verse. London. Heine-
mann. 1909. 16°. 146p.
Slippers of Cinderella. Fairy. 1 act
In Slippers of Cinderella, etc.
Hampden, J. ed. Seven modern
plays for younger players
Moses, M. J. ed. Another treasury
of plays for children

Robertson, William Henderson
Spring o' the year; a comedy in three
acts. N.Y. French. c1931. 12°. 150p.

**Robins, Gertrude, 1871-1917 (Mrs. L. B.
Reynolds)**
After the case
In Loving as we do, and other plays
Ilda's Honorable
In Loving as we do, and other plays
Loving as we do
In Loving as we do, and other plays
Return
In Loving as we do, and other plays

Robinson, Edward G. *joint author. See*
Swerling, Joseph and Robinson, Edward
G.

Robinson, Lennox, 1886-
Big house; four scenes in its life. Lon-
don. Macmillan. 1928. 12°. 112p. Ire-
land
Same in Plays
Canfield, C. ed. Plays of the
Irish renaissance
Crabbed youth and age. Comedy. 1 act
In Plays
Ever the twain, a comedy in three acts.
London. Macmillan. 1930. 12°. 157p.

Far-off hills, a comedy in three acts. Lon-
don. Chatto. 1931. 12°. 85p.
Same in Chandler, F. W. and Cordell,
R. A. eds. Twentieth cen-
tury plays
Give a dog—. A play in three acts. Lon-
don. Macmillan. 1928. 12°. 101p.
Same in Plays
Is life worth living? an exaggeration in
three acts. N.Y. Macmillan. 1933. 92p.
Portrait
In Plays
White blackbird, and Portrait
Round table. Comic tragedy. 3 acts
In Plays
White blackbird
In Plays
White blackbird, and Portrait
Whiteheaded boy. Comedy. 3 acts
In Plays of to-day. ser. 3

Rockwell, Ethel Gesner
It is I; a biblical drama. Boston. Baker.
1927. 12°. 27p. 7 episodes
Way; a Christmas pageant of peace.
Boston. Baker. c1927. 12°. 24p.

Rodenbach, Georges, 1855-1898
Veil. Belgian. 1 act
In Shay, F. ed. Fifty more contem-
porary one-act plays

Rogers, James Webb, 1822-1896
Madame Surratt, a drama in five acts.
Washington, D.C. Press of Judd &
Detweiler. [c1926] 4th ed. 8°. 135p.

Rogers, John William, jr. 1894-
Bumblepuppy, a comedy of climate in
one act. N.Y. French. c1927. 12°.
21p.
In Clark, B. H. and Nicholson, K. eds.
American scene
Isaacs, J. W. ed. Plays of Ameri-
can life and fantasy
Judge Lynch, a drama in one act. N.Y.
French. c1924. 12°. 22p. Negro
Same in Locke, A. LeR. and Gregory,
M. eds. Plays of Negro life
One act plays for stage and
study
Mary means what she says. N.Y. French.
1928. 12°. 24p. 1 act
Rescue of Cynthia Ann. Texas. 1 act
In One-act plays for stage and study.
ser. 5
Saved, a play in one act. N.Y. French.
1926. 12°. 31p.
Same in Clark, B. H. and Cook, T. R.
eds. One-act plays
Wedding presents; a play in one act.
N.Y. French. c1926. 12°. 18p.
Women folks; a pneumatic comedy in one
act. N.Y. French. 1927. 12°. 28p.

Rogers, Robert Emmons
Boy Will. Shakespeare. 1 act
In Cohen, H. L. ed. One-act plays by
modern authors. 1934 edition

Rolland, Romain, 1866-
Liluli. Farce. 1 act
In Plays of Romain Rolland
Montespan. Historical. 3 acts
In Plays of Romain Rolland

Palm Sunday; tr. from the French by Eugene Lohrke. N.Y. Holt. [1928] 12°. 147p. French revolution. 23 scenes

Revolt of the machines; or, Invention run wild; a motion picture fantasy; tr. by William A. Drake. Ithaca, N.Y. Dragon press. [1932] 12°. 57p.

Rölvaag, O. E. *See* Job, Thomas

Romains, Jules, pseud. (Louis Farigoule) 1885-

Peach (La scintillante). Comedy. 1 act
In Vernon, V. and F. eds. Modern one-act plays from the French

Six gentlemen in a row; in an English version by Harley Granville-Baker. London. Sidgwick. 1927. 12°. 30p.

Rose, Edward Everett, 1862-

Blarney stone, a comedy-drama in four acts. N.Y. French. c1933. 12° 99p.

Gold flame, a mystery comedy in four acts. Minneapolis, Minn. North-western press. c1933. 12°. 77p.

Irish eyes, a comedy-drama in three acts. N.Y. French. [c1933] 12°. 96p.

Maytime in Erin; comedy-drama in three acts. N.Y. French. c1933. 12°. 96p.

Rear car; a mystery play—from a new angle. N.Y. French. c1926. 12°. 107p.

Rosary (founded on an emblem of purity) a play in four acts. N.Y. French. c1926. 12°. 99p.

Rose of the Ghetto; a comedy drama in four acts. N.Y. French. c1927. 12°. 98p.

Rose, Edward Everett, 1862- **and Ford, Paul Leicester,** 1865-1902

Janice Meredith; a play in four acts; based on the novel "Janice Meredith" by Paul Leicester Ford. N.Y. French. c1927. 12°. 112p.

Rostand, Edmond, 1868-1918

Cyrano de Bergerac
In Tucker, S. M. ed. Modern continental plays
Tucker, S. M. ed. Twenty-five modern plays
Whitman, C. H. ed. Seven contemporary plays

Last night of Don Juan; a dramatic poem, tr. by T. Lawrason Riggs. Yellow Springs, Ohio. Kahoe & co. 1929. 8°. 123p.

Romancers. Romantic. 1 act
In Goldstone, G. A. ed. One-act plays
Webber, J. P. and Webster, H. H. eds. One-act plays for secondary schools

Two Pierrots, or The white supper. Fantasy. 1 act
In Vernon, V. and F. eds. Modern one-act plays from the French

White supper. *See* Two Pierrots, or The white supper

Rostand, Maurice, 1891-

He who did not kill, or The way to be loved. World war. 1 act
In Vernon, V. and F. eds. Modern one-act plays from the French

Rothery, Agnes Edwards (Mrs. Harry Rogers Pratt) 1888-

Miss Coolidge; a comedy in one act. Hartford, Conn. Haylofters. 1927. 12°. 39p.

Rouverol, Mrs. Aurania, 1885-

It never rains; a comedy of young love in three acts. N.Y. French. c1930. 12°. 109p.

Skidding; a comedy in three acts. Los Angeles. Playshop. c1928. 8°. 157p.

When's your birthday? a comedy in three acts (based on the novel "Paradise," by Alice Brown). N.Y. French. c1927. 12°. 102p.

Rowell, Adelaide Corinne, 1887-

Beloved, it is morn. 1 act
In Sanford, A. P. ed. Plays for graduation days

Hail the conquering hero! a comedy in three acts. Boston. Baker. 1921. 68p.

High heart. Confederate spy. 1 act
In Schauffler, R. H. and Sanford, A. P. eds. Plays for our American holidays. v. 3
Drama 17:173

Last frontier. 1 act
In Sanford, A. P. ed. One-act plays for women

Royde-Smith, Naomi Gwladys

Balcony. N.Y. Doubleday. 1928. 12°. Also London. Benn. Comedy. 3 acts

Mrs. Siddons. A play in four acts. London. Gollancz. 1931. 12°. 111p.

Rubinstein, Harold Frederick, 1892-

Dickens of Gray's Inn. Comedy. 1 act
In Hampden, J. ed. Three modern plays and a mime

Isabel's eleven; a comedy in four acts. N.Y. Doran. 1927. 12°. 101p.

Old boyhood. Comedy. 1 act
In Marriott, J. W. ed. One-act plays of to-day. ser. 5

Russell, Floyd Kymes

Clean up! Health. 1 act
In Schauffler, R. H. and Sanford, A. P. eds. Plays for our American holidays. v. 4

Russell, George William (pseud. A. E.) 1867-

Deirdre, a drama in three acts. Dublin. Maunsel. 1907. 12°. 53p. Legendary
Same in Canfield, C. ed. Plays of the Irish renaissance

Ruthenburg, Grace Dorcas

Death of Anulus. 1 act
In Sanford, A. P. ed. One-act plays for women

Gooseberry mandarin; a play in one act. N.Y. French. [c1928] 12°. 10p.
Same in Isaacs, E. J. ed. Plays of American life and fantasy

Hans Bulow's last puppet. 1 act
In Baker, G. P. ed. Yale one-act plays

O bright flame lifted! 1 act
In New plays for women and girls

Talking chair. Juvenile. 1 act
In Moses, M. J. ed. Ring up the curtain!

Ryan, Marion
Children of the way; an Easter play. N.Y.
Abingdon. 1933. 8p.
Ryerson, Florence
Cup of tea. Farce. 1 act
In Nicholson, Kenyon, ed. Appleton
book of short plays. ser. 2
Third angle. Comedy. 1 act
In Shay, F. ed. Fifty more contem-
porary one-act plays
**Ryerson, Florence and Clements, Colin,
1894-**
All on a summer's day. 1 act
In All on a summer's day, and six other
short plays
Hot lemonade; a comedy in one act.
N.Y. French. 1933. 10p.
Same in One-act plays for stage and
study. ser. 5
Letters. 1 act
In All on a summer's day, and six other
short plays
Sanford, A. P. ed. One-act plays
for women
Littlest shepherd, a Christmas interlude.
N.Y. French. [c1929] 8°. 13p. 1 act
Same in Shay, F. ed. Appleton book
of Christmas plays
Loop. Comedy. 1 act
In Johnson, T. ed. Diminutive come-
dies
Love is like that. 1 act
In All on a summer's day, and six other
short plays
Men folks. 1 act
In All on a summer's day, and six other
short plays
On the lot. St. Valentine's day. 1 act
In All on a summer's day, and six other
short plays
Schauffler, R. H. ed. Plays for our
American holidays. v. 1
Romantic interval. 1 act
In All on a summer's day, and six other
short plays
Storm. 1 act
In All on a summer's day, and six other
short plays
Willow plate. 1 act
In One-act plays for stage and study.
ser. 6
Sanford, A. P. Plays for graduation
days
Ryskind, Morrie, *joint author.* *See* Kauf-
man, George and Ryskind, M.
Ryttenberg, Anita
Rosamund at the tracks; a philosophical
melodrama in one act
In Poet Lore 39:436
Sabine, Lillian
Rise of Silas Lapham; a comedy in four
acts, from William Dean Howells'
story of the same name. N.Y. French.
c1927. 12°. 129p.
Salaman, Dora Clement
Chance of a lifetime. 1 act
In Tale of a cat and other plays
Flood time. 1 act
In Tale of a cat and other plays
Haunted road. 1 act
In Tale of a cat and other plays

Tale of a cat. 1 act
In Tale of a cat and other plays
Salten, Felix
Moral courage. The gravity of life. 1 act
In Shay, F. ed. Fifty more contem-
porary one-act plays
Sand, Maurice, 1823-1888
Candidate for Trepagny. Comedy. 1 act
In McPharlin, P. ed. Repertory of
marionette plays
Clemency of Titus. Puppet play. 1 act
In Maurice Sand's plays for marionettes
Flageolet. Puppet play. 1 act
In Maurice Sand's plays for marionettes
Rose queen of Viremollet. Puppet play.
1 act
In Maurice Sand's plays for marionettes
Spirit rappers. Puppet play. 1 act
In Maurice Sand's plays for marionettes
We dine at the colonel's. Puppet play.
1 act
In Maurice Sand's plays for marionettes
Sanford, Anne Putnam
Birthday party. Comedy. 1 act
In Schauffler, R. H. and Sanford, A. P.
eds. Plays for our American holi-
days. v. 4
Brother musicians. Comedy. 1 act
In Schauffler, R. H. and Sanford, A. P.
eds. Plays for our American holi-
days. v. 4
San Secundo, R. di
Stairs
In Katzin, W. ed. Eight European
plays
Sarg, Tony, *joint author.* *See* Williamson,
Hamilton and Sarg, Tony
Saunders, Allen
Three taps at twelve; a mystery melo-
drama in three acts. N.Y. French.
c1933. 12°. 93p.
Saunders, J. M. *joint author.* *See* Clements,
Colin and Saunders, J. M.
Saunders, Louise
Figureheads. Romantic. 1 act
In Goldstone, G. A. ed. One-act plays
Savage, George Milton
Small down payment. Farce. 1 act
In Hughes, G. ed. Short plays for
modern players
Savage, George Milton and Peltret, Edouard
Watch your step, a mystery farce in three
acts. N.Y. Longmans. 1931. 12°. 81p.
Savoir, Alfred
Going to the dogs (Chez les chiens).
1 act
In Vernon, V. and F. eds. Modern
one-act plays from the French
He, a comedy in three acts. N.Y. French.
c1933. 12°. 105p.
Schaffner, Herbert
Ghost bird; a mystery comedy in four
acts. Chicago. Denison. 1927. 12°.
142p.
Schayer, E. R.
Private Jones. 1 act
In Nicholson, K. ed. Hollywood plays
Schimmel, Robert C.
When Irish eyes are smiling; a comedy.
N.Y. Fitzgerald. 1933. 12°

Whispering pines; a comedy mystery in three acts. Boston. Baker. 1929. 12°. 93p.

Schnitzler, Arthur, 1862-
Actress and the count. Comedy. 1 scene
In Hands around
Affairs of Anatol. Romantic. 8 pts.
In Reigen, The affairs of Anatol and other plays
Count and the girl of the streets. Comedy. 1 scene
In Hands around
Dr. Graesler, tr. from the German by E. C. Slade. N.Y. Simon. 1930. 12°. 176p.
Episode; a play in one act
In Golden Bk 17:70
Gallant Cassian. Puppet play. 1 act
In Poet Lore 33:507
Girl of the streets and the soldier. Comedy. 1 scene
In Hands around
Green cockatoo. Grotesque. 1 act
In Reigen, The affairs of Anatol and other plays
Husband and the sweet young miss. Comedy. 1 act
In Hands around
Intermezzo. Comedy. 3 acts
In Steeves, H. R. ed. Plays from the modern theatre
Light-o' love. Comedy. 3 acts
In Tucker, S. M. ed. Modern continental plays
Tucker, S. M. ed. Twenty-five modern plays
Watson, E. B. and Pressey, B. eds. Contemporary drama. European plays. v. 1
Living hours. 1 act. Sacrifice
In Reigen, The affairs of Anatol and other plays
Parlor maid and the young man. Comedy. 1 scene
In Hands around
Poet and the actress. Comedy. 1 scene
In Hands around
Reigen (Hands around). 10 dialogues
In Reigen, The affairs of Anatol and other plays
Soldier and the parlor-maid. Comedy. 1 scene
In Hands around
Sweet young miss and the poet. Comedy. 1 scene
In Hands around
Young man and husband. Comedy. 1 scene
In Hands around
Young man and the young wife. Comedy. 1 scene
In Hands around

Schofield, Stephen
Marble god. 1 act
In Schofield, S. ed. Marble God, and other one-act plays

Scott, Duncan Campbell, 1862-
Pierre. 1 act
In Massey, V. ed. Canadian plays from Hart House theatre. v. 1

Scott, Mrs. Natalie V.
Zombi
In Isaacs, E. J. ed. Plays of American life and fantasy
Scott, Noel, 1889-
Joker; a play in four acts. N.Y. French. 1929. 8°. 67p.
Scribner, Edwin
Pat Piper's place, a comedy in three acts. Chicago. Denison. 1929. 12°. 163p.
Phoebe cleans house; a comedy in three acts. Chicago. Denison. [1930] 12°. 205p.
Smiling cow; a farce-comedy in three acts. Chicago. Denison. [1930] 12°. 164p.
Welcome to the old town; a comedy in three acts. Chicago. Denison. 1927. 12°. 189p.
Sée, Edmond, 1875-
Old friend (un ami de jeunesse). 1 act
In Vernon, V. and F. eds. Modern one-act plays from the French
Seiler, Conrad
Box seats. 1 act
In Husband of Xanthippe, and other short plays
Eyes. 1 act
In Husband of Xanthippe, and other short plays
Husband of Xanthippe. 1 act
In Husband of Xanthippe, and other short plays
In a window. 1 act
In Husband of Xanthippe, and other short plays
Lady in the sack. 1 act
In Husband of Xanthippe, and other short plays
Matrimony. 1 act
In Husband of Xanthippe, and other short plays
Shairp (Alexander) Mordaunt, 1887-
Green bay tree; a play in three acts. London. Allen. [1933] 12°. 89p. Social decadence
Same in Mantle, B. ed. Best plays of 1933-34 (abridged)
Sharpsteen, Ernest J.
Lifting Jimmy's jinx; a one-act comedy. Chicago. Denison. 1927. 12°. 16p.
Red thread of guilt; a mystery drama in four acts. Chicago. Denison. 1927. 12°. 112p.
Rural belle; a one-act comedy. Chicago. Denison. 1927. 12°. 17p.
Shaw, George Bernard, 1856-
Admirable Bashville; or Constancy rewarded. Comedy. 3 acts
In Complete plays
Translations and tomfooleries
Androcles and the lion. Comedy. 1 act
In Complete plays
Annajanska, the bolshevik empress. Satire. 1 act
In Complete plays
Apple cart: a political extravaganza. London. Constable. 1930. 12°. 78p. 2 acts
In Complete plays

Shaw, George Bernard—*Continued*
  Arms and the man. Comedy. 3 acts
    In Complete plays
  Augustus does his bit. Comedy. 1 act
    In Complete plays
  Back to Methuselah; a metabiological
      Pentateuch. 5 pts.
    In Complete plays
  Caesar and Cleopatra. Comedy. 5 acts
    In Complete plays
  Candida. Character. 3 acts
    In Complete plays
  Captain Brassbound's conversion. Com-
      edy. 3 acts
    In Complete plays
  Dark lady of the sonnets. Shakespeare.
      1 act
    In Complete plays
  Devil's disciple. Melodrama. 3 acts
    In Complete plays
  Doctor's dilemma. Satire. 5 acts
    In Complete plays
  Fanny's first play. Comedy. 3 acts
    In Complete plays
  Fascinating foundling. Comedy. 1 act
    In Complete plays
      Translations and tomfooleries
  Fatal gazogene. *See* Shaw, G. B. Pas-
      sion, poison and petrifaction
  Getting married. Comedy. 1 act
    In Complete plays
  Glimpse of reality. Tragedietta. 1 act
    In Complete plays
      Translations and tomfooleries
  Glimpses of the domesticity of Franklyn
      Barnabas. 1 act
    In Short stories, scraps and shavings
  Great Catherine. Comedy. 4 scenes
    In Complete plays
  Heartbreak house. English society. 3
      acts
    In Complete plays
  How he lied to her husband. 1 act
    In Complete plays
  Inca of Perusalem. William II of Ger-
      many. 1 act
    In Complete plays
  Jitta's atonement [tr. from S. Trebitsch]
      3 acts
    In Complete plays
      Translations and tomfooleries
  John Bull's other island. Comedy. 4 acts
    In Complete plays
  Major Barbara. Comedy. 3 acts
    In Complete plays
  Man and superman. Comedy. 4 acts
    In Complete plays
  Man of destiny. Napoleon. 1 act
    In Complete plays
  Misalliance. Comedy. 1 act
    In Complete plays
  Mrs. Warren's profession. Social. 4 acts
    In Complete plays
  Music cure. Farce. 1 act
    In Complete plays
      Translations and tomfooleries
  O'Flaherty, V. C. World war. 1 act
    In Complete plays
  On the rocks. Political comedy. 2 acts
    In Too true to be good, etc.

  Overruled. Comedy. 1 act
    In Complete plays
  Passion, poison and petrifaction; or, The
      fatal gazogene. Tragedy. 1 act
    In Complete plays
      Translations and tomfooleries
  Philanderer. Character. 4 acts
    In Complete plays
  Press cuttings. Topical sketch. 1 act
    In Complete plays
      In Translations and tomfooleries
  Pygmalion. Romantic. 5 acts
    In Complete plays
  Saint Joan. Historical. 5 scenes
    In Complete plays
  Shewing-up of Blanco Posnet. Melo-
      drama. 1 act
    In Complete plays
  Too true to be good. Political extrava-
      ganza. 3 acts
    In Too true to be good, etc.
  Village wooing. Comediettina. 3 con-
      versations. 2 acts
    In Too true to be good, etc.
  Widower's houses. Social. 3 acts
    In Complete plays
  You never can tell. Comedy. 4 acts
    In Complete plays

Shayer, John David, 1899-
  Resignation of Bill Snyder; a play in
      one act. N.Y. French. 1928. 12°. 28p.
    Same in Clark, B. H. and Cook, T. R.
      eds. One-act plays
        Clark, B. H. and Nicholson,
          K. eds. American scene

Sheldon, Edward Brewster, 1886-
  Romance. 3 acts and epilogue
    In Mantle, B. and Sherman, G. P. eds.
      Best plays of 1909-1919

Shepherd, Martin
  Ali the cobbler. Comedy. 1 act
    In Marriott, J. W. ed. Best one-act
      plays of 1932

Sheppard, Alfred Tresidder. *See* Hepworth,
  F. A.

Sherriff, Robert Cedric, 1896-
  Badger's Green, a play in three acts.
      London. Gollancz. 1930. 12°. 112p.
    Same in Six plays
  Journey's end; a play in three acts. N.Y.
      Brentano's. 1929. 12°. 204p. World
      war
    Same in Chandler, F. W. and Cordell,
      R. A. eds. Twentieth cen-
        tury plays
        Famous plays of to-day
        Mantle, B. ed. Best plays of
          1928-29 (abridged)
        Plays of a half-decade
        Twentieth century plays

Sherriff, Robert C. and De Casalis, Jeanne
  St. Helena; a play in twelve scenes. Lon-
      don. Gollancz. 1934. 12°. 254p. His-
      torical

Sherwood, Robert Emmet, 1896-
  Petrified forest. N.Y. Scribner. 1935. 12°.
      176p. Arizona. 2 acts
  Queen's husband. N.Y. Scribner. 1928.
      12°. 190p. Comedy

Reunion in Vienna; a play in three acts.
N.Y. Scribner. 1932. 12°. 205p. Comedy
Same in Famous plays of 1933-34
  Mantle, B. ed. Best plays of
  1931-32 (abridged)
Road to Rome. N.Y. Scribner. 1927. 12°.
178p. Comedy. 3 acts
Same in Mantle, B. ed. Best plays of
  1926-27 (abridged)
This is New York, a play in three acts.
N.Y. Scribner. 1931. 8°. 177p. Comedy
Waterloo bridge; a play in two acts. N.Y.
French. 1930. 8°. 173p. Melodrama

Shiels, George
Bedmates; a play in one act. Dublin.
Gael Co-operative Soc. 1922. 12°. 20p.
Cartney and Kevney. Comedy. 3 acts
In Two Irish plays
Mountain dew. 3 acts
In Two Irish plays
Paul Twyning. Comedy. 3 acts
In Professor Tim & Paul Twyning
Professor Tim. Comedy. 3 acts
In Professor Tim & Paul Twyning

Shipman, Louis Evan, 1869-
Ben Franklin; a comedy in four acts.
Boston. Baker. [c1933] 151p.

**Shively, Josephine, Maxwell, Ted, and
Maxwell, Virginia**
Runaway bride; a comedy drama in three
acts. Philadelphia. Penn. 1926. 12°.
78p.

Short, Marion
Betty engaged; a comedy in three acts.
N.Y. French. c1928. 12°. 71p.
Her alienated affections; a mock trial in
one act. N.Y. French. 1932. 12°. 35p.
Jade necklace, a modern comedy in three
acts. N.Y. French. 1929. 12°. 67p.
Lady Luck; comedy. 1 act
In New plays for women and girls
Lights of happyland; a one act play.
N.Y. French. c1922. 12°. 18p.
Miss Somebody Else; a comedy in four
acts. N.Y. French. 1918. 12°. 88p.
Nervous Miss Niles; a comedy in three
acts. N.Y. French. c1931. 12°. 85p.
Nobody's home, a comedy in three acts.
N.Y. French. c1931. 12°. 105p.
Peach tree road; a modern comedy in
three acts. N.Y. French. c1930. 8°.
88p.
Return of Hi Jinks; a comedy in four
acts. N.Y. French. c1916. 12°. 84p.
Return of Mr. Benjamin; a mystery play
in one act. N.Y. French. 1933. 25p.
She wouldn't stay put; a modern comedy
in one act. N.Y. French. c1933. 28p.
Touch-down, a comedy in four acts. N.Y.
French. 1913. 12°. 83p.

Short, Marion and Phelps, Pauline
Hidden guest; a comedy in three acts.
N.Y. French. c1926. 12°. 84p.
Home from college; a sketch for four
males. N.Y. French. 1915. 12°. 12p.
Nancy pretends; a modern comedy in
three acts. N.Y. French. 1927

Only me; a modern play in three acts.
N.Y. French. c1924. 12°. 96p.

Siegel, Max, *joint author.* *See* Gropper,
Milton Herbert and Siegel, Max

Sifton, Claire and Sifton, Paul
1931—a play. N.Y. Farrar. c1932. 12°.
172p.

Sifton, Paul
Belt. N.Y. Macaulay. 1927. 12°. 193p.
Labor

Sigurjónsson, Jóhann, 1880-
Eyvind of the hills (Bjoergejvind og
hans hustru). Tragedy. 4 acts
In Dickinson, T. H. ed. Chief contemporary dramatists. ser. 3

Silberer, Geza, 1876-
Caprice, a comedy in three acts by Sil-
Vara, pseud. Adapted by Philip
Moeller. N.Y. Doubleday. 1929. 12°.
173p.

Sil-Vara, pseud. *See* Silberer, Geza

Simpson, H.
Pan in Pimlico. 1 act
In Mayor, B. ed. Four one-act plays

Sinclair, Upton Beall, 1878-
Millennium, a comedy of the year 2000.
Pasadena, Cal. Northumberland press.
1929. 12°. 246p.
Oil! a play in four acts . . . (from the
novel by the author). Pasadena, Cal.
The Author. [c1929] 12°. 80p.

**Sitwell, Osbert, 1892- and Sitwell, Sache-
verell, 1877-**
All at sea; a social tragedy in three acts
for first-class passengers only. Garden City, N.Y. Doubleday. 1928. 12°.
199p.

Sklar, George and Maltz, Albert
Peace on earth; an anti-war play in 3
acts. N.Y. French. 1934. 12°. 120p.

Sklar, George, *joint author.* *See* Peters,
Paul and Sklar, George

Sladen-Smith, Francis, 1886-
Assyrian afternoon. 1 act
In Bourne, J. ed. 8 new one-act plays
of 1933
Crown of St. Felice; a play in one act.
Boston. Baker. 1928. 12°. 44p.
Same in Johnson, T. ed. Ten fantasies
for stage and study
Edward about to marry; an extravaganza
in one act. London. Gowans. 1926.
16°. 61p.
Golden fisherman. Chinese. 1 act
In Modern short plays. ser. 3
Guilty passion; a play. London. Gowans.
1932. 16°
Happy death. 1 act
In Bourne, J. ed. 8 new one-act plays
for 1934
Herald. London. Gowans. 1932. 23p.
Invisible duke; a Gothic farce in one
act. London. Gowans. 1927. 12°. 78p.
Same in Marriott, J. W. ed. One-act
plays of to-day. ser. 5
Man who wouldn't go to heaven; a play
in one act. Boston. Baker. 1929. 12°.
60p.

Sladen-Smith, Francis—*Continued*
Mrs. Noah gives the sign. 1 act
In Marriott, J. W. ed. Best one-act
plays of 1931
Resurrection of Joseph; a play in one
act. London. Gowans. 1931. 12°. 54p.
Sacred cat; a diversion in one act. Bos-
ton. Baker. 1928. 12°. 16p.
Same in Johnson, T. ed. Diminutive
comedies
St. Simeon Stylites. 1 act
In Herbert, A. P. ed. Four one-act
plays
Marriott, J. W. ed. One-act plays
of to-day. ser. 4
Mayor, B. ed. Four one-act plays
Wonderful tourist
In Bourne, J. ed. Eight new plays for
boys and girls
Wonderful Zoo; a play in a prologue,
eleven scenes and an epilogue. Lon-
don. Sidgwick. 1932. 92p.

Smith, Boyd
Patriarch, a play in three acts. N.Y.
French. [c1931] 12°. 145p.

Smith, Chard Powers
Hamilton, a poetic drama in three acts.
N.Y. Coward-McCann. 1930. 8°. 154p.

Smith, Dorothy Gladys. See Anthony, C. L.
pseud.

Smith, E. E. and Ireland, D. L.
Cottage on the moor. Roundheads. 1 act
In Webber, J. P. and Webster, H. H.
eds. One-act plays for secondary
schools

Smith, Edgar Valentine
'Lijah. 1 act
In Clark, B. H. and Nichoson, K. eds.
American scene
Phillips, Le R. and Johnson, T. eds.
Types of modern dramatic com-
position

Smith, Glanville
Deep, deep; a play in one act
In Players M 9:28

Smith, Harry James, 1880-1918
Mrs. Bumpstead Leigh. Comedy. 3 acts
In Mantle, B. and Sherman, G. P. eds.
Best plays of 1909-1919
They refuse to be resurrected; a fantasy
in one act. London. Allen. 1932. 12°
Same in Marriott, J. W. ed. Best one-
act plays of 1932

Smith, Ruth P.
At old Vincennes
In Sanford, A. P. ed. Lincoln plays

Smith, V.
Simple soul. 1 act
In Nicholson, K. ed. Hollywood plays

Sowerby, Githa
Bearskin. Juvenile. 1 act
In Little plays for little people
Before breakfast; a comedy in one act.
N.Y. French. c1913. 12°. 20p.
Fortunatus and Cassandra. Juvenile.
1 act
In Little plays for little people
King Cophetua and the beggar maid.
Juvenile. 1 act
In Little plays for little people

Magic wood, or, Civility costs nothing.
Juvenile. 1 act
In Plays for little people
Princess Tenderheart. Juvenile. 1 act
In Little plays for little people
Moses, M. J. ed. Ring up the cur-
tain!
Rose and the ring. Juvenile. 1 act
In Little plays for little people

Speirs, Russell
Change of mind. 1 act
In One-act plays for stage and study.
ser. 6
Grave. 1 act
In Poet Lore 40:113

Spence, Eulalie
Starter. Negro. 1 act
In Locke, A. Le R. and Gregory, M.
eds. Plays of Negro life

Spewack, Bella and Spewack, Samuel
Clear all wires! a play in three weeks.
N.Y. French. 1932. 12°. 246p. Comedy

Spewack, Samuel, *joint author. See* Cohen,
Bella and Spewack, Samuel; Spewack,
B. and S.

Spooner, Cecil and Blaney, Charles E.
My Irish Cinderella, a comedy in four
acts. N.Y. Longmans. 1930. 12°. 140p.

Squire, John Collings, *joint author. See*
Balderston, John Lloyd and Squire,
John, Collings

Staadt, Edward, d. 1932
Cabbages; a cartoon in one act. N.Y.
French. c1925. 12°. 54p. German-
American farmers
Wind in the south; an American comedy.
Minneapolis. c1933. 12°

Stahl, Max Edward
La Carota. 1 act
In Johnson, T. ed. Miniature plays for
stage or study

Stanley, Martha M. 1879-
Let and sub-let, a farce comedy of youth.
N.Y. French. 1930. 12°. 117p.
My son, a play in three acts. N.Y. French.
1929. 12°. 136p.

**Stanley, Martha M. and Matthews, Ade-
laide,** 1866-
First Mrs. Chiverick; a comedy in three
acts. N.Y. French. 1930. 12°. 106p.
Innocent Anne; a light comedy in four
acts. N.Y. French. 1930. 12°. 105p.
Nightie night, a farce in a prologue and
three acts. N.Y. French. c1929. 12°.
118p.
Puppy love; a farcical comedy in three
acts. N.Y. French. c1927. 12°. 158p.
Wasp's nest, a mystery comedy in three
acts. N.Y. French. c1929. 12°. 134p.
Where innocence is bliss, a light comedy
in four acts. N.Y. French. c1929. 8°.
73p.

Starling, Lynn
Meet the wife, a comedy in three acts . . .
revised and rewritten. N.Y. French.
1928. 8°. 80p.

Stayton, Frank, 1874-
Angelina's lover. A comedy in one act.
N.Y. French. c1903. 12°. 12p.

"The Joan Danvers"; a play in three acts. N.Y. French. c1926. 8°. 60p.

Mixed doubles; a farce in three acts. N.Y. French. c1927. 12°. 94p.

Stayton, G. Butler
In the days of Isaiah, a play in one act. N.Y. French. c1931. 12°. 28p. Biblical

These my brethren; a play in one act. N.Y. French. c1931. 12°. 23p.

Steele, Wilbur Daniel, 1886-
Giant's stair. Crime. 1 act
In Shay, F. ed. Fifty more contemporary one-act plays

Steell, Willis, 1866-
Fifth commandment. 1 act
In Johnson, T. ed. Miniature plays for stage or study

Stein, Gertrude
Four saints in three acts. N.Y. Random House. 1934. 12°. 57p.

Stenger, Georgia
Above all else, liberty. Historical. 1 act
In Schauffler, R. H. and Sanford, A. P. eds. Plays for our American holidays. v. 3

At the turn of tide. Puritan. 3 acts
In Schauffler, R. H. and Sanford, A. P. eds. Plays for our American holidays. v. 2

Light triumphant. 1 act
In Sanford, A. P. ed. Plays for graduation days

Stephens, James, 1882-
Julia Elizabeth, a comedy in one act. N.Y. Gaige. 1929. 8°. 24p.

Stephens, Nan Bagby
Charivari
In Isaacs, E. J. ed. Plays of American life and fantasy

Sterling, F.
Modern viking. Christmas
In Shay, F. ed. Appleton book of Christmas plays

Stern, Gladys Bronwyn, 1890-
Long lost father, a comedy. N.Y. Knopf. c1933. 12°. 265p.

Man who pays the piper; a play in a prologue and three acts. London. Heinemann. [1931] 12°. 109p.

Matriarch, a play in a prologue and three acts. N.Y. French. c1931. 8°. 84p.

Sterne, Emma Gelders
Jeanne d'Arc. Juvenile. 3 acts
In Moses, M. J. ed. Ring up the curtain!

Sternheim, Carl, 1878-
Place in the world
In Katzin, W. ed. Eight European plays

Stevens, Charles A.
Tangled web; a comedy in one act. N.Y. Longmans. 1933. 38p.

Stevens, Henry Bailey
All alone in the country; a farce in one act. Boston. Baker. [c1921] 12°. 19p.

Early frost. 1 act
In Johnson, T. ed. Miniature plays for stage or study

Johnny Appleseed and Paul Bunyan. A play of American folk-lore in three acts with prologue. Boston. Baker. [1930] 12°. 92p.

Tolstoy; a play in seven scenes. N.Y. Crowell. [c1928] 8°. 155p.

Stevens, Thomas Wood, 1880-
Duquesne Christmas mystery
In Shay, F. ed. Appleton book of Christmas plays

Joan of Arc, a pageant in prologue and nine scenes. N.Y. French. c1932. 12°. 122p.

Stewart, Charles Conger
Gasoline gypsies, a comedy in three acts. London. French. 1931. 12°. 104p.

Stewart, Donald Ogden, 1894-
Father William, a comedy of father and son. N.Y. Harper. 1929. 8°. 202p.

Rebound, a comedy in three acts. N.Y. French. 1931. 12°. 95p.
Same in Mantle, B. ed. Best plays of 1929-30 (abridged)

Stewart, Mary
Dream fairy and the spider. Fairy. 1 act
In Schauffler, R. H. and Sanford, A. P. eds. Plays for our American holidays. v. 2

Stiles, Hinson
Room with the black door; a play in one act
In Poet Lore 38 (i.e. 39 no. 1):101

Stinson, H. H.
Ace is trumped. 1 act
In Nicholas, K. ed. Hollywood plays

Stirling, W. Edward, joint author. *See* Young, Francis Brett and Stirling, W. Edward

Stoddard, Anne and Sarg, Tony
Don Quixote (Cervantes). Marionettes. 7 scenes
In Moses, M. J. ed. Another treasury of plays for children

Stoker, Edwin
Boomer. Revenge. 1 act
In Lewis, B. R. ed. University of Utah plays

Stokes, Richard Leroy, 1882-
Merry Mount; a dramatic poem for music in three acts of six scenes. N.Y. Farrar. [c1932] 8°. 133p.

Paul Bunyan; a folk comedy in three acts. N.Y. Putnam. 1932. 12°. 102p.

Stout, Oakley, 1872-
Harvest: a drama in three acts . . . with an introduction by Harold A. Ehrensperger. The winning play of 1928 Drama league—Longmans, Green and co. playwriting contest. N.Y. Longmans. 1929. 8°. 77p.

Stout, Wilbur
Dogwood bushes. Comedy. 1 act
In Koch, F. H. ed. Carolina folk comedies

Stout, Wilbur and Lay, Ellen
In Dixon's kitchen, a comedy of country courtship. 1 act
In Koch, F. H. ed. Carolina folk-plays. ser. 3

Strachan, Edna (Higgins)
Chinese water wheel. 1 act
In One-act plays for stage and study.
ser. 6
Weakness for nurses. Comedy
In Snook, L. O. ed. Comedies seven

Strindberg, Johan August, 1849-1912
Bond. Tragedy. 1 act
In Lucky Peter's travels and other
plays
Comrades. Comedy. 4 acts
In Tucker, S. M. ed. Modern con-
tinental plays
Tucker, S. M. ed. Twenty-five mod-
ern plays
Dance of death. Life's enigma. 2 pts.
In Easter and other plays
Dream play. Prologue and two scenes
In Easter and other plays
Easter. 3 acts
In Easter and other plays
Equals. 1 act
In Golden Bk 7:85
Erik XIV. Historical. 4 acts
In Master Olof and other plays
Father. Tragedy. 3 acts
In Lucky Peter's travels and other
plays
Ghost sonata. 3 scenes
In Easter and other plays
Gustav Vasa. Historical. 5 acts
In Master Olof and other plays
Lady Julie (Countess Julia). Tragedy.
1 act
In Lucky Peter's travels and other
plays
Lucky Peter's travels (Lucky Peter).
Allegorical. 5 acts
In Lucky Peter's travels and other
plays
Master Olof. Swedish reformation.
5 acts
In Master Olof and other plays
Playing with fire. 21 scenes
In Lucky Peter's travels and other
plays
Saga of the Folkungs. Swedish history.
5 acts
In Master Olof and other plays
There are crimes and crimes. Comedy.
4 acts
In Moses, M. J. ed. Dramas of modern-
ism and their forerunners
To Damascus; a dream trilogy
In Poet Lore 42:1 Spring '33

Strode, Hudson, 1893-
End of the dance; a play in one act.
Winner of the Samuel French prize
in the 1929 little theatre tournament.
N.Y. French. c1929. 12° 31p.

Strode, Hudson, 1893- and Hornthal, Larry
Dance below. Satire. 1 act [First produced as The jig]
In Shay, F. ed. Fifty more contemporary one-act plays

Strode, W. C. *See* Chetham-Strode, Warren

Strong, Mirjone
Culture. 1 act
In Sanford, A. P. ed. One-act plays
for women

Stuart, Aimée, 1890- and Stuart, Philip
Cat's cradle, a play in three acts. London.
Benn. 1929. 12°. 92p.
Clara Gibbings, a play in three acts.
London. Benn. 1929. 12°. 94p.
Her shop, a play in three acts. London.
Benn. 1929. 12°. 119p.
Nine till six; a play in three acts. Lon-
don. Benn. 1930. 12°. 121p.
Sixteen
In Famous plays of 1933-34
Supply and demand; a play in prologue
and three acts. London. Benn.
1931. 12°. 90p.

Stuart, Philip, *joint author*. *See* Stuart,
Aimée and Stuart, Philip

Stuckes, W.
Shanghai. 1 act
In Marriott, J. W. ed. Best one-act
plays of 1931

Sturges, Preston
Strictly dishonorable; a comedy in three
acts. N.Y. Liveright. 1929. 12°.
187p.
Same in Mantle, B. ed. Best plays of
1929-30 (abridged)

Sudermann, Hermann, 1857-1928
Far-away princess. Comedy. 1 act
In Golden Bk 5:625
Teja; a one-act play
In Golden Bk 6:493

Sullivan, Frank
Life is a bowl of Eugene O'Neills; a
dramatic satire in one act
In Golden Bk 18:60

Sutro, Alfred, 1863-
Cave of illusion; a play in four acts with
an introduction by Maurice Maeter-
linck. London. Richards. 1900
Living together, a play in four acts.
London. Duckworth. 1929. 12°.
102p.
Making a gentleman; a play in four acts.
London. Chiswick. 1909
Marriage has been arranged. Comedy.
1 act
In Pence, R. W. ed. Dramas by
present-day writers
Perfect lover; a play in four acts. N.Y.
French. 1906. 12°. 118p. Also pub-
lished under title Price of money
Uncle Anyhow; a comedy in three acts.
London. French. c1919. 12°. 84p.
Walls of Jericho. Social. 4 acts
In Marriott, J. W. ed. Great modern
British plays

Swan, Mark Elbert, 1871-
Judy walks in; a comedy of youth and
love, in three acts. N.Y. French.
c1928. 12°. 123p.
She walked in her sleep, a farce comedy
in three acts. Boston. Baker. 1929.
12°. 103p.

Swann, Mona
Saul and David. Biblical. 1 act
In Hampden, J. ed. Seven modern
plays for younger players

Swerling, Joseph and Robinson, Edward G.
Kibitzer; a comedy. N.Y. French. 1929. 12°. 168p. 3 acts

Synge, John Millington, 1871-1909
Deirdre of the sorrows. Tragedy. 3 acts
In Plays [1932]
Playboy of the western world. Comedy. 3 acts
In Plays [1932]
Riders to the sea. Sea. 1 act
In Plays [1932]
Canfield, C. ed. Plays of the Irish renaissance
Clark, B. H. ed. Representative one-act plays by British and Irish authors
Cohen, H. L. ed. One-act plays by modern authors. 1934 edition
Hampden, J. ed. Nine modern plays
Watson, E. B. and Pressey, B. eds. Contemporary drama. English and Irish plays. v. 1
Whitman, C. H. ed. Seven contemporary plays
Shadow of the glen. Comedy. 1 act
In Plays [1932]
Tinker's wedding. Comedy. 2 acts
In Plays [1932]

Szenes, Bela, 1894-
Budapest salesman should not read French illustrated magazines. Comedy. 1 act
In Shay, F. ed. Fifty more contemporary one-act plays

Taber, Gladys Bagg, 1899-
Lady of the moon, a comedy in three acts. Philadelphia. Penn. 1928. 75p. 12°
Miss Manda. Love. 1 act
In Poet Lore 38:412

Taber, Richard, *joint author.* See Gleason, James and Taber, Richard

Tagger, Theodore (Ferdinand Bruckner)
Races; a drama in three acts. tr. from the German . . . by Ruth Langner. N.Y. Knopf. 1934. 12°. 139p.

Talbot, A. J.
Betrothal of the princess; a play in doggerel. London. Gowans. 1930. 24°. 20p.
Same in Bystander. Christmas no. 1925
Cabinet minister's fireside, a comedy in one act. N.Y. French. c1932. 12°. 23p.
Casket scene up to date; a play in one act. London. Gowans. 1929. 24°. 21p.
Daniel in the lionesses' den; a comedietta in one act. London. Gowans. 1929. 16°. 20p.
Duke of Cul-de-Sac; a very modern melodrama. London. French. c1930. 12°. 16p.
Emily's excuse; a play in one act. London. Gowans. 1926. 16°. 25p.
In the outer darkness; a play in one act. London. Gowans. 1930. 24°. 20p.

Incorrigible. 1 act
In Schofield, S. ed. Marble God, and other one-act plays
Iron Duke; a chronicle play in seven scenes and an epilogue. London. Benn. 1926. 12°. 95p. Duke of Wellington
Murder in the foyer; a burlesque grand guignol in one scene. N.Y. French. c1932. 12°. 18p.
Old firm's awakening; a play in one act. London. Gowans. 1927. 16°. 18p.
Passing of Galatea. Fantasy
In Johnson, T. ed. Ten fantasies for stage and study
Quarter of an hour; a comedy in one act. N.Y. French. c1930. 12°. 21p.
Ray of reason; a farce in one act. London. Gowans. 1930. 16°. 40p.
Spartan girl; a doubtful tragedy by Euripides, adapted for modern costume and furnished with a brighter ending. N.Y. French. c1930. 12°. 19p.
Same in Marriott, J. W. ed. One-act plays of to-day. ser. 5
White jasmine; a fantasy in one act. London. Gowans. 1929. 16°. 31p.

Talbot, Francis Xavier
Born in Bethlehem. Nativity. 7 scenes
In Shining in darkness
He is risen. Easter scenes. 6 scenes
In Shining in darkness

Tarkington, Booth, 1869-
Beauty and the Jacobins; an interlude of the French Revolution. 1 act
In Cohen, H. L. ed. One-act plays by modern authors. 1934 edition
Help each other club; a one-act play. N.Y. Appleton. 1934. 26p.
Monsieur Beaucaire. Romantic. 3 acts
In Grove, J. ed. Omnibus of romance
Pence, R. ed. Dramas by present-day writers
Trysting place. Farce. 1 act
In Clark, B. H. and Nicholson, K. eds. American scene
Tucker, S. M. ed. Twelve one-act plays for study and production

Tarkington, Booth, 1869- and Wilson, Harry Leon, 1867-
Gibson upright. Labor. 3 acts
In Webber, J. P. and Webster, H. H. eds. Typical plays for secondary schools
How's your health? A comedy in three acts. N.Y. French. c1930. 12°. 105p.

Taylor, Helen Louise, 1908-
Angelus. Renunciation. 1 act
In One-act plays for stage and study. ser. 5

Taylor, Rex
Appearances. 1 act
In Nicholson, Kenyon, ed. Appleton book of short plays. ser. 2

Temple, Joan
Charles and Mary; a play on the life of Charles Lamb. London. Allen. [1930] 12°. 112p.

Tennyson, Alfred, Lord, 1809-1892
Devil and the lady. Edited by Charles
Tennyson. N.Y. Macmillan. 1931.
12°. 67p. Comedy. 3 acts
Falcon. Romantic. 1 act
In Webber, J. P. and Webster, H. H.
eds. One-act plays for secondary
schools

Terry, Joseph Edward Harold, 1885-
Collusion, a trifle in three acts. N.Y.
French. c1930. 8°. 79p.
General post, a comedy in three acts.
N.Y. Dutton. 1918. 8°. 128p.
Master Wayfarer. 1 act
In Marriott, J. W. ed. One-act plays
of to-day. ser. 3

Thomas, Albert Ellsworth, 1872-
No more ladies. Comedy. 3 acts
In Mantle, B. ed. Best plays of 1933-
34 (abridged)
Uncle Tom's cabin. Revised version;
based upon the dramatization of
George L. Aiken. N.Y. Appleton.
1934. 12°. 84p. 3 acts

Thomas, Augustus, 1857-
Man upstairs; a comedy in one act. N.Y.
French. 1933. 26p.

Thompson, Denman, 1833-1911
Old homestead; a play in four acts.
Boston. Baker. [c1927] 12°. 93p.

Thompson, Edward John, 1886-
Atonement; a play of modern India in
four acts. London. Benn. 1924.
12°. 128p.
Clouded mirror. Indian
In Thompson, E. J. and T. Three
Eastern plays
Floutern peasant
In Plays and pageants
Hell-ride of Brynhild
In Plays and pageants
Krishna Kumari, an historical drama in
four acts. London. Benn. 1924.
12°. 89p.
May pageant
In Plays and pageants
Queen of ruin. Indian
In Thompson, E. J. and T. Three East-
ern plays
Saul
In Plays and pageants

Thompson, J. F.
Warrior's husband. 1 act
In Nicholson, Kenyon, ed. Appleton
book of short plays. ser. 2

Thompson, Theodosia
Easter evening
In Thompson, E. J. and T. Three East-
ern plays

Thorne, Anthony
Thirteen o'clock; a play in three acts.
London. Benn. 1929. 12°. 69p.

Thornton, Clare
Marriage of Dotty. 1 scene
In Johnson, T. ed. More plays in
miniature

Thorp, Josephine
At the milestone. 1 act
In Sanford, A. P. ed. Plays for gradua-
tion days

Treasure chest. Fairy. 1 act
In Schauffler, R. H. and Sanford, A. P.
eds. Plays for our American
holidays. v. 2

Thrush, A.
Wisdom tooth. 1 act
In Bourne, J. ed. 8 new one-act plays
of 1933

Thurston, Althea
And the devil laughs. Satire. 1 act
In Lewis, B. R. ed. University of
Utah plays
Exchange. Satire. 1 act
In Lewis, B. R. ed. University of Utah
plays

Titheradge, Dion, 1889-
Barbarous work
In From "Folly to be wise"
Behind the curtain. N.Y. French. c1926.
12°. 81p.
Crooked Billet, a play in three acts. N.Y.
French. c1930. 8°. 88p.
For England
In Behind the curtain
Garrick revised
In Behind the curtain
Gooseberries in Piccadilly
In Behind the curtain
Great white sale
In From "Folly to be wise"
He who gets sacked
In From "Folly to be wise"
King can do no wrong
In From "Folly to be wise"
Lady Emily talks business
In From "Folly to be wise"
Little birds in their nests
In From "Folly to be wise"
Man proposes
In From "Folly to be wise"
Missing words
In From "Folly to be wise"
My lady Solomon
In Written on foolscap
No jazz to-night
In Behind the curtain
Permanent wave
In Behind the curtain
Relativity
In Behind the curtain
Speed!
In From "Folly to be wise"
Ups and downs from revue. N.Y. French.
c1926. 8°. 85p.
Same in Written on foolscap
Very devil
In Behind the curtain
Violin
In Behind the curtain
Zara the great
In Behind the curtain

Toler, Sidney
Her western Romeo; a comedy in three
acts. N.Y. French. c1928. 12°. 76p.
Miss Efficiency; a comedy drama in four
acts. N.Y. French. c1927. 12°. 122p.
Somebody's crooked; a comedy of
mystery in three acts. N.Y. French.
c1929. 12°. 78p.
Who's boss? A comedy in three acts.
N.Y. French. 1929. 12°. 90p.

Toller, Ernst, 1893-
Brokenbrow, a tragedy; tr. by Vera Mendel. London. Nonsuch. [1926] 8°. 50p.
Hoppla! a play in a prologue and five acts. English version by Hermon Ould. London. Benn. 1928. 12°. 141p.
Machine-wreckers; a drama of the English Luddites in a prologue and five acts. English version by Ashley Dukes. London. Benn. 1923. 12°. 113p.
Same in Moses, M. J. ed. Dramas of modernism and their fore-runners
Man and the masses
In Watson, E. B. and Pressey, B. eds. Contemporary drama: European plays

Tolstoi, Count Lyof N. 1828-1910
Live corpse. Conjugal. Six acts
In Chandler, F. W. and Cordell, R. A. eds. Twentieth century plays

Tomita, K.
Final refuge. 1 act
In Johnson, T. ed. Miniature plays for stage or study

Tompkins, Frank Gerow, 1879-
Letters. Comedy. 1 act
In Shay, F. ed. Fifty more contemporary one-act plays
Sham. Social satire. 1 act
In Goldstone, G. A. ed. One-act plays

Tompkins, J. M. S.
Deathless world. Religious. 1 act
In Eastman, F. ed. Modern religious dramas

Tompkins, Juliet Wilbor, 1871-
Once there was a princess; a comedy in three acts and a prologue. N.Y. French. c1927. 12°. 93p.

Toms, Robert M.
. . . and points west. Comedy. 1 act
In Players' book of one act plays. ser. 1

Toomer, Jean
Balo. Negro. 1 act
In Locke, A. Le R. and Gregory, M. eds. Plays of Negro life

Torrence, Frederic Ridgley, 1875-
Dance Calinda. Negro pantomime. 1 act
In Locke, A. Le R. and Gregory, M. eds. Plays of Negro life
Granny Maumee. Negro. 1 act
In Locke, A. Le R. and Gregory, M. eds. Plays of Negro life
Rider of dreams. Negro. 1 act
In Locke, A. Le R. and Gregory, M. eds. Plays of Negro life

Totheroh, Dan W. 1894-
Breaking of the calm; a play in one act. N.Y. French. [c1928] 12°. 15p.
Same in One-act plays for everyone
Distant drums, a play in three acts. N.Y. French. 1932. 12°. 163p.
Good vintage. Vengeance. 1 act
In Clark, B. H. and Nicholson, K. eds. American scene
One-act plays for everyone
Great dark. 1 act
In One-act plays

In the darkness. 1 act
In One-act plays for everyone
Lost princess; a fantasy in one act. (Sequel to Stolen prince). N.Y. French. 1933. 19p.
Same in One-act plays for everyone
One-act plays for stage and study. ser. 6
Mirthful marionettes. 1 act
In One-act plays for everyone
Pearls; a play in one act. N.Y. French. 1933. 19p.
Same in Cohen, H. L. ed. More one-act plays by modern authors
One-act plays for everyone
Stolen prince; a fantasy in one act. N.Y. French. 1933. 21p.
Same in Cohen, H. L. ed. More one-act plays by modern authors
Hampden, J. ed. Seven modern plays for younger players
One-act plays for everyone
Tune of a tune. Fantasy. 1 act
In One-act plays for everyone
One-act plays for stage and study. ser. 4
While the mushrooms bubble. 1 act
In One-act plays for everyone
Widdy's mite. 1 act
In One-act plays for everyone
One-act plays for stage and study. ser. 5

Totheroh, Dan, *joint author. See* Norris, K. and Totheroh, D.

Toy, Jane
Agatha; a romance of plantation days. 1 act
In Koch, F. H. ed. Carolina folk comedies

Tracy, H. E. H.
Understudy. Theatre. 1 act
In Eight one-act plays

Trask, Mrs. Kate Nichols, 1853-1922
Little town of Bethlehem; a play for the Christmastide in three parts. New York. French. 1929. 8°. 88p.

Treadwell, Sophie
Machinal. Tragedy. 10 episodes
In Mantle, B. ed. Best plays of 1928-29 (condensed)

Trebitsch, Siegfried, 1869-
Jitta's atonement. Comedy. 3 acts
In Shaw, G. B. Translations and tomfooleries

Tret'iakov, Sergei Mikhailovich, 1892-
Roar China; an episode in nine scenes; tr. from the Russian . . . N.Y. International pub. co. 1932. 87p.

Trevelyan, H. B.
Dark angel, a play of yesterday and to-day. London. Benn. 1928. 12°. 104p.

Trevelyan, Robert Calvery, 1872-
Bride of Dionysus, a music-drama, and other poems. N.Y. Longmans. 1912. 8°. 77p.
Cheiron. London. Woolf. 1927. 12°. 58p. 2 acts
Fand
In Three plays

Tears of dawn, a medieval fantasy in one act
  In Poet Lore 33:105
Three Thanksgivings. 1 act
  In Schauffler, R. H. and Sanford, A. P. eds. Plays for our American holidays. v. 2

Vildrac, Charles, 1882-
Art of making friends. (L'indigent) 1 act
  In Vernon, V. and F. eds. Modern one-act plays from the French
Michel Auclair; a play in three acts
  In [Leverton, G. H. ed. Plays for the college theatre. 1932]
Steamship Tenacity; a comedy in three acts
  In Dickinson, T. H. ed. Chief contemporary dramatists. ser. 3
  Tucker, S. M. ed. Twenty-five modern plays

Vinton, Iris
Just babies. 1 act
  In Sanford, A. P. ed. One-act plays for women

Vollmer, Lula
Sun-up; a play in three acts. Comedy
  In Tucker, S. M. ed. Twenty-five modern plays

Vollmoeller, K. 1848-
Uncle's been dreaming
  In Katzin, W. ed. Eight European plays

Vosper, Frank, 1899-
Lucky dip, a comedy in three acts. N.Y. French. c1931. 8°. 70p.
Marry at leisure, a comedy in three acts. N.Y. French. c1931. 8°. 76p.
Murder on the second floor; a play. N.Y. French. c1930. 16°. 81p. Mystery
People like us; a play. London. Putnam. [1929] 12°. 123p.

Waddell, Helen Jane
Abbé Prévost. London. Constable. c1933. 8°. 57p. Historical. 3 acts
Spoiled Buddha; a play in two acts. Dublin. Talbot press. 1919. 16°. 40p.

Wadhams, Neva M.
Fat, jolly old man. Christmas. 1 act
  In Curtis, A. ed. Christmas plays for one and all

Waldman, Seymour
Dead insist on living; a play in six scenes. N.Y. Gotham House. [c1931] 8°. 157p. Pessimism

Walker, Alice Johnstone, 1871-
Sanctuary knocker. 1 act
  In Sanford, A. P. ed. Plays for graduation days

Walker, Stuart
Birthday of the infanta (Oscar Wilde). 1 act
  In Moses, M. J. ed. Another treasury of plays for children
Medicine show. Comedy. 1 act
  In Clark, B. H. and Nicholson, K. eds. American scene

Nevertheless. Fantasy. 1 act
  In Webber, J. P. and Webster, H. H. eds. One-act plays for secondary schools
Seven gifts. Pantomime. 1 scene
  In Schauffler, R. H. and Sanford, A. P. eds. Plays for our American holidays. v. 1
  Shay, F. ed. Appleton book of Christmas plays

Wallace, Edgar, 1875-1932
Calendar, a racing play in three acts. N.Y. French. c1932. 8°. 88p.
Case of the frightened lady, a play in three acts N.Y. French. c1932. 8°. 73p.
Ringer, a play in four acts. N.Y. French. c1929. 8°. 79p.

Walter, Eugene
Easiest way. Problem. 4 acts
  In Mantle, B. and Sherman, G. P. eds. Best plays of 1909-1919

Warren, Edward Henry, 1873-
Shakespeare in Wall street. Boston. Houghton. 1930. 12°. 36p. Burlesque. 1 act

Warren, Prescott and Hutchins, Will
Day that Lincoln died, a play in one act. Boston. Baker. 1912. 12°. 16p.
  In Schauffler, R. H. and Sanford, A. P. eds. Plays for our American holidays. v. 3

Watkins, Maurine
Chicago. N.Y. Knopf. 1927. 12°. 111p. Comedy. 3 acts
  In Mantle, B. ed. Best plays of 1926-27 (abridged)

Watling, E. F.
All right on the night
  In Campion, C. et al. Stage door; ten sketches for revue
Community drama
  In Campion, C. et al. Stage door; ten sketches for revue
French as she is learnt
  In Campion, C. et al. Stage door; ten sketches for revue

Watters, George Manker and Hopkins, Arthur
Burlesque. Comedy. 3 acts
  In Mantle, B. ed. Best plays for 1927-28 (abridged)

Watts, Barbara
Princess and the players
  In Bourne, J. ed. Eight new plays for boys and girls

Watts, William
How heartsease cured the duke; a play in four acts. Boston. Four Seas. 1927. 12°. 38p.

Weaver, Mrs. Gustine Nancy (Courson) 1873-
Christmas pageant
  In Hop Run, and six other pageants
Hop-Run. Pageant
  In Hop-Run, and six other pageants
Memories: Mother's day play
  In Hop-Run, and six other pageants
Passion week: An Easter pageant
  In Hop-Run, and six other pageants

Weaver, G. N. C.—*Continued*
Patriotic pageant
  In Hop-Run, and six other pageants
Possibilities in rural church life. Pageant
  In Hop-Run, and six other pageants
Thanksgiving pageant. Pageant
  In Hop-Run, and six other pageants
Webber, James Plaisted
Frances and Francis. Subterfuge. 1 act
  In Webber, J. P. and Webster, H. H.
    eds. Typical plays for secondary
    schools
Golden arrow. 1 act
  In Johnson, T. ed. Ten fantasies for
    stage and study
Wedekind, Frank, 1864-1918
Heart of a tenor. 1 act
  In Smart Set anthology
Such is life. Mediaeval Italy. 5 acts
  In Dickinson, T. H. ed. Chief con-
    temporary dramatists. ser. 3
    Tucker, S. M. ed. Modern continen-
    tal plays
Weeks, Albert Loren
Cocktails. Comedy. 1 act
  In Players book of one act plays. ser. 1
Elsie. Comedy. 1 act
  In Players book of one act plays. ser. 1
Little brown jug. Comedy. 1 act
  In Players book of one act plays. ser. 1
Weinberg, Albert, 1889-
Lofty motives. Strategy. 1 act
  In Poet Lore 38:603
Weitzenkorn, Louis, 1893-
Five star final, a melodrama in three
    acts; preface by Herbert Bayard
    Swope. N.Y. French. 1931. 12°. 165p.
  In Mantle, B. ed. Best plays of 1930-
    31 (abridged)
Welff, E.
Three of a different kind. 1 act
  In Jagendorf, M. A. ed. Nine short
    plays
Wellington, Barbara
Is romance dead? 1 act
  In Johnson, T. ed. Ten fantasies for
    stage and study
Wells, C. F.
Apothecary. 1 act
  In Johnson, T. ed. Ten fantasies for
    stage and study
Werfel, Franz V. 1890-
Goat song (Bockgesang); a drama in
    five acts . . . tr. by Ruth Langner.
    Garden City, N.Y. Doubleday. 1926.
    12°. 161p.
Juarez and Maximilian; a dramatic his-
    tory in three phases and thirteen
    pictures; tr. by Ruth Langner. N.Y.
    Simon. 1927. 12°. 172p.
Paul among the Jews (a tragedy); tr.
    by Paul P. Levertoff. London. Dio-
    cesan house. [1928] 8°. 150p.
West, Rebecca. *See* Van Druten, John.
Return of the soldier
Wexley, John
Last mile; a play in three acts. N.Y.
    French. 1930. 12°. 128p. Death pen-
    alty
  Same in Mantle, B. ed. Best plays of
    1929-30 (abridged)

They shall not die. N.Y. Knopf. 12°.
    191p. Scottsboro case
  Same in Mantle, B. ed. Best plays of
    1933-34 (abridged)
Whipkey, Stella Dunaway
Door mats. 1 act
  In Poet Lore 40:92
White, Charlotte Reed
Group of plays about Ulysses and the
    Greeks. Classical
  In Schauffler, R. H. and Sanford, A. P.
    eds. Plays for our American holi-
    days. v. 4
White, Jessie Braham
Snow White and the seven dwarfs, a
    fairy tale play based on story of the
    brothers Grimm. N.Y. Dodd. 1913.
    24°. 236p.
  In Moses, M. J. ed. Another treasury
    of plays for children
White, Leonard C.
Perfect marriage. 1 act
  In Marriott, J. W. ed. Best one-act
    plays of 1931
White, Lucy
Bird child. Negro social. 1 act/
  In Locke, A. Le R. and Gregory, M.
    eds. Plays of Negro life
Whitehouse, Josephine Henry
Ambush; farce comedy. 1 act
  In Nicholson, K. ed. Appleton book
    of short plays. ser. 2
Daily bread. Domestic life. 1 act
  In Poet Lore 40:129
Indian summer, a comedy in one act
  In Poet Lore 39:455
Wied, Gustav Joannes, 1858-1914
2 x 2 = 5. Social revolt. 4 acts
  In Le Gallienne, E. ed. Eva Le Gal-
    lienne's civic repertory plays
Wight, Delano, 1882-
Colonel Washington, a play in seven
    scenes. Cambridge, Mass. Privately
    printed at Riverside press. 1933. 12°.
    133p.
Wight, Douglas
Under the oak. Chaucer's Pardoner's
    tale. 4 scenes
  In Hughes, G. ed. Short plays for
    modern players
Wilcox, Grace
Translated. 3 scenes
  In Poet Lore 41:251
**Wilde, Oscar (Fingall O'Flahertie Wills)
1856-1900**
Importance of being earnest. Comedy.
    3 acts
  In Steeves, H. R. ed. Plays from the
    modern theatre
    Tucker, S. M. ed. Twenty-five mod-
    ern plays
Salome. Tragedy. 1 act
  In Clark, B. H. ed. Representative
    one-act plays by British and Irish
    authors

Woman of no importance. Comedy. 4 acts
  In Cordell, R. A. ed. Representative modern plays

Wilde, Percival, 1887-
Alias Santa Claus; a play for children. N.Y. Appleton. 1927. 12°. 58p.
  In Schauffler, R. H. ed. Plays for our American holidays. v. 1
Catesby. Comedy. 1 act
  In One-act plays of Percival Wilde. ser. 1
Confessional. Ethical. 1 act
  In Eastman, F. ed. Modern religious dramas
    Goldstone, G. A. ed. One act plays
    Pence, R. W. ed. Dramas by present-day writers
    Tucker, S. M. ed. Twelve one-act plays for study and production
Dawn. Supernatural. 1 act
  In One-act plays of Percival Wilde. ser. 1
    Phillips, Le R. and Johnson, T. eds. Types of modern dramatic composition
Enchanted Christmas tree. 1 act
  In Shay, F. ed. Appleton book of Christmas plays
Finger of God. Ethical. 1 act
  In One-act plays of Percival Wilde. ser. 1
Gadgets. Mechanistic tragi-comedy. 1 act
  In Ten plays for little theatres
Great American drama. 1 act
  In Ten plays for little theatres
House of cards. Domestic tragedy. 1 act
  In One-act plays of Percival Wilde. ser. 1
Immoralia. 1 act
  In Three minute plays
In the net. Comedy. 1 act
  In One-act plays of Percival Wilde. ser. 1
Inn of discontent. Fantasy. 1 act
  In Sanford, A. P. ed. Plays for graduation days
Innocentia. 1 act
  In Three minute plays
Kings in Nomania. N.Y. Appleton. 1926. 12°. 75p.
  In One-act plays of Percival Wilde. ser. 1
Lady of dreams. Fantasy. 1 act
  In One-act plays of Percival Wilde. ser. 1
    Sanford, A. P. ed. One-act plays for women
Lift that failed. *See* Wilde, P. Lost elevator
Lost elevator. Improbable comedy. 1 act
  In One-act plays of Percival Wilde. ser. 1 (Lift that failed)
    Ten plays for little theatres
Lot's wife; a contribution to history. 1 act
  In Ten plays for little theatres

Mothers of men. Mother's Day. 1 act
  In Schauffler, R. H. ed. Plays for our American holidays. v. 4
Moving finger; a drama in one act. N.Y. French 1931. 26p.
  Same in One-act plays for stage and study. ser. 6
Musicalia. 1 act
  In Three minute plays
Noble lord. Comedy. 1 act
  In Schauffler, R. H. and Sanford, A. P. eds. Plays for our American holidays. v. 2
Out of the mouths of . . . ; a serio-comedy. 1 act
  In Ten plays for little theatres
Pawns. War. 1 act
  In One-act plays of Percival Wilde. ser. 1
Sequel. Comedy. 1 act
  In One-act plays of Percival Wilde
Short cut. Mine cave-in. 1 act
  In Ten plays for little theatres
Standish pride. Fantasy. 1 act
  In Ten plays for little theatres
Talisman. 1 act
  In One-act plays of Percival Wilde. ser. 1
Thing. Delusion. 1 act
  In Ten plays for little theatres
Traitor. Boer war. 1 act
  In One-act plays of Percival Wilde. ser. 1
Unseen host. War fantasy. 1 act
  In Webber, J. P. and Webster, H. H. eds. One-act plays for secondary schools
Vignette. Divorce. 1 act
  In Ten plays for little theatres
What never dies. 1 act
  In Ten plays for little theatres
    Hughes, G. ed. Short plays for modern players

Wilder, Thornton Niven, 1897-
And the sea shall give up its dead. Judgment day. 1 scene
  In Angel that troubled the waters, and other plays
Angel on the ship. Sea. 1 scene
  In Angel that troubled the waters, and other plays
    Church, V. W. ed. Curtain!
Angel that troubled the waters. Healing. 1 scene
  In Angel that troubled the waters, and other plays
Brother Fire. Italy. 1 scene
  In Angel that troubled the waters, and other plays
Centaurs. Ibsen. 1 scene
  In Angel that troubled the waters, and other plays
Childe Roland to the dark tower came. Death. 1 scene
  In Angel that troubled the waters, and other plays
Fanny Otcott. Morals. 1 scene
  In Angel that troubled the waters, and other plays

Wilder, Thornton Niven—*Continued*
Flight into Egypt. Holy family. 1 scene
In Angel that troubled the waters, and other plays
Happy journey to Trenton and Camden. 1 act
In Long Christmas dinner and other plays
Hast thou considered my servant Job? Biblical. 1 scene
In Angel that troubled the waters, and other plays
Leviathan. Fanciful. 1 scene
In Angel that troubled the waters, and other plays
Long Christmas dinner. Birth and death. 1 act
In Long Christmas dinner and other plays
Love and how to cure it; a play in one act. N.Y. French. c1932. 12°. 23p.
Same in Long Christmas dinner and other plays
Message and Jehanne. Comedy. 1 scene
In Angel that troubled the waters, and other plays
Mozart and the gray steward. Mozart. 1 scene
In Angel that troubled the waters, and other plays
Cohen, H. L. ed. One-act plays by modern authors. 1934 edition
Nascuntur poetae. Fate. 1 scene
In Angel that troubled the waters, and other plays
Now the servant's name was Malchus. Jesus. 1 scene
In Angel that troubled the water, and other plays
Penny that beauty spent. Romantic. 1 scene
In Angel that troubled the waters, and other plays
Proserpina and the devil, a play for marionettes. 1 scene
In Angel that troubled the waters, and other plays
Pullman car Hiawatha. 1 act
In Long Christmas dinner and other plays
Queens of France. Satire. 1 act
In Long Christmas dinner and other plays
Such things happen only in books. 1 act
In Long Christmas dinner and other plays

Williams, Emlyn
Late Christopher Bean; a comedy; an English adaptation of René Fauchois' Prenez garde à la peinture! London. Gollancz. 1933. 128p.

Williams, Jessie Lynch, 1871-
Why marry? Comedy. 3 acts
In Mantle, B. and Sherman, G. P. eds. Best plays of 1909-1919

Williams, Margery, *joint author. See* Hutchinson, Harold and Williams, Margery

Williams, Sarah M.
Turkey girl. Zuni indians. 1 act
In Lewis, B. R. ed. University of Utah plays

Willis, Richard
Confession. 1 act
In Four playlets
Six playlets
Cowards. 1 act
In Six playlets
Little old gent. 1 act
In Four playlets
Six playlets
Old grouch. 1 act
In Four playlets
Six playlets
Show must go on. 1 act
In Four playlets
Six playlets
Too much crime. 1 act
In Six playlets

Wilson, Alma
Company's coming, a farce-comedy in three acts. N.Y. French. c1931. 12°. 141p. (Copyright, 1915, under title, "The third leg")

Wilson, Frank H.
Sugar cane. Negro. 1 act
In Locke, A. LeR. and Gregory, M. eds. Plays of Negro life

Wilson, Harry Leon, *joint author. See* Tarkington, Booth and Wilson, Harry Leon
Photograph reveries; an entertainment in sixteen scenes. N.Y. French. c1933. 12°. 19p.

Wilson, Sue Ann
Festival of the harvest moon. Thanksgiving. 1 act
In Schauffler, R. H. and Sanford, A. P. eds. Plays for our American holidays. v. 2
Festival of Yankee Doodle. Fourth of July. 1 act
In Schauffler, R. H. and Sanford, A. P. eds. Plays for our American holidays. v. 3

Wilson, Theodora Wilson
Champion North. Comedy. 3 acts
In Five three-act plays

Winningham, C. C.
Murder will out. Comedy. 1 act
In Players book of one act plays. ser. 1

Winsloe, Christa
Children in uniform; a play in three acts; adapted from the same play as Mädchen in uniform. London. Gollancz. 1933. 96p. (German play was performed under title: Gestern und Heute.) Also Little, Brown. Boston. 1933
Same in Famous plays of 1932-33

Winter, John Keith
Rats of Norway; a play in three acts. London. Heinemann. [1933] 104p.

Shining hour; a play in three acts. Garden City, N.Y. Doubleday. 1934. 12°. 156p. Melodrama
Same in Mantle, B. ed. Best plays of 1933-34 (abridged)

Witherspoon, Frances
Other room. Ethical. 1 act
In Poet Lore 38:269

Witter, Gilbert
King Henry the Seventh [The missing play]. A play in four acts. Oxford. Shakespeare Head press. 1933. 12°. 144p. Historical

Wodehouse, P. G. *See* Molnar, F. Play's the thing

Wolff, Pierre, 1865-
Faithful! a sentimental fragment. (Fidèle) 1 act
In Vernon, V. and F. eds. Modern one-act plays from the French

Woollcott, Alexander and Kaufman, George S.
Dark tower; a melodrama. N.Y. Random House. 1934. 8°. 170p. 3 acts

Woolley, Olive Frank
Sara. Biblical. 1 act
In Lewis, B. R. ed. University of Utah plays

Worcester, Laurence G.
"After you, I'm next"; a play in three acts. Boston. Baker. c1927. 12°. 118p.
Cat o' nine tails; a mystery play in three acts. Boston. Baker. c1927. 12°. 121p.
Pink pajamas; a farce comedy in three acts. Philadelphia. Penn. 1927. 12°

Wormwood, Edyth M.
Doll that saved an army; an historical play in four scenes. Boston. Baker. 1916. 24p.
Same in Johnson, T. ed. Plays about George Washington

Wylie, Lauri, 1880-
She was right
In Campion, C. et. al. Stage door; ten sketches for revue

Wyspianski, Stanislaw
Meleager; a tragedy. tr. from the Polish by Florence Noyes and G. R. Noyes. Berkeley, Cal. Univ. of Cal. press. 1933. 77p.

Yeats, Jack Butler, 1871-
Apparitions
In Apparitions
Old sea road
In Apparitions
Rattle
In Apparitions
Scourge of the gulph. Marionette. 3 scenes
In McPharlin, P. ed. Repertory of marionette plays

Yeats, William Butler, 1865-
Cat and the moon. Ireland. 1 act
In Criterion 2:395
Countess Cathleen. London. Union Famine. [1924] 12°. 118p. 4 acts
Land of heart's desire. Symbolic. 1 act
In Clark, B. H. ed. Representative one-act plays by British and Irish authors
On Baile's strand. Legendary. 1 act
In Canfield, C. ed. Plays of the Irish renaissance
Only jealousy of Emer. Legendary. 1 act
In Canfield, C. ed. Plays of the Irish renaissance
Pot of broth. Comedy. 1 act
In Marriott, J. B. ed. One-act plays of to-day. ser. 3

Yerkes, Robert G.
Their appointed rounds. Melodrama. 1 act
In Players book of one-act plays. ser. 1

Yevreinow, Nikolai Nikolayevich. *See* Evreinov, Nicolai Nicolaevich

York, George
Christmas by request. 1 act
In Curtis, A. ed. Christmas plays for one and all

Young, Francis Brett, 1884- **and Armstrong, William**
Furnace; a play in four acts. N.Y. Knopf. 1929. 12°. 140p. Economic war

Young, Francis Brett and Stirling, W. Edward
Captain Swing, a romantic play of 1830. London. Gollancz. c1919. 12°. 95p.

Young, Stark
Addio. Romantic. 1 act
In Clark, B. H. and Nicholson, K. eds. American scene
King with the iron heart. Juvenile. 1 act
In Moses, M. J. ed. Another treasury of plays for children
Queen of Sheba. Insanity. 1 act
In Isaacs, E. J. ed. Plays of American life and fantasy
Rose windows. Comedy. 1 act
In Isaacs, E. J. ed. Plays of American life and fantasy
Twilight saint, a play in one act. N.Y. French. c1925. 12°. 17p.
In Cohen, H. L. ed. One-act plays by modern authors. 1934 edition

Zorrilla y Moral, Jose, 1855-1931
Dagger of the Goth. Tragedy. 1 act
In Poet Lore 40:426

Zweig, Stefan, 1881-
Ben Jonson's Volpone, a loveless comedy in 3 acts, freely adapted by Stefan Zweig, and translated from the German by Ruth Langner. N.Y. Viking. 1928. 12°. 187p.

TITLE AND SUBJECT INDEX

Title and Subject Index

Abbé Prévost. Waddell, H.
Abelard and Heloise. Hulley, L.
Aboard a slow train. Hare, W. B.
About face. Hoffman, P.
Above all else, liberty. Stenger, G.
Abraham Lincoln—a pageant. Fielden, A. D.
Abraham Lincoln, rail-splitter. Mackay, C. D'A.
Abraham Lincoln's birthday. Mackay, C. D'A.
Abram in Egypt. Reznikoff, C.
Absent-minded lady. Campion, C.
Ace is trumped. Stinson, H. H.
Acoma. Masters, E. L.
Across the border. Clements, C. C.
Across the Jordan. Culbertson, E. H.
Acting version of the Green Hat. Arlen, M.
Actress and the count. Schnitzler, A.
Acts of Saint Peter. Bottomley, G.
Ada beats the drum. Kirkpatrick, J. A.
Ada Wodderspoon. Ould, H.
Adam. Lewisohn, L.
Adam and Eve. Hulley, L.
Adam and Eve. Porras, A.
Adam the creator. Čapek, K. and Čapek, J.
Adam's opera. Ashton, W.
Adding machine. Rice, E. L.
Addio. Young, S.
Admirable Bashville; or, Constancy rewarded. Shaw, G. B.
Admirable Crichton. Barrie, J. M.
Admiral. Kennedy, C. R.
Admiral Christopher. Price, O. M.
Adolescent young. Phelps, P.
Adrea. Belasco, D.
Advantages of being shy. Hoffman, P.
Adventures of grandpa. Hare, W. B.
Affair of "The Sea Gull." Osgood, E.
Affairs of Anatol. Schnitzler, A.
Affairs of men. Beck, W.
After all. Van Druten, J.
After all these years. Beck, W.
After Euripides' Electra. Baring, M.
After midnight. Daixel, S.
After the funeral. Perez, I. L.
"After you, I'm next." Worcester, L. G.
Aftermath. Pride, L. B.
Afternoon. Johnson, P.
Agatha. Toy, J.
Age of accountability. Boatright, M. C.
Age of discretion. Berman, H.
Agnes. Hulley, L.
Ahasverus. Heijermans, H.
Airways, inc. Dos Passos, J. R.
Akhnaton. Phillpotts, A. E.
Alabama bound. Hare, W. B.
Aladdin. DuBois, T.
Alarm clock. Hopwood, A.
Albert: Prince Consort. Huxley, A.
Alcestis. Hankin, St. J.

Alchemy
　Dunsany, E. Jest of Hahalaba
Ali Baba and the forty thieves. Joseph, H. H.
Ali the cobbler. Shepherd, M.
Alias the deacon. Hymer, J. B. and Clemens, L.
Alice in everydayland. Van Delden, E. H.
Alice in Wonderland. LeGallienne, E. and Friebus, F.
Alice-sit-by-the-fire. Barrie, J. M.
Alien corn. Howard, S. C.
Alison's house. Glaspell, S.
All alone in the country. Stevens, H. B.
All at sea. Sitwell, O. and Sitwell, S.
All God's chillun got wings. O'Neill, E.
All on a summer's day. Ryerson, F. and Clements, C.
All right on the night. Watling, E. F.
All the king's horses. Openshaw, C. E.
Allison's lad. Dix, B. M.
All's vanity. Holbrook, M.
Almost a honeymoon. Ellis, W. W.
Along came Ruth. Day, H. F.
Alphabet tree. Olcott, V.
Amaco. Flavin, M.
Amateur detective. Janney, S.
Amazed evangelist. Mavor, O. H.
Ambassador of Capripedia. Huxley, A.
Ambitious guest (N. Hawthorne). Hartley, R. E. and Power, C. M.
Ambush. Hughes, R.
Ambush. Whitehouse, J. H.
Amende honorable. Housman, L.
America on trial. Eastman, F.
America triumphant. Mackay, C. D'A.
American comedy. Lloyd, H. C.
American revolution
　Frank, B. Twelve thousand
America's unfinished battles. Eastman, F.
Amnesia
　Giraudoux, J. Siegfried
Among the nightingales. Huxley, A. L.
Amy Robsart. Hugo, V.
Anaesthesia
　Cummings, E. E. Him
　Thrush, A. Wisdom tooth
Ananias and Sapphira. Hulley, L.
Anatomist. Mavor, O. H.
And Billy disappeared. Hare, W. B.
And home came Ted. Hare, W. B.
. . . and points west. Toms, R.M.
And so ad infinitum. See Čapek, K. and Čapek, J. World we live in
And so to bed. Fagan, J. B.
And the devil laughs. Thurston, A.
And the sea shall give up its dead. Wilder, T.
Andalusia
　Alvarez Quintero, S. and J. Four plays
Androcles and the lion. Shaw, G. B.
Angel cake. O'Ryan, A. W.

Laying the devil.   Drinkwater, J.
Lazarus laughed.   O'Neill, E.
Lazy-bones.   Denny, E.
Leading-strings.   Housman, L.
Lean years.   Reely, M. K.
Leap year.   Hickson, L. M.
Leap year bride.   Hickson, L. M.
Learn to give by giving.   Raymond, M.
Leave it to Psmith.   Beith, J. H. and Wodehouse, P. G.
Leave-taking.   Molnár, F.
'Lection.   Conkle, E. P.
Lee.   Masters, E. L.
Lee, Robert Edward
　Bate, R. A.   Robert Edward Lee
Left bank.   Rice, E. L.
Left overs.   Bagg, H.
Legend.   Johnson, P.
Legend of Saint Nicholas.   Dix, B. M.
Lenna looks down.   Halman, D. F.
Leonce and Lena.   Büchner, G.
Leopard lady.   Carpenter, E. C.
Let and sub-let.   Stanley, M. M.
Let 'em eat cake.   Kaufman, G. S. and Ryskind, M.
Let it burn.   Van der Veer, E. and Bigelow, F.
Let us be gay.   Crothers, R.
Let's get rich.   Reed, M. W.
Letter.   Maugham, W. S.
Letters.   Booth, H.
Letters.   Ryerson, F. and Clements, C.
Letters.   Tompkins, F. G.
Level crossing.   Campion, C.
Leviathan.   Wilder, T.
Liar and the unicorn.   Hughes, B.
Liars.   Aleichem, S.
Liars!   Bimko, F.
Liars.   Jones, H. A.
Liddy.   Gregson, J. R.
Lidia.   Archer, W.
Lie.   O'Connell, W.
Lies.   Molnár, F.
Life demands!   Berman, H.
Life is a bowl of Eugene O'Neills.   Sullivan, F.
Life of the Christmas party.   Curtis, A.
Life on the steppes.   Hughes, G.
Lift that failed.   See Wilde, P.   Lost elevator
Lifting Jimmy's jinx.   Sharpteen, E. J.
Light and shade.   Peach, L. du G.
Light comedian.   Ould, H.
Light-o'-love.   Schnitzler, A.
Light of the women.   Gunner, F.
Light triumphant.   Stenger, G.
Lighted candles.   Bland, M. and Duls, L.
Lights of happyland.   Short, M.
'Lijah.   Smith, E. V.
Likely story.   Housman, L.
Likes of her.   McEvoy, C.
Liliom.   Molnár, F.
Liluli.   Rolland, R.
Lily among thorns.   Sierra, G. and M.
Lily maid of Shulem.   Hulley, L.
Lima beans.   Kreymborg, A.
Limping along.   Kreymborg, A.
Lincoln, Abraham
　Masters, E. L.   Gettysburg
　Price, O.   Black Congo
　Rogers, J. W.   Madame Surratt

Sanford, A. P. ed.   Lincoln plays.   For contents see Appendix B
Warren, P. and Hutchins, W.   Day that Lincoln died
Links.   Heijermans, H.
Little accident.   Dell, F. and Mitchell, T.
Little birds in their nests.   Titheradge, D.
Little bit of fluff.   Ellis, W. W.
Little black Sambo.   Kaufman, H. S.
Little brown jug.   Weeks, A. L.
Little damozel.   Hoffe, M.
Little deserter.   Raymond, M.
Little dream.   Galsworthy, J.
Little flower.   Doran, M.
Little general.   Holbrook, M.
Little girl blue.   Heyward, D. H. and De Jagers, D.
Little Lady Dresden.   Price, O. M.
Little liberty.   Brighouse, H.
Little man.   Galsworthy, J.
Little Miss Fortune.   George, C.
Little Mr. Clown.   Joseph, H. H.
Little Mrs. Cummin.   Pryce, R.
Little new moon.   Riley, A. C.
Little old gent.   Willis, R.
Little princess.   Burnett, F. H.
Little shadows.   Brown, A. F.
"Little Square-toes."   Field, R. L.
Little things.   McMullen, J. C.
Little town of Bethlehem.   Trask, K. N.
Little vegetable men.   Griffith, E. G.
Little village.   Francis, J. O.
Littlest shepherd.   Ryerson, F. and Clements, C.
Live and grow wise.   Pohl, F. J.
Live corpse.   Tolstoi, L. N.
Living hours.   Schnitzler, A.
Living together.   Sutro, A.
Livingston, David
　Ould, H.   Pathfinder
La locandiera.   Goldoni, C.
Lofty motives.   Weinberg, A.
Lombardi, ltd.   Hatton, F. and Hatton, F.
London wall.   Van Druten, J.
Londonderry air.   Field, R. L.
Lone worlds!   Hirschbein, P.
Lonely of heart.   Coates, D.
Long Christmas dinner.   Wilder, T. N.
Long lost father.   Stern, G. B.
Long shadows.   Johnson, P.
Long voyage home.   O'Neill, E.
Look to the end.   Marks, J. A.
Looking-glass.   Firkins, O. W.
Loop.   Ryerson, F. and Clements, C.
Loose ankles.   Janney, S.
Lord Adrian.   Dunsany, E.
Lord Ashton's triumph.   Hulley, L.
Lord of life.   Biddle, A.
Lord of the manor.   Turner, J. H.
Lord's prayer.   Coppée, F.
Lord's will.   Green, P.
Lost elevator.   Wilde, P.
Lost princess.   Totheroh, D.
Lost saint.   Hyde, D.
Lost silk hat.   Dunsany, E.
Lot's wife.   Wilde, P.
Lotus-eaters.   Hulley, L.
Louder please.   Krasna, N.
Love and grow wise.   Pohl, F. J.
Love and how to cure it.   Wilder, T. N.
Love and lather.   Kester, K.

Mirage. Hulley, L.
Mirthful marionettes. Totheroh, D.
Misalliance. Shaw, G. B.
Miser of Eaglesmere. Hulley, L.
Miser of Rogafjord. Ould, H.
Miss Ant, Miss Grasshopper, and Mr. Cricket. Field, R. L.
Miss Baxter. Fulton, M.
Miss Coolidge. Rothery, A. E.
Miss Efficiency. Toler, S.
Miss Manda. Taber, G. B.
Miss Oliver's dollars. Callaway, E. H.
Miss Somebody Else. Short, M.
Miss Tassey. Baker, E.
Missing words. Titheradge, D.
Mistake at the manor. Frank, M. M.
Mr. Faint-heart. Beith, J. H.
Mr. Fox. Ashton, W.
Mr. Goodman and Mrs. Gracious. Neuville, L. de
Mr. Grant. Goodrich, A. F.
Mr. Hopkinson. Critchett, R. C.
Mr. Kelley from Kalamazoo. Janney, S.
Mr. Man. Miller, L.
Mr. Moneypenny. Pollack, C.
Mr. Pepys. Bax, C.
Mr. Pim passes by. Milne, A. A.
Mr. Prohack. Bennett, A. and Knoblock, E.
Mister Punch. Clement, C.
Mr. Sampson. Lee, C. J.
Mr. Scrooge. Miller, A.
Mr. Strahan's dinner party. Newton, A. E.
Mr. Susan Peters. Ford, H.
Mistress. Gnesin, M.
Mrs. Adis. Kaye-Smith, S. and Hampden, J.
Mrs. Bright's visitor. Hatch, M. R.
Mrs. Bumpstead Leigh. Smith, H. J.
Mrs. Dane's defence. Jones, H. A.
Mrs. Dot. Maugham, W. S.
Mrs. Hazenby's heath. Brown, C.
Mrs. Larkin's lodger. Paull, H. M.
Mrs. Leicester's school. Hoffman, P.
Mrs. Moonlight. Levy, B. W.
Mis' Nelly of N' Orleans. Eyre, L.
Mrs. Noah gives the sign. Sladen-Smith, F.
Mrs. Pat and the law. Aldis, M.
Mistress Penelope. Marble, T. L.
Mrs. Siddons. Royde-Smith, N. G.
Mrs. Warren's profession. Shaw, G. B
Mrs. Waterbury's millennium. Mavor, O. H.
Mixed doubles. Stayton, F.
Mob. Galsworthy, J.
Modern David Garrick. Andreas, E.
Modern magi. Brown, C. S.
Modern viking. Sterling, F.
Mon ami Pierrot. Fitzhugh, C.
Money. Gold, M.
Money for nothing. Howard, F. M.
Monkey Doodle Do. Hulley, L.
Monkey's paw. Parker, L. N.
Monomaniac. Hulley, L.
Monsieur Beaucaire. Tarkington, B.
Monsieur Tytgat. Ring, L. B.

Monte Carlo. Hulley, L.
Montespan. Rolland, R.
Moon. Broome, D. M.
Moon and the moonstruck. Phelps, P.
Moon in the yellow river. Johnston, D.
Moon of the Caribbees. O'Neill, E.
Moon rides high. Ould, H.
Moonbeam. Granville, E.
Mooney-Billings case
Golden, I. J. Precedent
Moonshine. Hopkins, A.
Moral courage. Salten, F.
Morality play for the leisured class. Balderston, J. L.
Morality plays
Levy, B. W. Devil passes
Morals and circumstance. Bloch, B.
More about apples. Phipps, A. H.
Morning glory. Housman, L.
Mother
Van der Veer, E. Shipping mother east
Mother and son. Mellon, E. E.
Mother o' mine. Hulley, L.
Mother of Washington. Phillips, L.
Mothers of men. Wilde, P.
Mothers they forgot. Parsons, M.
Mount Vernon. Holbrook, M.
Mountain dew. Shiels, G.
Mountain laurel. Cooksey, C.
Mountain wedding. Franklin, P.
Mountains of Bether. Fitzhugh, C.
Mountebanks. Gilbert, W. S.
Mourning becomes Electra. O'Neill, E.
Mousetrap. Darmady, J.
Moving finger. Wilde, P.
Mozart and the gray steward. Wilder, T. N.
Much ado about nothing. Hankin, St. J.
Mud & treacle. Levy, B. W.
Multabello road. Raymond, E.
Murder in the foyer. Talbot, A. J.
Murder! murder! murder! Hughes, B.
Murder on the second floor. Vosper, F.
Murder trial. Box, S.
Murder will out. Winningham, C. C.
Music cure. Shaw, G. B.
Musical box. Mayor, B.
Musical chairs. Mackenzie, R.
Musicalia. Wilde, P.
Mutiny. Anderson, L.
My China doll. George, C.
My dear! O'Connor, P.
My Dixie Rose. Bennett, M. K.
My double and how he undid me (E. E. Hale). Hartley, R. E. and Power, C. M.
My Irish Cinderella. Spooner, C. and Blaney, C. E.
My lady Solomon. Titheradge, D.
My lady's lace. Knoblock, E.
My Lady's Yule-tide. Meaker, I. J. and Perkins, E. E.
My son. Stanley, M.
My son Josiah. Curtis, A.
Mysterious money. Ford, H.
Mystery man. Ankrum, M. and Duffey, V.

Pahlen, Petr Aleksieevich
  Neumann, A. The patriot
Painful necessity. Housman, L.
Palace of truth. Gilbert, W. S.
Palm Sunday. Rolland, R.
Pan and the nymphs. Hulley, L.
Pan in Pimlico. Simpson, H.
Pandora's box. Vallance, R.
Pantaloon. Barrie, J. M.
Pantomime
  Armstrong, L. Van V. Doctor of lonesome folk
Parachute. Bell, F. E. E.
Pardoner's tale. Mavor, O. H.
Paris and Œnone. Binyon, L.
Paris bound. Barry, P.
Parlor maid and the young man. Schnitzler, A.
Parlor matches. Hare, W. B.
Parting. Bottomley, G.
Parting. Peach, L. du G.
Passing of Chow Chow. Rice, E. L.
Passing of Galatea. Talbot, A. J.
Passing of the Essenes. Moore, G.
Passion, poison and petrifaction; or The fatal gazogene. Shaw, G. B.
Passion week: an Easter pageant. Weaver, G. N.
Passion's furnace. Kosor, J.
Paste pearls. Downey, T. H.
Pat Piper's place. Scribner, E.
Patchwork. Brandon-Thomas, J. and Barrett, F. W.
Patchwork quilt. Field, R. L.
Pathfinder. Ould, H.
Patience. Hankin, St. J.
Patriarch. Smith, B.
Patriot. Dukes, A.
Patriot. Neumann, A.
Patriotic pageant. Weaver, G. N.
Patriotism
  McFadden, E. and Crimmins, A. Man without a country
  MacKaye, P. Washington and Betsy Ross
Patsy. Conners, B.
Paul among the Jews. Werfel, F. V.
Paul and Thekla. Goold, M. N.
Paul Bunyan. Stokes, R. L.
Paul Felice. Monkhouse, A. N.
Paul Twyning. Shiels, G.
Pawns. Wilde, P.
Pay as you enter. George, C.
Peace and quiet. Álvarez Quintero, S. and J.
Peace at home. Courteline, G.
Peace-makers. Housman, L.
Peace of Ferrara. Merivale, P.
Peace on earth. Sklar, G. and Maltz, A.
Peaceful valley. Kidder, E. E.
Peach. Romains, J.
Peach tree road. Short, M.
Pearl thief. Phelps, G. H. and Pitkin, M. I.
Pearl-tree. Trevelyan, R. C.
Pearls. Totheroh, D.
Pearls before swine. Meadon, J.
Pearly gates. Jennings, G. E.
Pease and beans. Phelps, P.
Peculiar old duffer. MacMullen, J. C.
Pedagogue. Loving, B.
Pedro the toreador. Carter, M.

Peggy. Crothers, R.
Pélléas and Mélisande. Maeterlinck, M.
Pen-and-ink. Mellon, E. E.
Penelope. Maugham, W. S.
Penny for a guy! Macnamara, M.
Penny that beauty spent. Wilder, T. N.
People. Glaspell, S.
People like us. Vosper, F.
Pepys, Samuel
  Bax, C. Mr. Pepys
  Fagan, J. B. And so to bed
  Firkins, O. W. King's vigil
Perfect alibi. *See* Milne, A. A. Fourth wall
Perfect husband. Francis, J. O.
Perfect lover. Sutro, A.
Perfect marriage. White, L.
Perfect pattern. Van der Veer, E.
Perfect wife. Douglass, V.
La Périchole. Offenbach, J.
Permanent wave. Titheradge, D.
Person responsible. Howard, F. M.
Personal appearance. Riley, Laurence
Personally or by letter. Beith, J. H.
Peter Pan; or, The boy who would not grow up. Barrie, J.
Peter the pied piper. Ould, H.
Petrified forest. Sherwood, R. E.
Petroushka. Mitcoff, E. Y.
Phantasms. Bracco, R.
Phantom lover. Kaiser, G.
Phantom lover. *See* Molnár, F. Tale of the wolf
Phantom treasure. Edmonds, R.
Pharaoh's daughter. Gaw, A. and E. T.
Pharaoh's daughter. Kotzebue, A. von
Philanderer. Shaw, G. B.
Philip goes forth. Kelly, G. E.
Philosopher of Butterbiggins. Chapin, H.
Phoebe cleans house. Scribner, E.
Phosphorus. Molnár, F.
Photograph reveries. Wilson, N. G.
Picking a winner. Janney, S.
Picnic. Green, P.
Pie and the tart. Jagendorf, M. A.
Pierre. Scott, D. C.
Pierrot and Columbine on Little West Jones street. Jagendorf, M. A.
Pierrot before the seven doors. Cantillon, A.
Pierrot of the minute. Dowson, E.
Pierrot's mother. Hughes, G.
Pigeon. Galsworthy, J.
Pigeons and people. Cohan, G. M.
Piker. Gordon, L. and Palmer, R. A.
Pine hill. Brooks, C. S.
Pink and patches. Bland, M.
Pink pajamas. Worcester, L. G.
Pinkie and the fairies. Robertson, W. G.
Pipe in the fields. Murray, T. C.
Piper. Peabody, J. P.
Piper laughs. Ould, H.
Pipes of Pan; or, The call of spring. Carpenter, E. C.
Pirates. Campbell, C. C.
Pirates of Key West. Hulley, L.
Pirates of Penzance; or, The slave of duty. Gilbert, W. S.
Place in the world. Sternheim, C.
Playboy of the western world. Synge, J. M.

When Irish eyes are smiling. Schimmel, R. C.
When knighthood was in flower. Kester, P.
When ladies meet. Crothers, R.
When the dawn is come. MacDonagh, T.
When the horns blow. Van der Veer, E.
When the ship goes down. McGuire, H.
When the whirlwind blows. Dane, E.
When toys talk. Robertson, M. F.
When your ship comes in. Carpenter, E. C.
When's your birthday? Rouverol, A.
Where ignorance is bliss. See Molnár, F. Guardsman
Where innocence is bliss. Stanley, M. M. and Matthews, A.
Where the cross is made. O'Neill, E.
Where's Peter? Loring, E.
While shepherds watch. Peach, L. du G.
While the mushrooms bubble. Totheroh, D.
Whipped cream. Davidson, M. L.
Whispering pines. Schimmel, R. C.
White asters. Price, O. M.
White blackbird. Robinson, L.
White carnations. Booth, H.
White chateau. Berkeley, R. C.
White cloud. Molnár, F.
White collars. Ellis, E.
White dresses. Green, P.
White hawk. Kemp, H.
White jasmine. Talbot, A. J.
White supper. See Rostand, E. Two Pierrot's, or The white supper
White wings. Barry, P.
Whiteheaded boy. Robinson, L.
Whittle. Hughes, G.
Who am I? Pierce, C. W.
Who killed me? Chantel, L.
Who won the war? Mechem, K.
Who's boss? Toler, S.
Whose money? Dickson, L. and Hickson, L. M.
Why be lonely? Lowndes, M. A. B. and F. S. A.
Why marry? Williams, J. L.
Why the bachelor? McOwen, B. J.
Why the chimes rang. McFadden, E. A.
Wicked uncles. Housman, L.
Widdy's mite. Totheroh, D.
Widow. Bottomley, G.
Widow by proxy. Cushing, C. C.
Widow of Wasdale Head. Pinero, A.
Widower's houses. Shaw, G. B.
Widow's eyes. Alvarez Quintero, S. and J.
Widow's third. Hulley, L.
Widow's wiles. Callaway, E. H.
Wife to a famous man. Martínez Sierra, G.
Wild boar. O'Brien, S.
Wild Decembers. Ashton, W.
Wild Westcotts. Morrison, A.
Wilde, Oscar
  Cohen, L. Oscar Wilde
Will. Barrie, J. M.
Will Shakespeare. Ashton, W.

Willow-plate. Ryerson, F. and Clements, C.
Willow tree. Benrimo, J. H. and Rhodes, H. G.
Wills and ways. Glover, H.
Wilson, Woodrow
  Ashton, W. Adam's opera
Wily one. Monkhouse, A.
Wind and the rain. Hodge, M.
Wind in the south. Staadt, E.
Wind o' the moon. Peach, L. du G.
Windblown. Harris, F. M.
Windows. Galsworthy, J.
Wings. Peabody, J. P.
Wings over Europe. Nichols, R. M. B. and Browne, M.
Winners all. Ehrlich, I. L.
Winterfeast. Kennedy, C. R.
Winter's night. Boyce, N.
Wireless and sich-like. Hyde, F. A.
Wireless can't lie. Brighouse, H. and Walton, J.
Wisdom tooth. Connelly, M. C.
Wisdom tooth. Thrush, A.
Wise fool. Hulley, L.
Wish shop. Brighouse, H.
Wishing-moon. Brown, A. F.
Witch. Molnár, F.
Witchcraft
  Price, O. M. Lantern light
Witch's daughter. Brighouse, H.
With all John's love. Lowndes, M. A. B.
Within the gates. O'Casey, S.
Wolf at the door. Hanlon, D. E.
Wolf of Gubbio. Peabody, J. P.
Wollstonecraft, Mary
  Peabody, J. P. Portrait of Mrs. W.
Woman. Kosor, J.
Woman at the well. Hulley, L.
Woman forgives. Nicholson, K.
Woman from the voe. Bottomley, G.
Woman of it. Andreas, E.
Woman of no importance. Wilde, O.
Woman of Paris. See Beaque, H. La Parisienne
Woman proposes. Housman, L.
Woman who understood men. Kirkpatrick, J.
Woman's honor. Glaspell, S.
Women do things like that. Brighouse, H. and Walton, J.
Women-folks. Kirkpatrick, J. A.
Women folks. Rogers, J. W.
Women have their way. Alvarez Quintero, S. and J.
Women's town. See Alvarez Quintero, S. and J. Women have their way
Wonder watch of the Jura. Olcott, V.
Wonderful tourist. Sladen-Smith, F.
Wonderful Zoo. Sladen-Smith, F.
Wooden kimono. Floyd, J.
Wooden leg. Dane, E.
Woolly lamb of God. Bond, F. F.
Words and music. Nicholson, K.
Workers at the loom. Dane, E.
Workhouse ward. Gregory, I. A.
World of light. Huxley, A. L.

World War
    Harnwell, A. J. and Meaker, I. J.   Knife
    Pilcher, V.   Searcher
    Price, O. M.   White asters
    Raynal, P.   Unknown warrior
    Roberts, C. E. B. and Forester, C. S.
      Nurse Cavell
    Sherriff, R. C.   Journey's end
    Wilde, P.   Mothers of men
World we live in.   Čapek, J. and K.
Worm.   Loving, B.
Worship the Nativity.   Farrar, J. C.
Would-be-gentleman.   Gregory, I. A.
Wozzeck.   Büchner, G.
Written on foolscap.   Titheradge, D.
Wrong door.   Housman, L.
Wurzel-Flummery.   Milne, A. A.
X-O: a night of the Trojan war.   Drink-
    water, J.
Xanthippe and Socrates.   Baring, M.
Yella.   McGuire, H.
Yellow fever
    Howard, S. C.   Yellow jack
Yellow jack.   Howard, S. C.
Yellow sands.   Phillpotts, E. and A. E.
Yeoman of the guard; or, The merryman
    and his maid.   Gilbert, W. S.
Yes and no.   Bates, A.
Yes, yes! go on.   Andreas, E. and Hurrie,
    J.

Yesterday.   Macnamara, M.
Yesterday's roses.   Larrimore, L.
Yolanda of Cyprus.   Rice, C. Y.
You and I.   Barry, P.
You never can tell.   Shaw, G. B.
Young Hale of Connecticut.   Price, O. M.
Young idea.   Coward, N. P.
Young Leonardo.   Tuttle, R. C.
Young love.   Roberts, C.
Young man and husband.   Schnitzler, A.
Young man and the young wife.   Schnitz-
    ler, A.
Young man with the cream tarts (R. L.
    Stevenson).   Hartley, R. E. and
    Power, C. M.
Young Washington at Mt. Vernon.   Mac-
    Kaye, P.
Young Woodley.   Van Druten, J.
Your kind indulgence.   Farjeon, H.
Your Uncle Dudley.   Lindsay, H. and
    Robinson, B.
Your uncle Dudley.   Paulton, E.
Yours unfaithfully.   Malleson, M.
Youth disposes.   Gregson, J. R.
Youth's highway.   Mackay, C. D'A.
Zara the great.   Titheradge, D.
Zee-Zee.   Murray, A.
Zombi.   Scott, N. V.
Zoo.   Arlen, M. and Smith, W.

APPENDIX

APPENDIXES

APPENDIX A

BOOKS BY ONE AUTHOR CONTAINING MORE THAN ONE PLAY

NOTE.—Single plays are not entered in this list. Full bibliographical information in regard to them may be found in the Author Index.

Alehin, Alexander Fedor
First sins and other one-act plays. Boston Expression Co. c1927 12° 95p

Álvarez Quintero, Serafín and Álvarez Quintero, Joaquín
Four comedies . . . in English versions by Helen and Harley Granville-Barker. N.Y. French 1932 12° 311p
Four plays . . . in English versions by Helen and Harley Granville-Barker. London Sidgwick 1927 12°

Anderson, Lee
Ten one act plays. N.Y. McKee 1928 194p

Anderson, Maxwell and Hickerson, Harold
Gods of the lightning. . . Outside looking in. N.Y. Longmans 1928 12° 187p

Andreas, Eulalie
Four one-act comedies. Hollywood, Cal. Playworker's studio [1924] 12° 80p

Archer, William
Three plays. . . . with a personal note by Bernard Shaw. London Constable [1927] 8° 268p

Ashton, Winifred
Recapture, a Clemence Dane (pseud) omnibus. London Heinemann 1932 12° 1283p

Atlas, Leopold
Wednesday's child and House we live in; two plays. N.Y. French 1934 12° 280p

Barrie, Sir James Matthew
Plays of J. M. Barrie, in one volume. N.Y. Scribner 1929 8° 871p
Shall we join the ladies? London Hodder 1929 12° 128p

Bax Clifford
Twelve short plays, serious and comic. London Gollancz 1932 12° 256p
Valiant ladies, three new plays. . . [London] Gollancz 1931 12° 320p

Beck, Warren
Six little theatre plays. Boston Baker [c1931] 12° 191p

Behrman, Samuel N.
Three plays. . . N.Y. Farrar c1934 12° 335p

Belasco, David
Six plays: Madame Butterfly, DuBarry, The darling of the gods, Adrea, The girl of the golden West: The return of Peter Grimm. . . Boston Little 1928 8° 503p

Bell, Florence E. E.
Four short plays. London Humphreys 1922 12° 104p

Bennett, Arnold
Three plays. London Chatto 1931 12° 117, 148, 179p

Berman, Henry
Life demands! and other plays. N.Y. Brentano's 1931 12° 362p

Biddle, (Frederick) Arnold
Two plays. N.Y. Macmillan 1933 62p

Binyon, Lawrence
Three short plays. . . London Sidgwick 1930 12° 46p

Bottomley, Gordon
Lyric plays. N.Y. Macmillan 1932 12° 166p
A parting and The return. N.Y. Macmillan 1928 12° 20p
Scenes and plays. N.Y. Macmillan 1929 8° 122p

Brandane, John, pseud. See MacIntyre, John

Bridie, James, pseud. See Mavor, Osborne Henry

Brighouse, Harold
Six fantasies. N.Y. French [1931] 12° 155p

Brody, Alter
Lamentations; four folkplays of the American Jew. . . N.Y. Coward-McCann 1928 8° 89p

Brooks, Charles Stephen
Tragedy of Josephine, and other one-act plays. N.Y. Harcourt 1931 12° 217p

Brown, Abbie Farwell
Lantern and other plays for children. Boston Houghton 1928 8° 152p

Büchner, Georg
Plays of Georg Büchner with an introduction by Geoffrey Dunlop. N.Y. Viking press 1928 12° 274p

Chekhov, A. P.
Plays of Anton Tchekov; tr. by Constance Garnett. . . N.Y. Modern library [1930] 12° 300p

Conkle, E. P.
Crick Botton plays; five mid-western sketches. N.Y. French 1928 12° 99p

Coward, Noel Pierce
Bitter sweet and other plays. . . Garden City, N.Y. Doubleday 1929 8° 314p
Collected sketches and lyrics. Garden City, N.Y. Doubleday 1932 8° 270p
Home chat, Sirocco, [and] "This was a man"; three plays with a preface. London Secker 1928 8° 271p
Play parade. Garden City, N.Y. Doubleday 1933 8° 576p
Plays of Noel Coward. First series. . . Garden City, N.Y. Doubleday 1928 8° 266p

Curtis, Agnes
Christmas comedies; a collection of one-act Christmas plays for teen-age young people. . . Chicago Denison c1927 12° 168p

Dearden, Harold
Three short plays. London Heinemann 1927 12° 69p

De la Roche, Mazo
Low life and other plays. Boston Little 1929 12° 109p

Dix, Beulah M.
Legend of Saint Nicholas and other plays. N.Y. French [c1927] 12° 266p

Dos Passos, John
Three plays. N.Y. Harcourt 1934 12° 298p

Dukes, Ashley
Five plays of other times. . . London Benn 1931 8°

Dunsany, Lord Edward
Seven modern comedies. N.Y. Putnam 1928 12° 126p

Eastman, Fred
Plays of American life. N.Y. French 1934 8° 258p

Edmonds, Randolph
Shades and shadows. Boston Meador 1930 8° 171p

Ervine, St. John Greer
Four one-act plays. . . N.Y. Macmillan 1928 12° 95p

Farjeon, Herbert
Happy New Year, a hard-hearted revue sketch in one act, and Your kind indulgence, a sketch in one act. London French [c1929] 12° 21p

Farrar, John Chipman
Indoor and outdoor plays for children, including The Magic sea shell. . . N.Y. Noble [c1933] 12° 201p. Published in 1923 under title: Magic sea shell and other plays for children

Feuchtwanger, Lion
Two Anglo-Saxon plays: The Oil Islands, Warren Hastings. . . tr. by Willa and Edwin Muir. N.Y. Viking 1928 12° 241p

Field, Rachel Lyman
Cross-stitch heart, and other plays. N.Y. Scribner 1927 12° 177p
Patchwork plays. . . Garden City, N.Y. Doubleday 1930 12° 139p

Firkins, Oscar W.
Bride of quietness, and other plays. Minneapolis. University of Minnesota press [c1932] 12° 241p
Revealing moment, and other plays. Minneapolis. University of Minnesota press [c1932] 12° 302p
Two passengers for Chelsea, and other plays. N.Y. Longmans 1928 8° 300p

Fitzhugh, Carroll
Mon ami Pierrot, and other plays. Boston Houghton 1928 8° 255p

Folmsbee, B.
Guki the moon boy, and other plays. . . N.Y. Harcourt [c1928] 8° 155p

Frank, F. K.
Three plays for a children's theatre. . . N.Y. Vinal 1926 12° 128p

Fyleman, Rose
Eight little plays for children. N.Y. Doran [c1925] 8° 94p

Galsworthy, John
Plays. London Duckworth 1929 8° 1150p
Plays. N.Y. Scribner 1928 8° 698p
Plays: seventh series: Escape, Exiled, The roof. London Duckworth [1930] 12° 100, 118, 129p

Garnett, Edward
Trial of Jeanne d'Arc, and other plays; with a foreword by John Galsworthy. N.Y. Viking 1931 12° 304p

Geddes, Virgil
Earth between and Behind the night, two plays. . . N.Y. French 1930 12° 226p
Four comedies from the life of George Emery Blum. Brookfield, Conn. Brookfield Players 1934 8° 166p
Native ground; a cycle of plays. N.Y. French 1932 12° 170p

Gerstenberg, Alice
Comedies all; short plays. N.Y. Longmans 1930 12° 238p

Gilbert, Sir William Schwenck
Best known works of W. S. Gilbert. . . N.Y. Illustrated Editions Co. [c1932] 8° 232p
Mikado, and other operas, with an introduction by Walter Prichard Eaton. N.Y. Macmillan 1929 12° 205p
New and original extravaganzas. . . Edited by Isaac Goldberg. Boston Luce [1931] 12° 180p
Plays and poems of W. S. Gilbert with a preface by Deems Taylor. . . N.Y. Random House 1932 12° 1218p
Savoy operas, being the complete text of the Gilbert and Sullivan operas as originally produced in the years 1875-1896. . . London Macmillan 1927 12° 698p

Glaspell, Susan
Trifles, and six other short plays (two of them written in collaboration with George Cram Cook). London Benn 1926 12° 150p

Glover, Halcott
Three comedies. . . London Routledge 1928 12° 256p
Wat Tyler, and other plays. N.Y. Viking 1927 12° 341p

Gogól, Nikolaí Vasíle'vich
The gamblers, and Marriage; tr. by Alexander Berkman. N.Y. Macauley Co. [c1927] 8° 210p
Government inspector, and other plays; tr. by Constance Garnett. N.Y. Knopf 1927 8° 288p

Green, Paul
House of Connelly and other plays. . . N.Y. French 1931 8° 308p
In the valley, and other Carolina plays. N.Y. French 1928 8° 308p
Lord's will, and other Carolina plays. . . N.Y. Holt 1925 12° xiii,264p

Gregory, Lady Isabella Augusta
Three last plays. N.Y. Putnam 1928 12° 280p

Gregson, James R.
The way of an angel, and other plays. London Schofield c1928 12° 144p

Hankin, St. J.
Dramatic sequels. N.Y. Minton 1926 12° 193p

Hartley, Roland English and Power, Caroline Marguerite
Short plays from great stories. N.Y. Macmillan 1928 12° 230p

Hemingway, Ernest
Men without women. N.Y. Scribner 1927 12° 232p [all are stories except Today is Friday]

Herne, James A.
Shore Acres and other plays. N.Y. French 1928 12°

Hodge, William Thomas
Plays. N.Y. French 1928 12° 2v

Housman, Laurence
Comments of Juniper; six plays from the life and legend of St. Francis of Assisi. . . London Sidgwick 1926 12° 99p
Palace plays. London Cape [1930] 12° 125p
Queen's progress. Palace plays (second series). London Cape [1932] 12° 160p
Victoria and Albert. Palace plays (third series). London Cape c1933 12° 191p
Ways and means; five one-act plays of village characters. London Deane n.d. 12° [72p]

Ye fearful saints! Plays of creed, custom and credulity. London Sidgwick [1932] 12° 157p

Howard de Walden, Thomas Evelyn Scott-Ellis
Five pantomimes. London E. Mathews 1930 8° 202p

Hughes, Glenn
New plays for mummers; ten dramatic burlesques. Seattle University of Washington Bookstore 8° 162p

Hughes, Richard Arthur Warren
Sisters' tragedy, and three other plays. London Heinemann 1924 12° 159p

Hulley, Lincoln
Dramas, in twenty volumes. Copyrighted by Lincoln Hulley. 1934. E. O. Painter printing co. Deland, Fla.

Jagendorf, M. A.
Pantomimes for the children's theatre. . . N.Y. Brentano's [c1926] 8° 239p

Johnson, Philip
Four plays; with a foreword by William Armstrong. London Benn c1929 228p

Johnston, Denis
Moon in the yellow river, and The old lady says "No!"; two plays. . . London Cape [1932] 12° 272p

Joseph, Helen (Haiman)
Ali Baba, and other plays for young people and puppets. . . N.Y. Harcourt [c1927] 12° 150p

Kaye-Smith, Sheila
Saints in Sussex; poems and plays. N.Y. Dutton [1927] 8° 135p

Kaye-Smith, Sheila and Hampden, John
Mrs. Adis, a tragedy in one act; with The mockbeggar, a comedy in one act. London. Nelson. [c1929]. 12°. 52p.

Kennedy, Charles Rann
Repertory of plays for a company of seven players and two short plays for smaller casts. Chicago Univ. of Chicago Press 1930 8° 698p
Repertory of plays for a company of three players. . . Chicago Univ. of Chicago Press [c1927] 8° 183p
Repertory of plays for a company of three players. v. 2 . . Chicago. Univ. of Chicago Press [c1933] 8° 219p

Lawson, John Howard
With a reckless preface; two plays. . . N.Y. Farrar 1934 12° 221p

Lenormand, Henry René
Three plays. . . London Gollancz 1928 12° 360p

Levy, B. W.
Art and Mrs. Bottle; and Mrs. Moonlight. N.Y. French 1932 12° 230p

Lloyd, R. E.
Two African plays. N.Y. Longmans 1932 184p

McFadden, Elizabeth Apthorp
Why the chimes rang and other plays for church and school. N.Y. French [1929] 8° 42p

MacIntyre, John (John Brandane, pseud.)
Glen is mine, and The lifting; two plays of the Hebrides. Boston Houghton [19- ?] 12° 236p
Treasure ship, Rory aforesaid, and The happy war; three plays. Boston Houghton 1928 12° 248p

Mackay, Constance D'Arcy
Youth's highway, and other plays for young people. . . N.Y. Holt c1929 12° 165p

MacKaye, Percy
Kentucky mountain fantasies; three short plays for an Appalachian theatre. N.Y. Longmans 1928 8° 173p

McMullen, J. C.
Evening of plays for men. An evening's entertainment of four one-act plays to be presented by an all male cast. Boston Baker [1930] 12° 55p

Marks, Jeannette Augustus
Merry, merry cuckoo, and other Welsh plays. N.Y. Appleton 1927 12° 226p

Martínez Sierra, Gregorio
Cradle song and other plays in English versions with an introduction by John Garrett Underhill. N.Y. Dutton 1929 8° 241p
Kingdom of God and other plays . . . in English versions with an introduction by Helen and Harvey Granville-Barker. N.Y. Dutton 1929 8° 297p

Masters, Edgar Lee
Gettysburg, Manila, Acoma. N.Y. Liveright 1930 12° 219p

Maugham, William Somerset
Plays. London Heinemann 1911 12° 2v

Mavor, Osborne Henry (James Bridie, pseud.)
Anatomist; Tobias and the angel; Amazed evangelist. London Constable 1931 12° 200p
Switchback; Pardoner's tale; Sunlight Sonata. Three plays. London Constable 1931 12° 155p

Mayor, Beatrice
Four plays for children. Oxford Blackwell 1926 12° 71p

Mellon, Evelyn Emig
Two prize plays and four others, each in one act. Boston Baker 1929 12° 141p

Milne, Alan Alexander
Four plays. N.Y. Putnam 1932 12° 272p

Molnár, Ferenc
Plays of Ferenc Molnár with a foreword by David Belasco. N.Y. Macy-Masius c1929 8° 823p
Plays of Molnár. English texts and introduction by Benjamin F. Glazer. London Jarrolds [1927] 8° 312p

Moore, Frank Frankfort
Kitty Clive, and other plays in one act. London Black 1929 12° 103p

Munro, Hector Hugh (Saki, pseud.)
Novels and plays of Saki. . . N.Y. Viking 1933 12° 452p
Square egg and other sketches with three plays. . . with a biography by his sister and an introduction by J. C. Squire. N.Y. Viking 12° 276p

Odets, Clifford
Three plays: Awake and sing; Waiting for Lefty; Till the day I die. N.Y. Random House 1935 12° 114,54,74p Also issued in 2 volumes pa.
Waiting for Lefty, and Till the day I die. N.Y. Random House 1935

Olcott, Virginia
Household plays for young people. N.Y. Dodd 1928 12° 275p
Industrial plays for young people. . . N.Y. Dodd 1927 12° 257p

O'Neill, E. G.
Nine plays, selected by the author. . . N.Y. Liveright 1932 8° 867p

Peabody, Josephine Preston
Collected plays of Josephine Preston Peabody (Mrs. Lionel S. Marks). . . Boston Houghton 1927 8° 790p

Peach, L. du Garde
Ever ready plays; may be acted without a stage, scenery, memorizing or rehearsing. N.Y. French c1926 12° 53p
More ever ready plays. . . N.Y. French c1926 12° 46p

Phillpotts, Eden
Three short plays. London Duckworth [1928] 16° 87p

Phillpotts, Eden and Phillpotts, Adelaide
Devonshire plays. . . London Duckworth [1927] 12° 124, 110, 143p

Pirandello, Luigi
One-act plays; ed. by Arthur Livingston. . . N.Y. Dutton 1928 12° 230p

Pohl, Frederick Julius
When things were new; nine plays. Brooklyn, N.Y. 1925 8° 206p

Price, Olive M.
Short plays from American history and literature. v. 1. N.Y. French 1925 12° 245p
Short plays from American history and literature. v. 2. N.Y. French 1928 257p

Pride, Leo Bryan
Shadow of the mine, and other plays of the coalfields. N.Y. French 1929 12° 181p

Ratcliffe, Mrs. Dorothy Una (Clough)
Blind man of Hiltune, and two other plays. N.Y. French c1930 12° 53p

Raymond, Sister Mary
Easy plays for amateurs. Caldwell, N.J. Sisters of St. Dominic 1933 12° 123p

Reznikoff, Charles
Chatterton, The black death, and Meriwether Lewis; three plays. [New York?] c1922 12° 44p
Coral, and Captive Israel; two plays. [New York city. For sale at the Sunwise turn] c1923 12° 40p
Nine plays. N.Y. Reznikoff [c1927] 8° 113p

Rice, Cale Young
Selected plays and poems. London Hodder [c1926] 8° 786p

Rice, E. E.
Plays of Elmer Rice. . . London Gollancz 1933 447p

Riggs, Lynn
Sump'n like wings, and A lantern to see by. N.Y. French 1928 12°

Ring, Mrs. Lina Barbara
Three plays under three flags. . . Boston Baker 1928 12° 117p

Robins, Gertrude
Loving as we do, and other plays. London Laurie [1914?]

Robinson, Lennox
Plays. N.Y. Macmillan 1928 12° 455p
White blackbird, and Portrait. Dublin Talbot press [1926] 12° 128p

Rolland, Romain
Plays of Romain Rolland. London Jarrolds [1927] 8° 252p

Ryerson, Florence and Clements, Colin
All on a summer's day, and six other short plays. N.Y. French 1928 12° 123p

Saki, pseud. See Munro, Herbert Hugh

Salaman, Dora Clement
Tale of a cat and other plays. London G. Allen [1931] 12° 27, 32, 27, 30p

Sand, Maurice
Maurice Sand's plays for marionettes, translated by Babette and Glenn Hughes. N.Y. French 1931 8° 103p

Schnitzler, Arthur
Hands around (Reigen). A cycle of ten dialogues. N.Y. Privately printed for members of the Schnitzler Society. 1929 8° 223p
Reigen, The affairs of Anatol and other plays. . . N.Y. Modern library 1933 316p

Seiler, Conrad
Husband of Xanthippe, and other short plays. Boston Baker [c1929] 12° 144p

Shaw, George Bernard
Complete plays of Bernard Shaw. . . London Constable [c1931] 8° 1131p
Short stories, scraps and shavings. N.Y. Dodd 1934 12° 305p
Too true to be good, Village wooing, and On the rocks. Three plays. N.Y. Dodd 1934 12° 343p
Translations and tomfooleries. N.Y. Brentano's 1926 12° 276p

Shiels, George
Professor Tim, and Paul Twyning; comedies in three acts. London Macmillan 1927 12° 222p
Two Irish plays: Mountain dew, a play in three acts and Cartney and Kevney, a comedy in three acts. . . London Macmillan 1930 12° 222p

Sowerby, Githa
Little plays for little people. . . N.Y. Hodder [1911] 8° 90p

Strindberg, August
Easter and other plays. London Cape 1929 8° 35p
Lucky Peter's travels and other plays. London Cape [1930] 8° 319p
Master Olof, and other plays. London Cape n.d. 12° 319p

Synge, John Millington
Plays. London G. Allen [1932] 35p

Talbot, Francis X.
Shining in darkness; dramas of the nativity and the resurrection. N.Y. Longmans 1932 12° 153p Pt. I. Born in Bethlehem. Pt. II. He is risen: Easter scenes

Thompson, Edward John
Plays and pageants. London Benn [1931] 12° 109p

Thompson, Edward John and Thompson, Theodosia
Three eastern plays, with a terminal essay on "Suttee" by Edward and Theodosia Thompson. London Allen [1927] 12° 128p

Titheradge, Dion
Behind the curtain. N.Y. French c1926 8° 81p
From "Folly to be wise." N.Y. French c1931 8° 80p
Written on foolscap. N.Y. French c1933 8° 46p

Totheroh, Dan
One-act plays for everyone. N.Y. French 1931 12° 2115p

Trevelyan, R. C.
Three plays: Sulla, Fand, The pearl tree. London Woolf 1931 12° 119p

Weaver, Mrs. Gustine Nancy (Courson)
  Hop-Run, and six other pageants. Cincinnati
    Powell & White 1927 12° 91p
Wilde, Percival
  One-act plays of Percival Wilde. First series.
    Ed. by J. W. Marriott. . . London Harrap
    [1933] 272p
  Ten plays for little theatres. Boston Little 1931
    12° 259p
  Three minute plays: Innocentia, Musicalia, Im-
    moralia. N.Y. Greenberg [c1927]

Wilder, Thornton
  Angel that troubled the waters, and other plays.
    N.Y. Coward-McCann 1928 8° 149p
  Long Christmas dinner and other plays in one
    act. N.Y. Coward-McCann 1931 8° 122p
Willis, Richard
  Four playlets. . . N.Y. R. Willis c1928 12° 69p
  Six playlets. . . N.Y. R. Willis [c1928] 12° 109p
Yeates, Jack Butler
  Apparitions, three plays. London Cape [1933]
    12° 157p

APPENDIX B

COLLECTIONS OF PLAYS BY MORE THAN ONE AUTHOR

Baker, George Pierce, ed.
Yale one-act plays. N.Y. French 1930 8° 204p
Contents:
Gnesin, M. Mistress
Ruthenburg, G. D. Han's Bulow's last puppet
Humphrey, M. Immersion
McGuire, H. Yella
Conkle, E. P. Minnie Field
Atlas, L. L. "L"

Block, Etta, tr.
One-act plays from the Yiddish. Second series
. . . authorized translation by Etta Block.
N.Y. Bloch 1929 12° 123p
Contents:
Hirschbein, P. Bebele
Hirschbein, P. Lone worlds!
Peretz, I. L. After the funeral
Raisin, A. Brothers
Bimko, F. Liars!
Peretz, I. L. Of an early morning
Peretz, I. L. Sisters

Bourne, John, ed.
8 new one-act plays for 1934. London Dickson
[1934] 12° 211p
Contents:
Bridie, J. Mrs. Waterbury's millennium
Sladen-Smith, F. C. Happy death, ltd.
Box, S. Fantastic flight
Coates, D. Lonely of heart
Grant, N. Hat trick
Kallas, A. Bath-sheba of Saaremaa
Popplewell, O. Pacifist
Bourne, J. Black night
8 new one-act plays of 1933. London Lovat Dickson
c1933 12° 160p
Contents:
Bax, C. Quaker's 'cello
Roberts, C. Last rib
Box, S. Symphonie pathétique
Sladen-Smith, F. Assyrian afternoon
Thrush, A. Wisdom tooth
Bourne, J. Puck's good deed for the day
Hepworth, F. A. Queen Dick
Coates, D. In our stars
Eight new plays for boys and girls. London
Dickson [1934] 12° 184p
Contents:
Sladen-Smith, F. Wonderful tourist
Gow, R. Miracle of Watling street
Hsiung, S. I. Mencius was a bad boy
Carter, M. Pedro the toreador
Watts, B. Princess and the players
Douglas, E. Green broom
Pellerin, J. Forgotten room
Bourne, J. Down the Crocus tunnel

Campion, Cyril, 1894-, Watling, E. F. and Wylie, Lauri, 1880-
Stage door, ten sketches for revue. N.Y. French
c1932 74p
Contents:
Campion, C. Absentminded lady
Campion, C. Editorial error
Campion, C. Oh! Mathilda!
Campion, C. Reformation
Campion, C. Level crossing
Watling, E. F. French as she is learnt
Watling, E. F. All right on the night
Watling, E. F. Community drama
Wylie, L. She was right

Canfield, Curtis, ed.
Plays of the Irish renaissance, 1880-1930. N.Y.
Ives Washburn 12° 436p
Contents:
Yeats, W. B. On Baile's strand
Yeats, W. B. Only jealousy of Emer
Russell, G. W. Deirdre
Gregory, I. A. Hyacinth Halvey
Hyde, D. Twisting of the rope
Fitzmaurice, G. Dandy dolls
Synge, J. M. Riders to the sea
Colum, P. Land
Murray, T. C. Birthright
Pearse, P. Singer
Martyn, E. Maeve
O'Casey, S. Juno and the paycock
Robinson, L. Big house

Chandler, Frank W. and Cordell, Richard A. eds.
Twentieth century plays. N.Y. Nelson 1934 8°
790p
Contents:
Pinero, A. W. Thunderbolt
Jones, H. A. Dolly reforming herself
Hankin, St. J. Last of the De Mullins
Ervine, St. J. John Ferguson
Sherriff, R. C. Journey's end
Robinson, L. Far-off hills
Coward, N. Private lives
Maugham, S. Breadwinner
Anderson, M. and Stallings, L. What price glory
O'Neill, E. Marco Millions
Rice, E. Street scene
Connelly, M. Green pastures
Crothers, R. As husbands go
Tolstoy, L. Live corpse
Lenormand, H. R. Coward
Chlumberg, Hans. Miracle at Verdun
Molnár, F. Swan
Čapek, K. and J. And so ad infinitum
Pirandello, L. Each in his own way

Church, Mrs. Virginia Woodson
Curtain! A book of modern plays. N.Y. Harper
1932 12° 504p
Contents:
Bennett, A. Great adventure
Milne, A. A. Great Broxopp
O'Neill, E. Emperor Jones
Nichols, R. and Brown, M. Wings over Europe
Green, P. Man who died at twelve o'clock
MacKaye, P. Napoleon crossing the Rockies
Wilder, T. N. Angel on the ship
Dunsany, Lord. Lost silk hat
Morley, C. Good theatre
Church, V. What men live by
Millay, E. St. V. Aria da capo

Clark, Barrett H. and Cook, Thomas R. eds.
One-act plays. Boston Heath 1929 12° 288p
Contents:
Conkle, E. P. Sparkin'
Norris, K. and Totheroh, D. Kelly kid
Riggs, L. Knives from Syria
O'Neill, E. Ile
Rogers, J. W. Saved
Shayer, J. D. Resignation of Bill Snyder
Green, P. No 'count boy
Nicholson, K. and Pendray, G. E. Organ
Field, R. Bargains in Cathay
Gold, M. Money
Hughes, B. Backstage
O'Dea, M. Song of Solomon

Clark, Barrett Harper and Nicholson, Kenyon, eds.
American scene . . N.Y. Appleton 1930 8°
694p
Contents:
Field, R. Greasy luck
O'Neill, E. Bound east for Cardiff
MacKaye, P. Chuck
Clark, J. A. Quarry
Dransfield, J. Blood o' kings
Crocker, B. Last straw
Gold, M. Money
Brooks, G. S. No cause for complaint
Halvey, P. Wanderlust
Dreiser, T. Girl in the coffin
Baumer, M. Town
Green, P. No 'count boy
Smith, E. V. 'Lijah
Cornelius, O. F. Tie that binds
Rogers, J. W. Bumblepuppy
Walker, S. Medicine show
Levinger, E. E. Cow with wings
Tarkington, B. Trysting place
Ferber, E. Eldest
Ilsley, S. M. Feast of the holy innocents
Pride, L. B. Barbarians
Eastman, F. Bread
Glaspell, S. Trifles
Conkle, E. P. Minnie Field
Carver, A. J. Cajun
Young, S. Addio
Shaver, J. D. Resignation of Bill Snyder
Riggs, L. Reckless

Clark and Nicholson. American scene—*Cont.*
Clements, C. Across the border
Pendray, G. E. Organ
Mack, O. Last day for grouse
Culbertson, E. H. End of the trail
Pieratt, A. Day's end
Totheroth, D. Good vintage

Cohen, Helen Louise, ed.
One-act plays by modern authors. N.Y. Harcourt 1934 (enlarged ed.) 12° 539p
Contents:
Rogers, R. E. Boy Will
O'Neill, E. Ile
Downs, O. Maker of dreams
Dowson, E. Pierrot of the minute
Brighouse, H. Maid of France
MacKaye, P. Gettysburg
Gregory, A. Spreading the news
Synge, J. Riders to the sea
Marks, J. Welsh honeymoon
Dunsany, E. Night at the inn
Milne, A. A. Wurzel-Flummery
Young, S. Twilight saint
Maeterlinck, M. Intruder
Egerton, Alix. Masque of the two strangers
Galsworthy, J. Little man
Peabody, J. P. Fortune and men's eyes
Tarkington, B. Beauty and the Jacobins
Chekhov, A. Proposal
Brooks, C. S. Old trouper
Kelly, G. Flattering word
Wilder, T. N. Mozart and the gray steward

Cordell, Richard Albert, ed.
Representative modern plays; British and American, from Robertson to O'Neill. N.Y. Nelson 1929 8° 654p
Contents:
Robertson, T. W. Caste
Gilbert, W. S. Sweethearts
Wilde, O. Woman of no importance
Jones, H. A. Mrs. Dane's defence
Pinero, A. W. Iris
Bennett, A. Great adventure
Dane, C. Bill of divorcement
Maugham, W. S. Circle
Milne, A. A. Success
O'Casey, S. Juno and the paycock
Fitch, C. Climbers
Ade, G. College widow
Crothers, R. Expressing Willie
Hughes, H. Hell bent fer heaven
Kaufman, G. S. and Connelly, M. Beggar on horseback
O'Neill, E. Diff'rent

Curtis, Agnes, ed.
Christmas plays for one and all; a collection of one-act plays for all ages, from primary grades to the teen ages. Chicago Denison 1930 12° 183p
Contents:
Morris, H. Book children's Christmas
Curtis, A. Bringing up the Christmas baby
York, G. Christmas by request
Curtis, A. Christmas comes but once a year
Curtis, A. Christmas secret
Wadhams, N. M. Fat, jolly old man
Curtis, A. Is there a Santa Claus?
Curtis, A. My son Josiah
Curtis, A. Santa Claus messenger
Clough, G. E. Santa Claus on trial

Dickinson, Thomas H. ed.
Chief contemporary dramatists. Third series. Boston Houghton c1930 8° 698p
Contents:
O'Neill, E. Emperor Jones
Green, P. In Abraham's bosom
Howard, S. Silver cord
Milne, A. A. Dover road
O'Casey, S. Juno and the paycock
Wedekind, F. Such is life
Kaiser, G. From morn to midnight
Hoffmansthal, H. von. Electra
Vildrac, C. Steamship Tenacity
Lenormand, H. R. Time is a dream
Pirandello, L. Naked
Benelli, S. Love of the three kings
Alvarez Quintero, S. and J. Malvaloca
Martinez Sierra, G. and M. Lily among thorns
Andreev, L. He who gets slapped
Yevreinov, N. N. Theatre of the soul
Molnár, F. Liliom
Čapek, K. R.U.R.
Ansky, S. Dybbuk
Sigurjónsson, J. Eyvind of the hills

Dickon goes to the fair, and other plays.
N.Y. Doran c1927 12° 204p
Contents:
Alden, A. W. Dickon goes to the fair
Commons, Mrs J. R. Merman's pipe
Kingsbury, S. R. Voice of Montezuma
Burt, O. F. W. Midsummer night

Eastman, Fred, ed.
Modern religious dramas. N.Y. Holt c1928 8° 326p
Contents:
Gale, Z. Neighbors
Wilde, P. Confessional
Church, V. What men live by
Hall, H. and Middlemas, R. Valiant
Eastman, F. Bread
Eastman, F. America's unfinished battles
Tompkins, J. M. S. Deathless world
Larkin, M. El Cristo
Goodman, K. S. Dust of the road
MacNair, I. T. Color line
Cook, C. R. Golden rule in courtship
Brown, C. S. Modern magi
Bowie, W. R. Christmas pageant of the Holy Grail

Eight one-act plays. London Rich [1933] 12° 197p
Contents:
Bennett, A. Snake charmer
Bell, J. J. Thirst
Brunton, F. C. Blind man's bluff
Box, Sydney. Murder trial
Byron-Webber, Ronald. 100—not out
Beresford, Hugh and Seale, C. S. St.B. Second guest
Tracy, H. E. H. Understudy
Kemp, Harry. Boccaccio's untold tale

Famous plays of 1931. London Gollancz [1932] 12° 672p
Contents:
Besier, R. Barretts of Wimpole street
Fagan, J. B. Improper duchess
Delafield, E. M. To see ourselves
Van Druten, J. After all
Van Druten, J. London wall
Anthony, C. L. Autumn crocus

Famous plays of 1932. London Gollancz 1932 12° 654p
Contents:
Mackenzie, R. Musical chairs
Van Druten, J. Somebody knows
Rice, E. See Naples and die
Bax, C. Rose without a thorn
Van Druten, J. There's always Juliet
Hart, M. and Kaufman, G. Once in a lifetime

Famous plays of 1932-33. London Gollancz 1933 12° 727p
Contents:
Winsloe, Christa. Children in uniform
Chlumberg, Hans. Miracle at Verdun
Anthony, C. L. Service
Van Druten, J. Behold, we live
Rice, E. Counsellor-at-law

Famous plays of 1933. London Gollancz 1934 12° 702p
Contents:
Fauchois, R. Late Christopher Bean
Daviot, G. Richard of Bordeaux
Armstrong, A. Ten-minute alibi
Chetham-Strode, W. Sometimes even now
Howard, S. Alien corn
Kaufman, G. S. and Ryskind, M. Of thee I sing

Famous plays of 1933-34. London Gollancz 1934 12° 712p
Contents:
Lipscomb, W. P. and Minney, J. R. Clive of India
Hodge, Merton. Wind and the rain
Sherwood, R. E. Reunion in Vienna
Daviot, G. Laughing woman
Stuart, Aimee and Philip. Sixteen
Van Druten, J. Distaff side

Famous plays of to-day. London Gollancz 1930 12° 671p
Contents:
Sherriff, R. C. Journey's end
Van Druten, J. Young Woodley
Hoffe, M. Many waters
Berkeley, R. Lady with the lamp
Dukes, A. Such men are dangerous
Levy, B. W. Mrs. Moonlight

Johnson, T.—*Continued*
More plays in miniature. For two or three
characters. Boston Baker 1929 12° 143p
Contents:
Dane, E. His only way
Clements, C. C. Spring!
Halman, D. Famine and the ghost
Baring, M. Xanthippe and Socrates
Fairbanks, S. v. K. Other voice
Dobson, A. Secrets of the heart
Baring, M. Drawback
Thornton, C. Marriage of Dotty
Hunting, E. S. Double dummy
Pain, Mrs. B. Vicious circle
Bates, A. Yes and no
Riddle, G. Come here
Anon. At the ferry
Dobson, A. "Au revoir"
Cobb, G. C. Just advertise
Dane, E. Wooden leg
Plays about George Washington. Boston Baker
[c1931] 12° 128p
Contents:
Holmes, E. D. Capture of Major André
Holmes, E. D. Capture of the British sen-
tinel at Stony Point
Mather, C. C. Dispatches for Washington
Wormwood, E. M. Doll that saved an army
Cooke, C. C. Friends in need
Cavanah, F. Glorious wish
Marble, T. L. Mistress Penelope
Parsons, M. G. Prophecy
Van Derveer, C. Spirit of '76
Holbrook, M. Stitch in time
Ten fantasies for stage and study. . . Boston
Baker [c1932] 12° 160p
Contents:
Wellington, Barbara. Is romance dead?
Talbot, A. J. Passing of Galatea
Hickenlooper, M. "St. Anselm only carved
one soul"
Wells, C. F. Apothecary
Sladen-Smith, F. Crown of St. Felice
Hoffman, P. Man of the moment
Webber, J. P. Golden arrow
Dane, E. Workers at the loom
Fyleman, Rose. In Arcady
Going, C. B. Twilight of the moon
Washington anniversary plays. . . Boston Baker
1931 12° 192p
Contents:
MacKaye, P. George Washington at the Dela-
ware
Bates, E. W. Evacuation of Boston
Phillips, L. Mother of Washington
Holbrook, M. Backwoods
Holbrook, M. Brandywine
Holbrook, M. Mount Vernon
Fitch, C. Nathan Hale (Act 3)
Harris, M. P. Pageant of inauguration
Price, O. M. Sandman's pack o' dreams
Hare, W. B. Colonial garden party
Katzin, W. ed.
Eight European plays . . . preface by Barrett H.
Clark. N.Y. Brentano's 1927 8° 426p
Contents:
French:
Bernard, J. J. Glamour
Bernard, J. J. Martine
Italian:
San Secondo, R. di. Stairs
German:
Kaiser, G. Fire in the opera house
Harlan, W. Nüremburg egg
Mann, H. Madame Legros
Sternheim, C. Place in the world
Vollmoeller, K. Uncle's been dreaming
Koch, Frederick H. ed.
Carolina folk comedies. . . N.Y. French 1931
12° 311p
Contents:
Coffin, G. W. Magnolia's man
Fussler, I. Ever' snitch
Toy, J. Agatha
Stout, W. Dogwood bushes
Dortch, H. Companion-mate Maggie
O'Connell, W. Lie
Bailey, L. C. Cloey
Peet, T. New moon
Carolina folk-plays. ser. 3. N.Y. Holt [c1928]
12° 267p
Contents:
Cox, W. N. The scuffletown outlaws
Bailey, L. C. Job's kinfolks
Stout, W. In Dixon's kitchen

Coffin, G. W. A shotgun splicin'
Bland, M. Lighted candles
Green, P. Quare medicine
Le Gallienne, Eva, ed.
Eva Le Gallienne's civic repertory plays. .
N.Y. Norton 1928 8° 327p
Contents:
Ibsen, H. Hedda Gabler
Goldoni, C. La locandiera
Wied, G. 2x2=5
Chekhov, A. P. Three sisters
**Locke, Alain Le Roy and Gregory, Montgomery,
eds.**
Plays of Negro life; a source book of native
American drama. . . N.Y. Harper 1927 12°
430p
Contents:
O'Neill, E. Dreamy kid
Torrence, R. Rider of dreams
Culbertson, E. H. Rackey
Green, P. No 'count boy
Richardson, W. Flight of the natives
Green, P. White dresses
Green, P. In Abraham's bosom
Wilson, F. H. Sugar cane
Mathews, J. 'Cruiter
Spence, E. Starter
Rogers, J. W. Judge Lynch
Torrence, R. Granny Maumee
White, L. Bird child
Toomer, J. Balo
Johnson, G. D. Plumes
Richardson, W. Broken banjo
Duncan, T. Death dance
O'Neill, E. Emperor Jones
Torrence, R. Dance Calinda
Bruce, R. Sahdji, an African ballet
McDermott, John Francis, ed.
Modern plays. . . N.Y. Harcourt [c1932] 8°
427p
Contents:
Ibsen, H. Doll's house
Čapek, K. R.U.R.
Maugham, W. S. Circle
Milne, A. A. Mr. Pim passes by
O'Neill, E. Emperor Jones
Hughes, H. Hell bent fer heaven
Howard, S. They knew what they wanted
McPharlin, Paul, ed.
Repertory of marionette plays. Chosen and trans-
lated . . . by Paul McPharlin. N.Y. Viking
1929 8° 372p
Contents:
Yeats, J. B. Scourge of the gulph
Fool, T. School, or Thou shalt not commit
Dondo, M. Every dog has his day
Mourguet, L. Coq brothers
Duranty, L. E. Cataclysterium's medicine
Neuville, L. de. Mr. Goodman and Mrs.
Gracious
Sand, M. Candidate for Trepagny
Bouchor, M. Noël, or The mystery of the
nativity
Maeterlinck, M. Death of Tintagiles
Bonneschky. Doctor Faustus
Goethe, J. W. von. Junk-dump fair
Pocci, F. von. Casper among the savages
Mitcoff, E. Y. Petroushka
Drum dance. *See* Chinese plays
Mantle, Burns, ed.
Best plays of 1926-27. N.Y. Dodd 1927 12° 563p
Contents:
Dunning, P. and Abbott, G. Broadway
Anderson, M. Saturday's children
Watkins, M. Chicago
Maugham, W. S. Constant wife
Sherwood, R. E. Road to Rome
Wodehouse, P. G. Play's the thing
Howard, S. Silver cord
Martínez Sierra, G. and M. Cradle song
Kelly, G. Daisy Mayme
Green, P. In Abraham's bosom
Best plays of 1927-28 and the Yearbook of the
drama in America. N.Y. Dodd 1928 8° 588p
Contents:
O'Neill, E. Strange interlude
Kaufman, G. S. and Ferber, E. Royal family
Watters, G. M. and Hopkins, A. Burlesque
Abbott, G. and Bridgers, Anne. Coquette
Kelly, G. Behold the bridegroom
Heyward, D. and DuB. Porgy
Barry, P. Paris bound
Galsworthy, J. Escape
Cormack, B. Racket
O'Casey, S. Plough and the stars

Massey, Vincent, ed.
　Canadian plays from Hart House theatre. Toronto
　　Macmillan 1926, 1927 12° 2v
　Contents:
　　v. 1: Denison, M. Brothers in arms
　　Denison, M. Weather breeder
　　Scott, D. C. Pierre
　　Osborne, M. Point of view
　　Borsook, H. Three weddings of a hunchback
　　MacKay, I. E. Second lie
　　Denison, M. Balm
　　Cooke, B. Translation of John Snaith
　　v. 2: Aikins, C. God of gods
　　MacKay, L. A. Freedom of John Guichet
　　Reid, L. Trespassers

Mayor, Beatrice, ed.
　Four one-act plays. Oxford Blackwell 1923 12°
　Contents:
　　Herbert, A. P. Double demon
　　Sladen-Smith, F. St. Simeon Stylites
　　Mayor, B. Thirty minutes in a street
　　Simpson, S. Pan in Pimlico

Modern short plays. First series. London Uni-
　versity of London press 1933 12° 160p
　Contents:
　　Drinkwater, J. Robin Hood and the pedlar
　　Raleigh, W. Riddle
　　Gregory, Lady. Travelling man
　　Binyon, L. Paris and Œnone
　　Munro, H. H. Death-trap
　　Phillpotts, E. Something to talk about
　　Dunsany, E. Tents of the Arabs

Modern short plays. Second series. London Uni-
　versity of London press 1931 12° 158p
　Contents:
　　Phillpotts, E. Purple bedroom
　　Milne, A. A. Wurzel-Flummery
　　Dunsany, E. Gods of the mountain
　　Ould, H. Joan the maid
　　Ratcliffe, D. U. Desormais
　　Gilbert, B. Eldorado

Modern short plays. Third series. London Uni-
　versity of London press 12° 117p
　Contents:
　　Malleson, M. Man of ideas
　　Munro, H. H. Karl-Ludwig's widow
　　Ratcliffe, D. U. Mary of Scotland in Wensley-
　　　dale
　　Dane, E. When the whirlwind blows
　　Brighouse, H. Oak settle
　　Sladen-Smith, F. Golden fisherman
　　Baring, M. King Alfred and the neat-herd

Moses, Montrose J. ed.
　Dramas of modernism and their forerunners,
　　edited with introductions and bibliographies. . .
　　Boston Little 1931 8° 741p
　Contents:
　　Chekhov, A. Cherry orchard
　　Gorky, M. Night's lodging (Lower depths)
　　Andreyev, L. He who gets slapped
　　Kaiser, G. From morn to midnight
　　Toller, E. Machine-wreckers
　　Lenormand, H. R. Dream doctor
　　Pirandello, L. Right you are! (If you think
　　　so)
　　Čapek, K. and J. Adam the creator
　　Molnár, F. Liliom
　　Strindberg, A. There are crimes and crimes
　　Maugham, W. S. Circle
　　Milne, A. A. Truth about Blayds
　　Nichols, R. and Browne, M. Wings over
　　　Europe
　　Kelly, G. Craig's wife
　　Howard, S. Silver cord
　Ring up the curtain! a collection of plays for
　　children. Boston Little 1932 8° 398p
　Contents:
　　Riley, A. C. D. Ten minutes by the clock
　　Brooks, E. S. Land of Nod
　　Mackay, C. D. Nimble-wit and fingerkin
　　Farrar, J. House gnomes
　　du Bois, T. Aladdin
　　Kaufman, H. S. Little black Sambo
　　Gregory, A. Talking dragon
　　Ruthenburg, G. D. Talking chair
　　Sterne, E. G. Jeanne d'Arc
　　Ford, J. E. Snickerty Nick
　　Robertson, W. G. Masque of May morning
　　Sowerby, G. Princess Tenderheart

**New plays for women and girls; fifteen one-act
　plays.** N.Y. French 1932 8° 314p
　Contents:
　　Ruthenburg, G. D. O bright flame lifted!
　　Hughes, G. For the love of Michael
　　Hughes, B. First white woman
　　Kirkpatrick, J. Green eyes from Romany
　　Phelps, P. I know George Washington
　　Phelps, P. Night club girl
　　Hoffman, P. Mrs. Leicester's school
　　Riley, A. C. D. Uplifting Sadie
　　Cameron, M. One of those days
　　Short, M. Lady Luck
　　Van der Veer, E. and Bigelow, F. Let it burn
　　Kreymborg, A. I'm not complaining
　　Brighouse, H. Wish shop
　　Giorloff, R. "Lavender and red pepper"
　　Gale, Z. Clouds

Nicholson, Kenyon, ed.
　Appleton book of short plays (second series). . .
　　N.Y. Appleton 1927 8° 332p
　Contents:
　　Ferber, E. Eldest
　　Divine, C. Post mortems
　　Carb, D. Samson à la mode
　　Thompson, J. F. Warrior's husband
　　Whitehouse, J. H. Ambush
　　Cohen, O. R. Melancholy dame
　　Ryerson, F. Cup of tea
　　Bloch, B. Gas, air and Earl
　　Taylor, R. Appearances
　　Ehrlich, I. L. 'Twas ever thus
　　Murfin, J. Prince Gaby
　　Emery, G. Delilah
　Hollywood plays; twelve one-act plays from the
　　repertory of the Writers' club of Hollywood,
　　California. . . N.Y. French 1930 8° 312p
　Contents:
　　Stinson, H. H. Ace is trumped
　　Smith, V. Simple soul
　　Hughes, R. On the razor edge
　　Schayer, E. R. Private Jones
　　Geraghty, T. J. Pound of flesh
　　Marion, F. Cup of life
　　Heath, E. P. Bird in the hand
　　Blackmore, M. To die with a smile
　　Fulton, M. Miss Baxter
　　Ahearn, T. J. Twelve before three
　　Cohn, A. A. Semper fidelis
　　Ingersoll, P. G. Troupers

One-act plays for stage and study. Fourth se-
　ries. Twenty-two contemporary plays never
　before published in book form, by American,
　English and Irish dramatists. Preface by Paul
　Green. N.Y. French 1928 8° 370p
　Contents:
　　Nicholson, K. Snake eater
　　Kummer, C. So's your old antique!
　　Brooks, G. S. Fortinbras in plain clothes
　　Hughes, B. Three players, a fop and a duchess
　　Brighouse, H. Witch's daughter
　　Ford, H. In-laws
　　Riggs, L. Reckless
　　Basshe, E. J. Invitation
　　Kirkpatrick, J. Wedding
　　Glick, C. Fourth Mrs. Phillips
　　Halman, D. F. Lenna looks down
　　Totheroh, D. Tune of a tune
　　Kreymborg, A. Brother Bill
　　Davies, M. C. Cobweb kings
　　Conkle, E. P. Things is that-a-way
　　Monkhouse, A. Wily one
　　Murray, T. C. Pipe in the fields
　　Ehrlich, I. L. Cured
　　Dondo, M. Miracle of Saint Martin
　　Clements, C. and Saunders, J. M. Love in
　　　a French kitchen
　　O'Brien, S. Christmas eve
　　Green, P. Blue thunder

One-act plays for stage and study. Fifth series.
　Preface by Elmer L. Rice. N.Y. French 1929
　　12° 341p
　Contents:
　　Rice, E. L. Diadem of snow
　　Armstrong, L. Van V. Late Captain Crow
　　Baumer, M. It's an ill wind
　　Brighouse, H. Stoker
　　Farrar, J. Wedding rehearsal
　　Hughes, B. No more Americans
　　Hughes, G. Art and Mrs. Palmer
　　Rogers, J. W. Rescue of Cynthia Ann
　　Guinan, J. Black Oliver
　　Kaye-Smith, S. and Hampden, J. Mrs. Adis
　　Totheroh, D. Widdy's mite

Taylor, H. L. Angelus
Kreymborg, A. Limping along
Van der Veer, E. Babouscka
Ryerson, F. and Clements, C. Hot lemonade
Green, C. M. Jumpin' the broom
Giorloff, R. Maizie
Pride, L. B. Haunted coal mine
Nicholson, K. Words and music
Medcraft, R. First dress-suit
Davies, M. C. Tables and chairs

One-act plays for stage and study. Sixth series.
Twenty-one contemporary one-act plays never
before published in book form, by American,
English and Irish dramatists. N.Y. French
1931 8° 377p
Contents:
Kaufman, G. S. Still alarm
Bennett, A. Snake charmer
Brighouse, H. Ghost of Windsor Park
Pertwee, R. Speaking terms
Hughes, B. Murder! murder! murder!
Kennedy, C. O. Men, women and goats
Gregory, Lady. Colman and Guaire
Ryerson, F. and Clements, C. Willow plate
Kirkpatrick, J. Woman who understood men
Medcraft, R. Poetry and plaster
Field, R. Bad penny
Totheroh, D. Lost princess
Strachan, E. H. Chinese water wheel
Drummond, A. M. Traffic signals
Hughes, G. Babbitt's boy
Crocker, B. Josephine
Van der Veer, E. Saint Cyprian and the devil
Hanlon, D. E. Wolf at the door
Jagendorf, M. Pie and the tart
Speirs, R. Change of mind
Wilde, P. Moving finger

Pence, Raymond W. ed.
Dramas by present-day writers. N.Y. Scribner
c1927 12° 690p
Contents:
Davies, M. C. Slave with two faces
Drinkwater, J. Cophetua
Dunsany, J. Night at an inn
Galsworthy, J. Loyalties
Glaspell, S. Trifles
Gregory, Lady. Spreading the news
Jacobs, W. W. and Hubbard, P. Love passage
Jones, H. A. Goal
Mackay, C. D'A. Counsel retained
Morley, C. Thursday evening
O'Neill, E. "Ile"
Sutro, A. Marriage has been arranged
Wilde, P. Confessional
Bennett, A. and Knoblock, E. Milestones
Kaufman, G. S. and Connelly, M. Merton
of the movies
Tarkington, B. Monsieur Beaucaire

Phillips, Le Roy and Johnson, Theodore, eds.
Types of modern dramatic composition; an an-
thology of one act plays for schools and col-
leges, with an introductory essay by George
Pierce Baker. Boston Ginn 1927 12° 418p
Contents:
Norris, K. and Totheroh, D. Kelly kid
Berkeley, R. Dweller in the darkness
Nicholson, K. Wanderlust
Delano, E. B. and Carb, D. Grandma pulls the
strings
Fyleman, R. Cabbages and kings
Finnegan, E. Fool of a man
Wilde, P. Dawn
Housman, L. Bethlehem
Malleson, M. Maurice's own idea
Hubbard, P. Crumbs that fell
Smith, E. V. 'Lijah
Gibbs, A. H. Meredew's right hand
Glaspell, S. Trifles
Crothers, R. Peggy
Gale, Z. Uncle Jimmy
Halman, D. F. Closet
Cowles, A. Killer
Reeley, M. K. Lean years
Cantillon, A. Pierrot before the seven doors
Moseley, K. P. Daggers and diamonds

Players' book of one act plays; seventeen plays
written and produced by the Players of De-
troit. First series. N.Y. McKee 1928 12°
345p
Contents:
Toms, R. M. . . . and points west
Pike, C. S. Glorious martyr
Pike, C. S. String of pearls

Weeks, A. L. Little brown jug
Weeks, A. L. Elsie
Weeks, A. L. Cocktails
Anderson, L. Is peculiar
Anderson, L. Mutiny
Anderson, L. Strategy
Neebe, J. H. Fog
Neebe, J. H. Guts
Yerkes, R. G. Their appointed rounds
Winningham, C. C. Murder will out
Meadon, J. Vespers
Meadon, J. Pearls before swine
Murphy, T. F. Mary Brice
Phelps, G. H. and Pitkin, M. J. Pearl thief

Plays of a half-decade. London Gollancz c1933
12° 1008p
Contents:
Sherriff, R. C. Journey's end
Van Druten, J. Young Woodley
Berkeley, R. Lady with a lamp
Hoffe, M. Many waters
Besier, R. Barretts of Wimpole street
Fagan, J. B. Improper duchess
Delafield, E. M. To see ourselves
Van Druten, J. After all
Anthony, C. L. Autumn crocus
Mackenzie, R. Musical chairs
Bax, C. Rose without a thorn

Plays of the Moscow Art theatre musical studio
. . . tr. by George S. and Gilbert Seldes. .
N.Y. Brentano's c1925 12°
Contents:
Le Cocq, A. C. Daughter of Madame Angot
Lipskeroff, C. Carmencita and the soldier
Offenbach, J. La Périchole

Plays of to-day. Ser. 3. London Sidgwick 1930
12° 443p
Contents:
Dukes, A. Man with a load of mischief
Mayor, B. Pleasure garden
Munro, C. K. At Mrs. Beam's
Quintero bros. Hundred years old
Robinson, L. Whiteheaded boy

Prize plays of 1927-28. . . . Philadelphia Penn
[1930] 8° 2v
Contents:
v. 1: Larrimore, Lida. Yesterday's roses
Murray, Amie. Zee-Zee
Mackay, I. E. Two too many
Ranck, Carter. Weakest link
Bagg, Helen. Left overs
v. 2: Larrimore, Lida. Third floor front
Dyar, R. E. Horseshoe luck
Longnecker, E. B. References
Loring, Emilie. Where's Peter?
Parke, J. H. It runs in the family

Prize plays of 1928. Philadelphia Penn 1928 12°
414p
Contents:
Larrimore, L. Third floor front
Dyar, R. E. Horseshoe luck
Longenecker, E. B. References
Loring, E. Where's Peter?
Parke, J. H. It runs in the family

Rascoe, Burton and Conklin, Groff
Smart Set anthology. N.Y. Reynal [c1934] 8°
840p
Contents:
Conrad, J. One more day
O'Neill, E. Long voyage home
Wedekind, F. Heart of a tenor

Richardson, Willie, ed.
Plays and pageants from Negro life. Washing-
ton Associated pub. [c1930] 8° 373p
Contents:
Plays:
Duncan, T. M. Sacrifice
Cuney-Hare, Maud. Antar of Araby
Matheus, John. Ti Yette
Miller, May. Graven images
Miller, May. Riding the goat
Richardson, W. House of sham
Richardson, W. Black horseman
Richardson, W. King's dilemma
Pageants:
Burke, I. M. Two races
Guinn, D. C. Out of the dark
Gunner, Frances. Light of the women
McCoo, E. J. Ethiopia at the bar of justice

Sanford, Mrs. Anne Putnam, ed.
Lincoln plays. N.Y. Dodd 1933 12° 249p
Contents:
  Barton, L.   New Salem days
  Marschall, P.   Grandpa tells about Lincoln
  Fielden, A. D.   Abraham Lincoln—a pageant
  Parsons, M.   Massa Linkum's sojer
  Smith, R. P.   At old Vincennes
  Harnwell, A. J.   Her name was Anne
One-act plays for women. N.Y. Dodd 1934 12°
236p
Contents:
  Wilde, P.   Lady of dreams
  Rowell, A. C.   Last frontier
  Ruthenburg, G. D.   Death of Anulus
  Emerson, J.   Screen
  Corneau, P. B.   Clock
  Vinton, I.   Just babies
  Strong, M.   Culture
  Barton, L.   Susan should marry
  Holbrook, M.   All's vanity
  Holbrook, M.   Kid gloves
  Clements, C.   Siege
  Ryerson, F. and Clements, C.   Letters
  Corneau, P. B.   Retired
Plays for graduation days. N.Y. Dodd 1930 8°
322p
Contents:
  Clements, C.   Mister Punch
  Thorpe, J.   At the milestone
  Parsons, M.   Graduation gifts
  Stenger, G.   Light triumphant
  Gilbert, B.   May madness
  Holbrook, M.   Better mouse trap
  Van der Veer, E.   Perfect pattern
  Corneau, B. B.   Last voyage of Odysseus
  Rowell, A. C.   Beloved, it is morn
  Ryerson, F.   Willow plate
  Walker, A. J.   Sanctuary knocker
  Students N.D. university.   Shakespeare, the
    playmaker
  Wilde, P.   Inn of discontent

**Schauffler, Robert Haven and Sanford, A. P.
eds.**
Plays for our American holidays. . . N.Y. Dodd
1928 12° 4v
Contents:
v. 1: Christmas
  Walker, S.   Seven gifts
  Wilde, P.   Alias Santa Claus
  Meaker, I. J. and Perkins, E. E.   My lady's
    yule-tide
  Lyon, E. S.   Synthetic Santa
  Oglesbee, D. H.   Ten fingers of François
  Donahue, V. and Holmes, L. T.   Elves and
    the shoemaker
  Van der Veer, E.   Boy on the meadow
  Brighouse, H.   Maid of France
St. Valentine's Day
  Price, O. M.   Gifts of the gods
  Ryerson, F. and Clements, C.   On the lot
  Giorloff, R.   Jazz and minuet
St. Patrick's Day
  Lyon, E. S.   Shamrock
  Gregory, I. A.   Bogie men
  Aldis, M.   Mrs. Pat and the law
Easter
  Bates, E. W.   Tree of life
  Bellamy, F. L.   Darkness and dawn
  Colby, G.   First Easter bunny
Hallowe'en
  Parsons, M.   Elfin knight of Hallowe'en
  Parsons, M.   Hansel and Gretel
  Glassie, A. B.   Meadow gold
v. 2: New Year's Day
  Arkwright, R.   Baby New Year
  Olcott, V.   Cave of the fates
  Van der Veer, E.   When the horns blow
Twelfth Night
  Knox, E. L.   Twelfth night festivities
Arbor Day
  Thorp, J.   The treasure chest
  Edgar, M. S.   Conspiracy of spring
  Grimball, E. B.   The snow queen
April Fool's Day
  Clements, C.   Two plum puddings
  Olcott, V.   An April fool
  Bolton, I.   The king of Sherwood
  Wilde, P.   The noble lord
May Day
  Stewart, M.   The dream fairy and the spider
  Burrows, E.   A garden Cinderella
  Cummins, S. L.   The sleeping beauty

Thanksgiving
  Wilson, S. A.   Festival of the harvest moon
  Vilas, F. Van V.   The three Thanksgivings
  Meaker, I. J. and Harnwell, A. J.   Sojourners
Forefathers' Day
  Stenger, G.   At turn of tide
  Marble, A.   Faith of our fathers
v. 3: Lincoln's Birthday
  Mackay, C. D'A.   Abraham Lincoln: rail-splitter
  Warren, P. and Hutchins, W.   Day that Lincoln
    died
Washington's Birthday
  MacKaye, P.   George Washington at the Dela-
    ware
  Burgess, K. S.   God winks
  Archer, W.   George Washington's wedding
Flag Day
  MacKaye, P.   Washington and Betsy Ross
  McFadden, E. A. and Crimmins, A.   Man
    without a country
Memorial Day
  Price, O. M.   Boy in blue
  Rowell, A. C.   High heart
Independence Day
  Eldridge, F. M.   Growth of a nation
  Wilson, S. A.   Festival of Yankee Doodle
Thomas Jefferson's Day
  Stenger, G.   Above all else, liberty
Armistice Day
  Harnwell, A. J. and Meaker, I. J.   Knife
  Moses, G. C.   Tree of memory
  Gribble, H. W.   Message
v. 4: Mother's Day
  Van der Veer, E.   Shipping mother east
  Parsons, M.   Mother they forgot
  Wilde, P.   Mothers of men
  Lewis, D. B. W.   At the mule
Children's Day
  Branch, A. B.   St. Francis and the wolf
  White, C. R.   Group of plays about Ulysses
Labor Day
  Reely, M. K.   Daily bread
  Greene, P. and E.   Fixin's
  Dunsany, E.   Evil kettle
Columbus Day
  Fenzi, F.   Jewels of Isabella
  Parsons, M.   Sailing west to find the east
Health Week
  Griffith, E. G.   Little vegetable men
  Griffith, E. G.   House the children built
  Russell, F. K.   Clean up!
  Pemberton, A.   Nelagony, or Good Water
Music Week
  Sanford, A. P.   Brother musicians
  Cooke, J. F.   Scenes from the life of Richard
    Wagner
Book Week
  Sanford, A. P.   Birthday party
  Morley, C.   On the shelf
Red Cross Week
  Anonymous.   Taking the picnic to the Shut-in
  Jordan, E. B.   What becomes of it
  Muse, G. A.   Close call

Schofield, Stephen, ed.
Marble god, and other one-act plays. . . N.Y.
Bretano's 1927 12° 116p
Contents:
  Pakington, M.   House with the twisty windows
  Nesbit, C. M.   Net
  Talbot, A. J.   Incorrigibles
  Schofield, S.   Marble god

Shay, Frank, ed.
Appleton book of Christmas plays. . . N.Y.
Appleton 1929 8° 252p
Contents:
  Goodman, K. S.   Dust of the road
  Ryerson, F. and Clements, C.   Littlest shepherd
  O'Brien, S.   Christmas eve
  Harper, H.   Christmas tale
  Sterling, E.   Modern viking
  Van Der Veer, E.   Boy on the meadow
  Doyle, A.   Exile
  Wilde, P.   Enchanted Christmas tree
  Stevens, T. W.   Duquesne Christmas mystery
  Dickens, C.   Christmas carol
  Walker, S.   Seven gifts

Six plays. London Gollancz 1931 12° 672p
Contents:
  Connelly, M.   Green pastures
  Rice, E.   Street scene
  Sherriff, R. G.   Badger's green
  George, E.   Down our street
  Bax, C.   Socrates
  Glaspell, S.   Alison's house

Watson, E. B. and Pressey, B.—*Continued*
  European plays. v. 1:
    Ibsen, H. Doll's house
    Becque, H. Vultures
    Curel, F. de. Fossils
    Hauptmann, G. Beaver coat
    Schnitzler, A. Light o' love
  Contemporary drama: English and Irish plays.
    N.Y. Scribner 1931 12° 446p
    Milne, A. A. Mr. Pim passes by
    Maugham, W. S. Circle
    Galsworthy, J. Loyalties
    Barrie, J. M. Dear Brutus
    O'Casey, S. Juno and the paycock
  Contemporary drama: Enropean plays. N.Y.
    Scribner 1934 12° 425p
  Contents:
    Chekhov, A. Cherry orchard
    Andreyev, L. He who gets slapped
    Toller, E. Man and the masses
    Čapek, K. R.U.R.
    Pirandello, L. Henry IV

Webber, James Plaisted and Webster, Hanson Hart, eds.
  One-act plays for secondary schools. Boston
    Houghton c1933 12° 308p
  Contents:
    Milne, A. A. Boy comes home
    Brighouse, H. Followers
    Alvarez Quintero, S. and J. Sunny morning
    Tennyson, A. Falcon
    Price, G. Coming of fair Annie
    Rostand, E. Romancers
    Knoblock, E. My lady's lace
    Coppée, F. Lord's prayer
    Smith, E. E. and Ireland, D. L. Cottage on the
      moor
    Leighton, G. R. Solemn pride
    Drinkwater, J. X=O: a night of the Trojan
      war
    Gregory, I. A. Rising of the moon
    Walker, S. Nevertheless

    Kreymborg, A. Manikin and Minikin
    Mackay, C. D'A. Beau of Bath
    Wilde, P. Unseen host
    Branch, A. H. Shoes that danced
    Arkell, R. Colombine
  Typical plays for secondary schools. Boston
    Houghton c1929 12° 343p
  Contents:
    Baring, M. Rehearsal
    Frank, M. M. Mistake at the manor
    Mackay, C. D'A. Prince of court painters
    Webber, J. P. Frances and Francis
    Chapin, H. Augustus in search of a father
    Kotzebue, A. von. Pharaoh's daughter
    Cheng-Chin Hsuing. Thrice promised bride
    Healey, F. Copper pot
    Gilbert, W. S. Sweethearts
    Tarkington, B. Gibson upright
    Gregory, Lady. Dragon

White, Bessie F. trans. Nine one-act plays from
  the Yiddish. Boston Luce 1932 235p
  Contents:
    Leivick, H. Golem
    Gordin, J. Captain Dreyfus
    Levin, Z. Doctor's first operation
    Daixel, S. After midnight
    Peretz, I. L. Sewing of the wedding gown
    Berkowitz, I. D. Landsleit
    Libin, Z. Colleagues
    Pinski, D. Sorrows
    Aleichem, S. Gymnazie

Whitman, Charles Huntington, ed.
  Seven contemporary plays. Boston Houghton
    [1931] 12° 565p
  Contents:
    Ibsen, H. Enemy of the people
    Hauptmann, G. Sunken bell
    Tchekov, A. Cherry orchard
    Rostand, E. Cyrano de Bergerac
    Galsworthy, J. Strife
    Synge, J. M. Riders to the sea
    O'Neill, E. Beyond the horizon